Small Business Made Simple

Sole Proprietorship
Small Business
Start-Up Kit

Sole Proprietorship

Small Business Start-Up Kit

by Daniel Sitarz
Attorney-at-Law

Nova Publishing Company
Small Business and Consumer Legal Books and Software
Carbondale, Illinois

ISBN-1-892949-08-3   Book w/CD   ($29.95)
Library of Congress Catalog Card Number 99-28052

Library of Congress Cataloging-in-Publication Data
        Sitarz, Dan, 1948-
        Sole Proprietorship : small business start-up kit / Daniel Sitarz
        P. cm-(Small business made simple)
        ISBN 1-892949-08-3
        1. Sole Proprietorship—United States. 2. Small business-Law and Legislation-United States.
        I. Title. II. Title: Small Business Start-up kit. III. Series
        KF1355.Z9 S58 2000   346.73'0652-dc21   CIP 99-28052

Nova Publishing Company is dedicated to providing up-to-date and accurate legal information to the public. All Nova publications are periodically revised to contain the latest available legal information.

2nd Edition; 2nd Printing   April, 2007
2nd Edition; 1st Printing: December, 2005
1st Edition; 1st Printing: January, 2000

This publication is designed to provide accurate and authoritative information in regard to the subject matter covered. It is sold with the understanding that the publisher and author are not engaged in rendering legal, accounting, or other professional services. If legal advice or other expert assistance is required, the services of a competent professional person should be sought.
                —From a Declaration of Principles jointly adopted by a Committee of
                the American Bar Association and a Committee of Publishers

DISCLAIMER

Nova Publishing Company   Distributed by:
Small Business and Consumer Legal Books and Software   National Book Network
1103 West College St.   4501 Forbes Blvd., Suite 200
Carbondale, IL 62901   Lanham, MD 20706
Editorial: (800) 748-1175   Orders: (800) 462-6420
www.novapublishing.com   Free shipping on internet orders

Nova Publishing Company Green Business Policies

Nova Publishing Company is committed to preserving ancient forests and natural resources. Our company's policy is to print all of our books on recycled paper, with no less than 30% post-consumer waste de-inked in a chlorine-free process. In addition, all Nova books are printed using soy-based inks. As a result, for the printing of this book, we have saved:

    19.6 trees • 5,669 gallons of water • 3,320 kilowatt hours of electricity • 48.6 pounds of pollution

Nova Publishing Company is a member of Green Press Initiative, a nonprofit program dedicated to supporting publishers in their efforts to reduce their use of fiber obtained from endangered forests. For more information, go to www.greenpressinitiative.org. In addition, Nova uses all compact fluorescent lighting; recycles all office paper products, aluminum and plastic beverage containers, and printer cartridges; uses 100% post-consumer fiber, process-chlorine-free, acid-free paper for 95% of in-house paper use; and, when possible, uses electronic equipment that is EPA Energy Star-certified. Finally, all carbon emissions from office energy use are offset by the purchase of wind-energy credits that are used to subsidize the building of wind turbines on the Rosebud Sioux Reservation in South Dakota (see www.nativeenergy.com/coop).

Table of Contents

List of Forms

Business Start-up Checklist
Business Start-up Checklist (text and PDF form)

Business Plan
Business Plan Worksheet (text and PDF form)
Executive Summary (text and PDF form)

Marketing Plan
Business Marketing Worksheet (text and PDF form)

Financial Plan
Business Financial Worksheet (text and PDF form)
Estimated Profit and Loss Statement (PDF form)
Current Balance Sheet (PDF form)

Pre-Start-up
Pre-Start-up Worksheet (text and PDF form)
Pre-Start-up Checklist (text and PDF form)

Sole Proprietorship Plan
Sole Proprietorship Plan Checklist (text and PDF form)
Sample Sole Proprietorship Plan (text form)

Registration of Sole Proprietorship Name
Statement of Intention to Conduct Business Under an Assumed or Fictitious Name (text and PDF form)

Employee Documents
General Employment Contract (text and PDF form)
Independent Contractor Agreement (text and PDF form)
Contractor/Subcontractor Agreement (text and PDF form)

Business Financial Recordkeeping
Financial Recordkeeping Checklist (text and PDF form)

Business Accounts
Income Chart of Accounts (PDF form)
Expense Chart of Accounts (PDF form)
Balance Sheet Chart of Accounts (PDF form)
Sample Chart of Accounts (PDF form)
Current Asset Account (PDF form)
Physical Inventory Report (PDF form)
Periodic Inventory Report (PDF form)
Cost of Goods Sold Report (PDF form)
Fixed Asset Account (PDF form)
Accounts Payable Record (PDF form)
Long-Term Debt Record (PDF form)
Weekly Expense Record (PDF form)
Monthly Expense Summary (PDF form)
Annual Expense Summary (PDF form)

Weekly Cash Report (PDF form)
Monthly Cash Report Summary (PDF form)
Weekly Income Record (PDF form)
Monthly Income Summary (PDF form)
Annual Income Summary (PDF form)
Monthly Credit Sales Record (PDF form)
Credit Sales Aging Report (PDF form)
Invoice (PDF form)
Statement (PDF form)
Past Due Statement (PDF form)
Credit Memo (PDF form)

Business Payroll

Quarterly Payroll Time Sheet (PDF form)
Employee Payroll Record (PDF form)
Payroll Depository Record (PDF form)
Annual Payroll Summary (PDF form)
Payroll Checklist (text and PDF form)

Taxation of Sole Proprietorships *(All IRS forms are PDF forms)*

Sole Proprietorship Tax Forms Checklist (text and PDF form)
Sole Proprietorship Tax Schedules (text and PDF form)
IRS Form SS-4: *Application for Employer Identification Number*
IRS Form 940: *Employer's Annual Federal Unemployment (FUTA) Tax Return*
IRS Form 941: *Employer's Quarterly Federal Tax Return*
IRS Form W-2: *Wage and Tax Statement*
IRS Form W-3: *Transmittal of Wage and Tax Statements*
IRS Form W-4: *Employee's Withholding Allowance Certificate*
IRS Form 1040-SE: *Self-Employment Tax*
IRS Schedule C: *Profit or Loss from Business*
IRS Schedule C-EZ: *Net Profit from Business*
IRS Form 8829: *Expenses for Business Use of Your Home*

Additional Legal Forms *(all additional forms are PDF and text forms)*

Contract
Extension of Contract
Modification of Contract
Termination of Contract
Assignment of Contract
Consent to Assignment of Contract
Notice of Assignment of Contract
Notice of Breach of Contract
General Release
Mutual Release
Specific Release
Release of Mechanic's Lien
Receipt in Full
Receipt on Account
Receipt for Goods
Commercial Lease
Assignment of Lease
Consent to Assignment of Lease

Notice of Assignment of Lease
Amendment of Lease
Extension of Lease
Sublease
Consent to Sublease
Notice of Breach of Lease
Landlord's Notice to Terminate Lease
Personal Property Rental Agreement (Simple)
Personal Property Rental Agreement (Complex)
Contract for Sale of Personal Property
Bill of Sale, with Warranties
Bill of Sale, without Warranties
Bill of Sale, Subject to Debt
Contract for Sale of Real Estate
Option to Buy Real Estate
Quitclaim Deed
Warranty Deed

Preface

These various business guides are prepared by business professionals who feel that small business owners deserve the clearest and most understandable information available to assist them in starting and running their businesses. The business references in this series are designed to provide concrete information to small business owners to allow them to understand and start their own businesses with a minimum of outside assistance.

With the proper information, the average person in today's world can easily understand and operate a small business and apply many areas of law. However, each year many thousands of small businesses fail because their owners have been unable to manage their financial, legal, or management affairs properly.

However, in an endeavor as complex as starting a business, it is not always prudent to attempt to handle every legal, financial, or accounting situation which arises without the aid of a competent professional. Although the information presented in this book will give readers a basic understanding of the areas of law, business, and accounting covered, it is not intended that this text entirely substitute for experienced assistance in all situations. Throughout this book there are references to those particular situations in which the aid of a lawyer or other professional is strongly recommended.

Regardless of whether or not a lawyer or accountant is ultimately retained in certain situations, the information in this handbook will enable the reader to understand the framework of starting a business in this country. To try and make that task as easy as possible, technical legal jargon has been eliminated whenever possible and plain English used instead. When it is necessary in this book to use a legal term which may be unfamiliar to most people, the word will be defined when first used. A glossary of business, legal, and accounting terms most often encountered is also included at the end of this book.

Introduction

How to Use This Book

This book is designed to be used as a workbook to start your own business as a sole proprietorship. You will work through various worksheets, complete various checklists, and prepare numerous forms. In each chapter of this book, you will find an introductory section that will give you an overview of the types of situations in which the worksheets, checklists, or forms in that chapter will generally be used. This explanation will, generally, include a listing of the information that must be compiled to complete the form. The forms are not designed to be torn out of this book (especially if this is a library's copy!). It is expected that the forms may be used on more than one occasion. By using the copies of the forms that are contained on the attached CD-ROM, it is possible to easily fill in the forms and prepare them for filing or use. If you do not have access to a computer, the preferable manner for using these forms is to make a photocopy of the form, fill in the information that is necessary, and then retype the form in its entirety on white letter-sized paper. The trend in the legal profession is to move entirely to letter-sized (8½" x 11") paper. In fact, many court systems (including the entire Federal court system) now refuse to accept documents on legal-sized paper.

It is recommended that you review the table of contents of this book in order to gain a broad overview of the range and type of legal, business, and accounting documents that are available. Then, before you prepare any of the forms for use, you should carefully read the introductory information and instructions in the chapter in which the particular form is contained. Try to be as detailed and specific as possible as you fill in these forms. The more precise the description, the less likely that later disputes might develop over what was actually intended by the language chosen. The forms can be carefully adapted to a particular situation that may confront your sole proprietorship.

The careful preparation and use of the legal, business, and accounting forms in this book should provide the typical business sole proprietorship with most of the documents necessary for day-to-day operations. If in doubt as to whether a particular form will work in a specific application, please consult a competent lawyer. It may also be wise to consult with an experienced accountant as you begin to organize the sole proprietorship. The tax laws regarding sole proprietorships are somewhat complex and must be carefully complied with in order to obtain the maximum tax benefits.

How to Use the Forms-on-CD

Over 100 of the worksheets, checklists, and legal, business, tax, and accounting forms from this book have been provided on the enclosed Forms-on-CD for your use if you have access to a computer. Please note that the Forms-on-CD also includes a number of forms that are not included in this book. The forms on the Forms-on-CD are provided in two separate formats. First, all of the legal and business forms are provided in text-only format. These files all have the file extension> .txt. In addition, all of the accounting and Internal Revenue Service tax forms and most of the business and legal forms are provided in Adobe® PDF format. These files all have the file extension> .pdf.

System Requirements

There are a few system requirements in order to use the Forms-on-CD:

- A PC with an i486 or Pentium processor
- Windows 95, Windows 98, Windows NT 4.0 with Service Pak 3.0 or later, Windows ME, Windows 2000, or Windows EX
- 8 MB RAM on Windows 95 or Windows 98 (16 recommended)
- 16 MB RAM on Windows NT (24 recommended)
- 20 MB of available hard-drive space to install the software

How to Install the Forms-on-CD
For PCs:

1. Insert the enclosed CD in your computer. The installation program should start in a few seconds. Follow the onscreen dialog boxes and make the appropriate choices.
2. If the CD installation does not start automatically, click on the Windows START box, then select RUN, then BROWSE, then select your computer's CD drive, then select the file "Install.exe." Finally, click OK to run the installation program.
3. Open the "Readme.doc" document (which should be visible on your Windows desktop). Print out and follow the instructions on this document.

For MACs:

1. Insert the enclosed CD in your computer and copy the folder "Forms for MACs" to your hard drive.
2. Copy the folder "Forms-for-Macs" to your hard drive. All of the PDF and text-only forms are included in this folder.
3. If you do not already have the Adobe Acrobat Reader program installed on your hard drive, you will need to download the version of this software that is appropriate for your particular MAC operating system from www.adobe.com. Note: The latest versions of the MAC operating system (OS-X) has PDF capabilities built into it.

CHAPTER 1
Deciding to Start Business as a Sole Proprietorship

One of the first decisions that potential business owners must confront is how their business should be structured and operated. This crucial decision must be made even before the business has actually begun operations. The legal documents that will generally accompany the formation of a business can follow many different patterns, depending on the particular situation and the type of business to be undertaken.

Initially, the type of business entity to be used must be selected. There are many basic forms of business operating entities. The five most common forms are:

- Sole proprietorship
- Partnership
- Limited liability company
- C-Corporation
- S-corporation

The choice of entity for a particular business depends on many factors. Which of these forms of business organization is chosen can have a great impact on the success of the business. The structure chosen will have an effect on how easy it is to obtain financing, how taxes are paid, how accounting records are kept, whether personal assets are at risk in the venture, the amount of control the "owner" has over the business, and many other aspects of the business. Keep in mind that the initial choice of business organization need not be the final choice. It is often wise to begin with the simplest form, the sole proprietorship, until the business progresses to a point where another form is clearly indicated. This allows the business to begin in the least complicated manner and allows the owner to retain total control in the important formative period of the business. As the business grows and the potential for liability and tax burdens increase, circumstances may dictate a re-examination of the business structure. The advantages and disadvantages of the five choices of business operation are detailed below.

Sole Proprietorship

Setting up a sole proprietorship is the focus of this book. A *sole proprietorship* is both the simplest and the most prevalent form of business organization. An important reason for this is that it is the least regulated of all types of business structures. Technically, the sole proprietorship is the traditional unincorporated one-person business. For legal and tax purposes, the business is the owner. It has no existence outside the owner. The liabilities of the business are personal to the owner and the business ends when the owner dies. On the other hand, all of the profits are also personal to the owner and the sole owner has full control of the business.

Disadvantages

Perhaps the most important factor to consider before choosing this type of business structure is that all of the personal and business assets of the sole owner are at risk in the sole proprietorship. If the demands of the creditors of the business exceed those assets which were formally placed in the name of the business, the creditors may reach the personal assets of the owner of the sole proprietorship. Legal judgments for damages arising from the operation of the business may also be enforced against the owner's personal assets. This unlimited liability is probably the greatest drawback to this type of business form. Of course, insurance coverage of various types can lessen the dangers inherent in having one's personal assets at risk in a business. However, as liability insurance premiums continue to skyrocket, it is unlikely that a fledgling small business can afford to insure against all manner of contingencies and at the maximum coverage levels necessary to guard against all risk to personal assets.

A second major disadvantage to the sole proprietorship as a form of business structure is the potential difficulty in obtaining business loans. Often in starting a small business, there is insufficient collateral to obtain a loan and the sole owner must mortgage his or her own house or other personal assets to obtain the loan. This, of course, puts the sole proprietor's personal assets in a direct position of risk should the business fail. Banks and other lending institutions are often reluctant to loan money for initial small business start-ups due to the high risk of failure for small businesses. Without a proven track record, it is quite difficult for a small business owner to adequately present a loan proposal based on a sufficiently stable cash flow to satisfy most banks.

A further disadvantage to a sole proprietorship is the lack of continuity that is inherent in the business form. If the owner dies, the business ceases to exist. Of course, the assets and liabilities of the business will pass to the heirs of the owner, but the expertise and knowledge of how the business was successfully carried on will often die with the owner. Small sole proprietorships are seldom carried on profitably after the death of the owner.

Advantages

The most appealing advantage of the sole proprietorship as a business structure is the total control the owner has over the business. Subject only to economic considerations and certain legal restrictions, there is total freedom to operate the business however one chooses. Many people feel that this factor alone is enough to overcome the inherent disadvantages in this form of business.

Related to this is the simplicity of organization of the sole proprietorship. Other than maintenance of sufficient records for tax purposes, there are no legal requirements on how the business is operated. Of course, the prudent businessperson will keep adequate records and sufficiently organize the business for its most efficient operation. But there are no outside forces dictating how such internal decisions are made in the sole proprietorship. The sole owner makes all decisions in this type of business.

As was mentioned earlier, the sole proprietorship is the least regulated of all businesses. Normally, the only license necessary is a local business license, usually obtained by simply paying a fee to a local registration authority. In addition, it may be necessary to file an affidavit with local authorities and publish a notice in a local newspaper if the business is operated under an assumed or fictitious name. This is necessary to allow creditors to have access to the actual identity of the true owner of the business, since it is the owner who will be personally liable for the debts and obligations of the business. Information on the registration of a sole proprietorship name is contained in Chapter 10.

Finally, it may be necessary to register with local, state, and federal tax bodies for I.D. numbers and for the purpose of collection of sales and other taxes. Other than these few simple registrations, from a legal standpoint little else is required to start up a business as a sole proprietorship.

A final and important advantage to the sole proprietorship is the various tax benefits available to an individual. The losses or profits of the sole proprietorship are considered personal to the owner. The losses are directly deductible against any other income the owner may have and the profits are taxed only once at the marginal rate of the owner. In many instances, this may have distinct advantages over the method by which partnerships are taxed or the double taxation of corporations, particularly in the early stages of the business. Information on the taxation of sole proprietorships is contained in Chapter 15.

Partnership

A *partnership* is a relationship existing between two or more persons who join together to carry on a trade or business. Each partner contributes money, property, labor, and/or skill to the partnership and, in return, expects to share in the profits or losses of the business. A partnership is usually based on a partnership agreement of some type, although the agreement need not be a formal document. It may even simply be an oral understanding between the partners, although this is not recommended.

A simple joint undertaking to share expenses is not considered a partnership, nor is a mere co-ownership of property that is maintained and leased or rented. To be considered a partnership for legal and tax purposes, the following factors are usually considered:

- The partners' conduct in carrying out provisions of the partnership agreement
- The relationship of the parties
- The abilities and contributions of each party to the partnership
- The control each partner has over the partnership income and the purposes for which the income is used

Disadvantages

The disadvantages of the partnership form of business begin with the potential for conflict between partners. Of all forms of business organization, the partnership has spawned more disagreements than any other. This is generally traceable to the lack of a decisive initial partnership agreement that clearly outlines the rights and duties of the partners. This disadvantage can be partially overcome with a comprehensive partnership agreement. However, there is still the seemingly inherent difficulty many people have in working within the framework of a partnership, regardless of the initial agreement between the partners.

A further disadvantage to the partnership structure is that each partner is subject to unlimited personal liability for the debts of the partnership. The potential liability in a partnership is even greater than that encountered in a sole proprietorship. This is due to the fact that in a partnership the personal risk for which one may be liable is partially out of one's direct control and may be accrued due to actions on the part of another person. Each partner is liable for all of the debts of the partnership, regardless of which partner may have been responsible for their accumulation.

Related to the business risks of personal financial liability is the potential personal legal liability for the negligence of another partner. In addition, each partner may even be liable for the negligence of an employee of the partnership if such negligence takes place during the usual course of business of the partnership. Again, the attendant risks are broadened by the potential for liability based on the acts of other persons. Of course, general liability insurance can counteract this drawback to some extent to protect the personal and partnership assets of each partner.

Again, as with the sole proprietorship, the partnership lacks the advantage of continuity. A partnership is usually automatically terminated upon the death of any partner. A final accounting and a division of assets and liabilities is generally necessary in such an instance unless specific methods under which the partnership may be continued have been outlined in the partnership agreement.

Finally, certain benefits of corporate organization are not available to a partnership. Since a partnership cannot obtain financing through public stock offerings, large infusions of capital are more difficult for a partnership to raise than for a corporation. In addition, many of the fringe benefit programs that are available to corporations (such as certain pension and profit-sharing arrangements) are not available to partnerships.

Advantages

A partnership, by virtue of combining the credit potential of the various partners, has an inherently greater opportunity for business credit than is generally available to a sole proprietorship. In addition, the assets which are placed in the name of the partnership may often be used directly as collateral for business loans. The pooling of the personal capital of the partners generally provides the partnership with an advantage over the sole proprietorship in the area of cash availability. However, as noted above, the partnership does not have as great a potential for financing as does a corporation.

As with the sole proprietorship, there may be certain tax advantages to operation of a business as a partnership, as opposed to a corporation. The profits generated by a partnership may be distributed directly to the partners without incurring any "double" tax liability, as is the case with the distribution of corporate profits in the form of dividends to the shareholders. Income from a partnership is taxed at personal income tax rates. Note, however, that depending on the individual tax situation of each partner, this aspect could prove to be a disadvantage.

For a business in which two or more people desire to share in the work and in the profits, a partnership is often the structure chosen. It is, potentially, a much simpler form of business organization than the corporate form. Less start-up costs are necessary and there is limited regulation of partnerships. However, the simplicity of this form of business can be deceiving. A sole proprietor knows that his or her actions will determine how the business will prosper, and that he or she is, ultimately, personally responsible for the success or failure of the enterprise. In a partnership, however, the duties, obligations, and commitments of each partner are often ill-defined. This lack of definition of the status of each partner can lead to serious difficulties and disagreements. In order to clarify the rights and responsibilities of each partner and to be certain of the tax status of the partnership, it is good business procedure to have a written partnership agreement. All states have adopted a version of the *Uniform Partnership Act*, which provides an outline of partnership law. Although state law will supply the general boundaries of partnerships and even specific partnership agreement terms if they are not addressed by a written partnership agreement, it is better for a clear understanding of the business structure if the partner's agreements are put in writing.

Limited Liability Company

The limited liability company is a hybrid type of business structure. It contains elements of both a traditional partnership and a corporation. The limited liability company form of business structure is relatively new. Only in the last few years has it become available as a form of business in all 50 states and Washington D.C. Its uniqueness is that it offers the limited personal liability of a corporation and the tax benefits of a partnership. A limited liability company consists of one or more members/owners who actively manage the business of the limited liability company. There may also be nonmember managers employed to handle the business.

Disadvantages

In as much as the business form is still similar to a partnership in operation, there is still a potential for conflict among the members/owners of a limited liability company. Limited liability companies are formed according to individual state law, generally by filing formal Articles of Organization of a Limited Liability Company with the proper state authorities in the state of formation. Limited liability companies are, generally, a more complex form of business operation than either the sole proprietorship or the standard partnership. They are subject to more paperwork requirements than a simple partnership but somewhat less than a corporation. Limited liability companies are also subject to far more state regulations regarding both their formation and their operation than either a sole proprietorship or a partnership. In all states, they are also required to pay fees for beginning the company, and in some states, annual franchise fees of often hundreds of dollars are assessed for the right to operate as a limited liability company.

Similar to traditional partnerships, the limited liability company has an inherent lack of continuity. In recent years, however, an increasing number of states have allowed limited liability companies to exist for a perpetual duration, as can corporations. Even if the duration of a limited liability company is perpetual, however, there may be difficulties if the sole member of a one-member limited liability company becomes disabled or dies. These problems can be overcome to some extent by providing, in the Articles of Organization of the limited liability company, for an immediate reorganization of the limited liability company with the deceased member's heirs or estate becoming members of the company. In addition, similar to partnerships, it may be difficult to sell or transfer ownership interests in a limited liability company.

Advantages

The members/owners in such a business enjoy a limited liability, similar to that of a shareholder in a corporation. In general, the members' risk is limited to the amount of their investment in the limited liability company. Since none of the members will have personal liability and may not necessarily be required to personally perform any tasks of management, it is easier to attract investors to the limited liability company form of business than to a traditional partnership. The members will share in the potential profits and in the tax deductions of the limited liability company, but will share in fewer of the financial risks involved. Since the limited liability company is generally taxed as a partnership, the profits and losses of the company pass directly to each member and are taxed only at the individual level.

A further advantage of this type of business structure is that it offers a relatively flexible management structure. The company can be managed either by members/owners themselves or by managers who may or may not be members. Thus, depending on needs or desires, the limited liability company can be a hands-on, owner-managed company or a relatively hands-off operation for its members/owners with hired managers actually operating the company.

A final advantage is that limited liability companies are allowed more flexibility than corporations in how profits and losses are actually allocated to the members/owners. Thus, one member/owner may be allocated 50 percent of the profits (or losses) even though that member/owner only contributed 10 percent of the capital to start the company.

Corporations

A corporation is a creation of law. It is governed by the laws of the state where it was incorporated and of the state or states in which it does business. In recent years it has become the business structure of choice for many small businesses. Corporations are, generally, a more complex form of business operation than either a sole proprietorship or partnership. Corporations are also subject to far more state regulations regarding both their formation and operation. The following discussion is provided in order to allow the potential business owner an understanding of this type of business operation.

The corporation is an artificial entity. It is created by filing Articles of Incorporation with the proper state authorities. This gives the corporation its legal existence and the right to carry on business. The Articles of Incorporation act as a public record of certain formalities of corporate existence. Adoption of corporate *bylaws*, or internal rules of operation, is often the first business of the corporation, after it has been given the authority to conduct business by the state. The bylaws of the corporation outline the actual mechanics of the operation and management of the corporation.

There are two basic types of corporations: C-corporations and S-corporations. These prefixes refer to the particular chapter in the U.S. Tax Codes that specify the tax consequences of either type of corporate organization. In general, both of these two types of corporations are organized and operated in similar fashion. There are specific rules that apply to the ability to be recognized by the U.S. Internal Revenue Service as an

S-corporation. In addition, there are significant differences in the tax treatment of these two types of corporations. These differences will be clarified later in this chapter under the heading "S-Corporations." The basic structure and organizational rules below apply to both types of corporations, unless noted.

C-Corporation

In its simplest form, the corporate organizational structure consists of the following levels:

• **Shareholders:** who own shares of the business but do not contribute to the direct management of the corporation, other than by electing the directors of the corporation and voting on major corporate issues

• **Directors:** who may be shareholders, but as directors do not own any of the business. They are responsible, jointly as members of the board of directors of the corporation, for making the major business decisions of the corporation, including appointing the officers of the corporation

• **Officers:** who may be shareholders and/or directors, but, as officers, do not own any of the business. Officers (generally the president, vice president, secretary, and treasurer) are responsible for day-to-day operation of the corporate business

Disadvantages

Due to the nature of the organizational structure in a corporation, a certain degree of individual control is necessarily lost by incorporation. The officers, as appointees of the board of directors, are answerable to the board for management decisions. The board of directors, on the other hand, is not entirely free from restraint, since it is responsible to the shareholders for the prudent business management of the corporation.

The technical formalities of corporation formation and operation must be strictly observed in order for a business to reap the benefits of corporate existence. For this reason, there is an additional burden and expense to the corporation of detailed recordkeeping that is seldom present in other forms of business organization. Corporate decisions are, in general, more complicated due to the various levels of control and all such decisions must be carefully documented. Corporate meetings, both at the shareholder and director levels, are more formal and more frequent. In addition, the actual formation of the corporation is more expensive than the formation of either a sole proprietorship or partnership. The initial state fees that must be paid for registration of a corporation with a state can run as high as $900.00 for a minimally capitalized corporation. Corporations are also subject to a greater level of governmental regulation than any other type of business entity. These complications have the potential to overburden a small business struggling to survive.

Finally, the profits of a corporation, when distributed to the shareholders in the form of dividends, are subject to being taxed twice. The first tax comes at the corporate level. The distribution of any corporate profits to the investors in the form of dividends is not a deductible business expense for the corporation. Thus, any dividends that are distributed to shareholders have already been subject to corporate income tax. The second level of tax is imposed at the personal level. The receipt of corporate dividends is considered income to the individual shareholder and is taxed as such. This potential for higher taxes due to a corporate business structure can be moderated by many factors, however.

Advantages

One of the most important advantages to the corporate form of business structure is the potential limited liability of the founders of and investors in the corporation. The liability for corporate debts is limited, in general, to the amount of money each owner has contributed to the corporation. Unless the corporation is essentially a shell for a one-person business or unless the corporation is grossly under-capitalized or under-insured, the personal assets of the owners are not at risk if the corporation fails. The shareholders stand to lose only what they invested. This factor is very important in attracting investors as the business grows.

A corporation can have a perpetual existence. Theoretically, a corporation can last forever. This may be a great advantage if there are potential future changes in ownership of the business in the offing. Changes that would cause a partnership to be dissolved or terminated will often not affect the corporation. This continuity can be an important factor in establishing a stable business image and a permanent relationship with others in the industry.

Unlike a partnership, in which no one may become a partner without the consent of the other partners, a shareholder of corporate stock may freely sell, trade, or give away his or her stock unless this right is formally restricted by reasonable corporate decisions. The new owner of such stock is then a new owner of the business in the proportionate share of stock obtained. This freedom offers potential investors a liquidity to shift assets that is not present in the partnership form of business. The sale of shares by the corporation is also an attractive method by which to raise needed capital. The sale of shares of a corporation, however, is subject to many governmental regulations on both the state and federal levels.

Taxation is listed both as an advantage and as a disadvantage for the corporation. Depending on many factors, the use of a corporation can increase or decrease the actual income tax paid in operating a corporate business. In addition, corporations may set aside surplus earnings (up to certain levels) without any negative tax consequences. Finally, corporations are able to offer a much greater variety of fringe benefit programs to employees and officers than any other type of business entity. Various retirement, stock option, and profit-sharing plans are only open to corporate participation.

S-Corporation

The S-corporation is a certain type of corporation that is available for specific tax purposes. It is a creation of the Internal Revenue Service. S-corporation status is not relevant to state corporation laws. Its purpose is to allow small corporations to choose to be taxed, at the Federal level, like a partnership, but to also enjoy many of the benefits of a corporation. It is, in many respects, similar to a limited liability company. The main difference lies in the rules that a company needs to meet in order to qualify as an S-corporation under Federal law.

In general, to qualify as an S-corporation under current IRS rules, a corporation must meet certain requirements:

- It must not have more than 100 shareholders
- All of the shareholders must, generally, be individuals and U.S. citizens
- It must only have one class of stock
- Shareholders must consent to S-corporation status
- An election of S-corporation status must be filed with the IRS

The S-corporation retains all of the advantages and disadvantages of the traditional corporation except in the area of taxation. For tax purposes, S-corporation shareholders are treated similarly to partners in a partnership. The income, losses, and deductions generated by an S-corporation are "passed through" the corporate entity to the individual shareholders. Thus, there is no "double" taxation of an S-corporation. In addition, unlike a standard corporation, shareholders of S-corporations can personally deduct any corporate losses.

The decision of which business entity to choose depends upon many factors and should be carefully studied. If the choice is to operate a business as a sole proprietorship, this book will provide an array of easy-to-use legal forms that will, in most cases, allow the business owner to start and operate the corporation with minimal difficulty while meeting all of the legal paperwork requirements.

CHAPTER 2
Business Start-up Checklist

Following is the first of many checklists that are provided in this book in order to help you organize your preparation for starting a business. This initial checklist provides an overview of the entire process of starting a business and, in many ways, is your blueprint for your personal business start-up. It incorporates references to many other forms, worksheets, and checklists from throughout this book. Keep this list handy as you proceed through the process of starting your own Sole Proprietorship.

Business Start-up Checklist

- ☐ Read through this entire book to understand the process of starting a Sole Proprietorship

- ☐ Install the software and forms from the Forms-on-CD if you will be using a computer to complete the forms (Introduction)

- ☐ Complete the Business Plan Worksheet (Chapter 3)

  - ☐ Prepare your written Business Plan

- ☐ Complete the Business Marketing Worksheet (Chapter 4)

  - ☐ Prepare your written Marketing Plan

- ☐ Prepare the Business Financial Worksheet (Chapter 5)

  - ☐ Prepare your written Financial Plan

- ☐ Prepare your written Executive Summary (Chapter 3)

  - ☐ Compile your final Business Plan package

- ☐ Complete the Pre-Start-up Worksheet (Chapter 8)

- [ ] Review the Pre-Start-up and Document Filing Checklists

- [ ] Prepare your Sole Proprietorship Plan (Chapter 9)

- [ ] File and publish Intention to Conduct Business Under Fictitious or Assumed Name (with state or local authorities, if required-Chapter 10)

- [ ] Prepare Employment Contracts for any employees of business (Chapter 11)

- [ ] Set up Business Accounting System Chart of Accounts (Chapter 13)

- [ ] Prepare Income/Expense/Asset/Liability Accounts (Chapter 13)

- [ ] Open Business Bank Account

- [ ] Set up business payroll (Chapter 14)

- [ ] Set up Company tax payment schedules (Chapter 15)

CHAPTER 3
Developing a Business Plan

One of the most important and often overlooked aspects of starting a business is the process of preparing a Business Plan. It is through preparation of a formal business plan than you begin the process of refining what your business will actually be and, more importantly, how you can make it successful from the start. To develop a useful plan, you will need to research your business idea and determine how it can be developed into a feasible and successful business. You will use your business plan for many purposes: for your own use to continually fine-tune your actual business start-up; for obtaining financing, even it is only from family members; and for presenting your business ideas to potential shareholders, employees, investors, suppliers, and anyone else with whom you may be doing business. Your plan needs to be dynamic and detailed. If you prepare your plan with care and attention, it will help guide you through the process of starting a successful business. If you take shortcuts in researching, thinking about, and preparing your plan, your path to business success will become an everyday struggle.

This book has divided the preparation of your business plan into three separate parts. In this chapter, you will develop your overall plan. However, in the two following chapters, you will also develop plans that will become an integral part of your business plan. Chapter 4 concentrates on the plans to market your business service or product. Chapter 5 provides a worksheet and instructions for preparing and implementing a strategy for financing your business. Together, the three plans that you create will comprise your total Business Plan package. Finally, after completing all three sections, you will prepare an Executive Summary. The instructions for preparing the summary are at the end of this chapter. With the information you will have gathered and set down in your plan, starting a successful business will be simplified and streamlined. Each of these three chapters has a similar format. A worksheet is presented into which you will enter information that you have gathered or researched. Crucial business decisions will need to be made, even at this early stage, in order for you to honestly assess your chances for success. After completing the worksheet, you will use the compiled information to complete a written (printed) plan. If you are using a computer, all three of the Business Plan Worksheets are included on the Forms-on-CD. You may enter your answers to the questions directly on the text forms which you can open in your own word-processing program or you may print out the PDF version forms and complete them by hand (Note: these particular PDF worksheet forms can not be completed on a computer). This will allow you to quickly and easily compile the answers that you will use to finalize your Business Plan. Following this first worksheet are more detailed instructions for preparing your Business Plan.

Business Plan Worksheet

Preliminary Business Concept Analysis

In one sentence, describe your business concept: _____
_____

What is your business service or product? _____
_____
_____

How long do you estimate that it will take to develop this service or product to the point of being ready for the public? _____
_____

What are the estimated costs of development of this product or service? _____
_____

Why do you think that this business concept will succeed? _____
_____
_____

Who is your target market? _____
_____

Is this market readily identifiable? _____
_____

What are the buying patterns of this market? _____
_____

Is there sufficient advance interest in this type of product or service? _____
_____

What are your expected annual sales/revenue volumes?
- Year one: $ _____
- Year two: $ _____
- Year three: $ _____
- Year four: $ _____
- Year five: $ _____

Company Description

What is your company's mission? _____

_____

What is the type of business entity of your company?   *Sole Proprietorship*

What will the physical location of your company be? _____

_____

Where will be the company's main place of doing business? _____

Will there be any additional locations for the company? _____

_____

What geographic areas will your company serve? _____

What are the long-term plans for the business? (Expand, go public, sell to competitor, etc.)

_____

_____

Industry Analysis

In what industry will your company operate? _____

What is the overall size of the industry? _____

What is the growth rate of the industry? _____

What are any seasonal or business cycles in the industry? _____

_____

What have been the main technological advances in the past five years? _____

_____

What are projected technological advances in the industry for the next five years? _____

_____

Do any industry standards apply to your business? _____

_____

Are there any government regulatory approvals or requirements? _____

_____

Are there any local or state licenses necessary for the service or product? _____
_____

What are the main trade or business associations in your industry? _____
_____

To which associations do you currently belong? _____
_____

Product or Service Analysis

Description of product or service: _____
_____

What is the main purpose of the product or service? _____
_____

Is it a luxury item or a necessity? _____

What are the unique features of your product or service? (Cost, design, quality, capabilities, etc.) _____
_____
_____

What is the life of the product or service? _____

How does this product/service compare with the state-of-the-art for the industry? _____
_____

In what stage is the development of the product? (Idea, model, prototype, full production, etc.) _____

Describe the company's facilities: _____
_____

How will the product be produced or the service provided? _____
_____

Is it labor- or material-intensive to produce or supply? _____
What types of quality control will be in place in the business? _____
What components or supplies are necessary to produce or supply this product? _____
_____

Are there any special technical considerations? _____
Has the service or product been the subject of any engineering or design tests? _____
_____

What are the maintenance or updating requirements for the product/service? _____
_____

Can the product be copyrighted, patented, or trade- or service-marked? _____
_____

Are there other products, services, or spin-offs that will be developed and marketed in future years? _____
_____

Are there any known dangers associated with the manufacture, supply, or use of the product/ service? _____

What types of liabilities are posed by the product, service, or any other business operations?
    To employees: _____
    To customers: _____
    To suppliers: _____
    To distributors: _____
    To the public: _____

Are there any litigation threats posed by this business? _____

Are there any other problems or risks inherent in this type of business? _____
_____

What types of insurance coverage will be necessary for the business? _____
_____

What are the costs of the needed insurance coverage? _____

What steps will be taken to minimize any potential liabilities, dangers, or risks? _____
_____
_____

Business Operations

Describe the type of facilities that your business will need to operate: _____
_____

Estimate the cost of acquiring and maintaining the facilities for two years: _____
_____

Describe your production plan or service plan: _____
_____
_____

How will orders be filled and your product or service delivered? _____
_____

Will you work through any wholesalers or distributors? _____
_____

Who will be the main wholesalers/distributors? _____
_____

Describe the equipment or machinery that you will need for your business: _____
_____
_____

Who will be the main suppliers of this equipment? _____
_____

What are the estimated costs of obtaining this equipment? _____

What type of inventory will you need? _____

Who will be the main suppliers of the inventory? _____
_____

Estimate the costs of obtaining sufficient inventory for the first two years of operation:
_____

Management Analysis

What will be the organizational structure of the company? (Include an organizational chart)
_____

Who will manage the day-to-day affairs of the company? _____

Describe the management style of the central manager: _____
_____

What are the qualifications of the main management? _____

What type of workforce will be necessary for your business? _____
_____

How many employees will be needed?

    Initially: _____

    First year: _____

    Second year: _____

    Third year: _____

    Fourth year: _____

    Fifth year: _____

What are the job descriptions of the employees? _____

What job skills will the employees need? _____

Are employment and hiring/firing procedures and guidelines in place? _____

What will be the hourly wages or salaries of the employees?

    Salaried: _____

    Full-time: _____

    Part-time: _____

Will any fringe benefits be provided to employees?

    Sick pay: _____

    Vacation pay: _____

    Bonuses: _____

    Health insurance or benefits: _____

    Profit-sharing or stock options: _____

    Other benefits: _____

Estimate the annual cost for employee compensation for the first two years of operations:

_____

Will you need to contract with lawyers, accountants, consultants, designers, or specialists?

_____

Who will be the outside contractors you will use? _____

_____

Estimate the annual cost of outside contractors for the first two years of operations:

_____

Is the business bookkeeping system set up and working? _____

Are business bank accounts set up? _____

Are there administrative policies set up for billings, payments, accounts, etc.? _____

Supporting Documentation

Do you have any professional photos of the product, equipment, or facilities? _____
_____

What contracts have already been signed? _____

Does the company hold any patents, trademarks, or copyrights? _____
_____

Have the company's name registration papers been filed with the county? _____
_____

Do you have any samples of advertising or marketing materials? _____

Do you have references and resumés from each of the principals in the business? _____
_____

Do you have personal financial statements from each of the principals in the business?
_____

Have you prepared a time line chart for the company's development for the first five years?
_____

Have you prepared a list of the necessary equipment, with a description, supplier, and cost
of each item noted? _____

Have you prepared current and projected balance sheets and profit/loss statements? _____

Preparing Your Business Plan

Once you have completed the previous worksheet and the worksheets in the next two chapters (relating to marketing and financial plans), you will need to prepare your final Business Plan and complete the Executive Summary. The Executive Summary is, perhaps, the most important document in the entire Business Plan, for it is in this short document that you will distill your entire vision of your company. Do not attempt to prepare the Executive Summary until you have completed all of the other worksheets and plans, for they will provide you with the insight that you will need to craft an honest and enthusiastic Executive Summary for your company.

To prepare your Business Plan, carefully read through the answers you have prepared for the Business Plan Worksheet to obtain a complete overview of your proposed business. Your task will be to carefully put the answers to the questions on the worksheet into a narrative format. If you have taken the time to fully answer the questions, this will not be a difficult task. If you have supplied the answers to the worksheet questions on the computer file version of the worksheet, you should be able to easily cut and paste your Business Plan sections together, adding only sentence and paragraph structure and connecting information. Keep the plan to the point but try to convey both a broad outline of the industry that you will be operating in and a clear picture of how your particular company will fit into that industry and succeed. Emphasize the uniqueness of your company, product, or service, but don't intentionally avoid the potential problems that your business will face. An honest appraisal of your company's risks and potential problems at this stage of the development of your company will convey to investors and bankers that you have thoroughly and carefully investigated the potential for your company to succeed.

For each subsection of the Business Plan Worksheet, use the answers to the questions to prepare your written plan. You may rearrange the answers within each section if you feel that it will present a clearer picture to those who will be reading your Business Plan. Try, however, to keep the information for each section in its own discreet portion of the Business Plan. You will use this same technique to prepare the written Marketing and Financial Plans in the following two chapters. Once you have prepared your written Business, Marketing, and Financial Plans, you are ready to prepare your Executive Summary.

Preparing Your Executive Summary

It is in the Executive Summary that you will need to convey your vision of the company and its potential for success. It is with this document that you will convince investors, suppliers, bankers, and others to take the risks necessary to back your dreams and help you to make them a reality. The Executive Summary portion of your Business Plan should be about one to three pages long. It should be concise, straightforward, and clearly written. Don't use any terms or technical jargon that the average person cannot understand. You may go into more detail in the body of the Business Plan itself, but keep the Executive Summary short and to the point. This document will be a distillation of the key points in your entire Business Plan. It is in the Executive Summary that you will need to infuse your potential backers with your enthusiasm and commitment to success. However, you will need to remain honest and forthright in the picture that you paint of your business and its competition. Use the following outline as a guide to assist you in preparing your Executive Summary. You will, of course, be using the information that you have included in your written Business, Marketing, and Financial Plans to prepare the Executive Summary. After completing your Executive Summary, there are some brief instructions to assist you in compiling your entire Business Plan package.

Executive Summary

Business Plan of _____

Executive Summary

In the year _____ , _____ was formed as a sole proprietorship in the State of _____ .

The purpose of the company is to: _____
_____
_____ .

Our mission statement is as follows: This company is dedicated to providing the highest quality _____ to a target market of _____ . Our long-term goals are to: _____
_____ .

Industry Analysis

The industry in which this company will operate is: _____
_____ .

The annual gross sales of the _____ industry are approximately $ _____ .

Continue with a brief explanation of how your company will fit into this industry: _____
_____

Product or Service Analysis

The product/service that this company will provide is: _____ .

It is unique in its field because: _____ .

Continue with a brief explanation of product/service: _____
_____
_____ .

Business Operations

Prepare a brief explanation of how the business will operate to obtain and deliver the product/ service to the market. Include short explanations of strategies you will use to beat the competition: _____

_____

_____ .

Management of the Company

The company will be managed by: _____

_____ .

Include a brief summary of the management structure and the qualifications of the key management personnel and how their expertise will be the key to the success of the company:

_____

_____

_____ .

Market Strategy

The target market for this product/service is: _____

_____ .

Prepare a brief analysis of your market research and marketing plans and why your product/ service is better than any competitors: _____

_____

_____ .

Financial Plans

In this section, briefly review the data on your Current Balance Sheet and Estimated Profit and Loss Statements and describe both the annual revenue projections and the company's immediate and long-term needs for financing: _____

_____

_____

_____ .

Compiling Your Business Plan

1. Prepare a Title page filling in the necessary information:

> Business plan of (*name of Sole Proprietorship*),
> Formed in the State of (*name of state*)
> Address:
> Phone:
> Fax:
> Internet:
> E-mail:
> Date:
> Prepared by (*name of preparer*)

2. Include a Table of Contents listing the following items that you have:

- Executive Summary
- Business Plan
    - Business Concept and Objectives
    - Industry Analysis
    - Product/Service Analysis
    - Business Operations
    - Management Analysis
- Marketing Plan
    - Target Market Analysis
    - Competitive Analysis
    - Sales and Pricing Analysis
    - Marketing Strategy
        - Advertising and Promotion
        - Publicity and Public Relations
- Financial Plan
    - Financial Analysis
    - Estimated Profit/Loss Statement
    - Current Balance Sheet
- Appendix
    - Photos of Product/Service/Facilities
    - Contracts
    - Bank Account Statements
    - Personal Financial Statements of Principals
    - Proposed List of Equipment/Supplies/Inventory
    - Proposed Time Line for Company Growth

3. Neatly print or type the necessary Business/Marketing/Financial Plans.

4. Compile all of the parts of your Plan and have multiple photocopies made.

5. Assemble all of the parts into a neat and professional folder or notebook.

Congratulations! Your completed Business Plan will serve as an essential guide to understanding your business and will allow potential backers, investors, bankers, and others to quickly see the reality behind your business goals.

CHAPTER 4
Developing a Marketing Plan

An integral part of the process of starting a business is preparing a Marketing Plan. Whether the business will provide a service or sell a product, it will need customers in some form. Who those customers are, how they will be identified and located, and how they will be attracted to the business are crucial to the success of any small business. Unfortunately, it is also one part of a business start-up that is given less than its due in terms of time and effort spent to fully investigate the possibilities. In this chapter, a Business Marketing Worksheet is provided to assist you in thinking about your business in terms of who the customers may be and how to reach them. In many ways, looking honestly at who your customers may be and how to attract them may be the most crucial part of starting your business, for if your understanding of this issue is ill-defined or unclear, your business will have a difficult time succeeding.

In order to create your written Marketing Plan, simply follow the same process that you used in creating your Business Plan in Chapter 3. Take the answers that you have supplied on the following worksheet and edit them into a narrative for each of the four sections of the worksheet:

- Target Market Analysis
- Competitive Analysis
- Sales and Pricing Analysis
- Marketing Strategy

By following this process, you should be able to create a clear and straightforward description of your own business's marketing objectives and methods.

Business Marketing Worksheet

Target Market Analysis

What is the target market for your product/service? _____
_____

What types of market research have you conducted to understand your market? _____
_____

What is the geographic market area you will serve? _____

Describe a typical customer:
    Sex: _____
    Marital status: _____
    Age: _____
    Income: _____
    Geographic location: _____
    Education: _____
    Employment: _____

Estimate the number of potential people in the market in your area of service: _____
_____

What is the growth potential for this market? _____

How will you satisfy the customers' needs with your product/service? _____
_____

Will your product/service make your customers' life more comfortable? _____

Will your product/service save your customers' time or money or stress? _____

Competitive Analysis

Who are your main competitors? _____

Are there competitors in the same geographic area as your proposed business? _____
_____

Are the competitors successful and what is their market share? _____

How long have they been in business? _____

Describe your research into your competitors' business operations: _____
_____

Are there any foreseeable new competitors? _____

What are the strengths and/or weaknesses of your competitor's product/service? _____
_____

Why is your product/service different or better than that of your competitors? _____
_____
_____

What is the main way that you will compete with your competitors (price, quality, technology, advertising, etc.)? _____
_____

How will your customers know that your product/service is available? _____
_____

What is the main message that you want your potential customers to receive? _____
_____

Why is your product/service unique? _____
_____

How will you be able to expand your customer base over time? _____
_____

Sales and Pricing Analysis

What are your competitors' prices for similar products/services? _____

Are your prices higher or lower, and why? _____

Will you offer any discounts for quantity or other factors? _____

Will you accept checks for payment? _____

Will you accept credit cards for payment? _____

Will you have a sales force? Describe: _____

What skills or education will the sales force need? _____

Will there be sales quotas? _____

Will the sales force be paid by salary, wages, or commission? _____

Are there any geographic areas or limitations on your sales or distribution? _____
_____

Will you sell through distributors or wholesalers? Describe: _____

Will there be dealer margins or wholesale discounts? _____

Do you have any plans to monitor customer feedback? Describe: _____
_____

Do you have warranty, guarantee, and customer return policies? Describe: _____
_____

Will any customer service be provided? Describe: _____
_____

What is your expected sales volume for the first five years?
    Year one: _____
    Year two: _____
    Year three: _____
    Year four: _____
    Year five: _____

Marketing Strategy

What is your annual projected marketing budget? _____

Have your company's logo, letterhead, and business cards already been designed?
_____

Do you have a company slogan or descriptive phrase? _____

Has packaging for your product/service been designed? _____

Has signage for your facility been designed? _____

Describe your advertising plans:

    Signs: _____

    Brochures: _____

    Catalogs: _____

    Yellow Pages: _____

    Magazines: _____

    Trade journals: _____

    Radio: _____

    Television: _____

    Newspapers: _____

    Internet: _____

    Trade shows: _____

    Videos: _____

    Billboards: _____

    Newsletters: _____

Have advertisements already been designed? _____

Have you prepared a media kit for publicity? _____

Describe your plans to receive free publicity in the media via news releases or new product/ service releases:

    Radio: _____

    Television: _____

    Newspapers: _____

    Magazines: _____

    Internet: _____

Have you requested inclusion in any directories, catalogs, or other marketing vehicles for your industry? _____

Describe any planned direct mail campaigns: _____

Describe any planned telemarketing campaigns: _____

Describe any internet-based marketing plans:

    E-mail account: _____

    Website: _____

Will there be any special or seasonal promotions of your product/service? _____

How will your customers actually receive the product/service? _____

CHAPTER 5
Developing a Financial Plan

The third crucial part of your initial Business Plan entails how your business will obtain enough money to actually survive until it is successful. The failure of many small businesses relates directly to underestimating the amount of money needed to start *and* continue the business. Most business owners can, with relative ease, estimate the amount of money needed to start a business. The problem comes with arriving at a clear estimate of how much money will be necessary to keep the business operating until it is able to realistically support itself. If you can honestly determine how much is actually necessary to allow the business time to thrive before you can take out profits or pay, the next challenge is to figure out where to get that amount of money. To help you arrive at a clear picture of your business's finances, a Business Financial Worksheet follows. This worksheet will lead you through a number of questions to help you determine the amount of money needed and where it might be obtained. Following the worksheet are instructions on preparing both a Estimated Profit and Loss Statement and a Current Balance Sheet. Both of these financial forms will help you actually put some real numbers into your plans.

When you have completed the Business Financial Worksheet and your two financial forms, you will again need to prepare a written Financial Plan from your worksheet answers and the data that you have compiled on your Profit and Loss Statement and Balance Sheet. Use the same technique that you used in Chapters 3 and 4 to convert your answers to a narrative. After your written Financial Plan is completed, you will need to return to the instructions at the end of Chapter 3, complete your Executive Summary, and compile your completed parts into your entire final Business Plan package. You may then use your formal plan for presentations to prospective investors, bankers, family, or friends as you go in search of the assistance you will need to make your business a success. You will also need to develop a financial recordkeeping system. This and other accounting-related details are explained in Chapters 12 through 14.

Business Financial Worksheet

Describe the current financial status of your company: _____
_____
_____

Income and Expenses

Estimate the annual expenses for the first year in the following categories:
Advertising expenses: _____
Auto expenses: _____
Cleaning and maintenance expenses: _____
Charitable contributions: _____
Dues and publications: _____
Office equipment expenses: _____
Freight and shipping expenses: _____
Business insurance expenses: _____
Business interest expenses: _____
Legal and accounting expenses: _____
Business meals and lodging: _____
Miscellaneous expenses: _____
Postage expenses: _____
Office rent/mortgage expenses: _____
Repair expenses: _____
Office supplies: _____
Sales taxes: _____
Federal unemployment taxes: _____
State unemployment taxes: _____
Telephone/internet expenses: _____
Utility expenses: _____
Wages and commissions: _____

Estimate the first year's annual income from the following sources:
Sales income: _____
Service income: _____
Miscellaneous income: _____

Estimate the amount of inventory necessary for the first year: _____
_____

Estimate the amount of inventory that will be sold during the first year: _____
_____

Estimate the Cost of Goods Sold for the first year: _____

Using the above information, complete the Estimated Profit and Loss Statement as explained later.

Assets and Liabilities

What forms of credit have already been used by the business? _____
_____

How much cash is available to the business? _____

What are the sources of the cash? _____

What types of bank accounts are in place for the business and what are the balances?
_____
_____

What types of assets are currently owned by the business?
    Current assets: _____
    Inventory: _____
        Cash in bank: _____
        Cash on hand: _____
    Accounts receivable: _____
    Fixed and depreciable: _____
    Autos/trucks: _____
        Buildings: _____
        Equipment: _____
        Amount of depreciation taken on any of above: _____
    Fixed non-depreciable: _____
        Land: _____
    Miscellaneous: _____
        Stocks/bonds: _____

What types of debts does the business currently have?
    Current liabilities: _____
        Taxes due: _____
        Accounts payable: _____
        Short-term loans/notes payable: _____
        Payroll accrued: _____
        Miscellaneous: _____

Long-term liabilities: _____
    Mortgage: _____
    Other loans/notes payable: _____

Financial Needs

Based on the estimated profits and losses of the business, how much credit will be necessary for the business?
    Initially: _____
    First year: _____
    Second year: _____
    Third year: _____
    Fourth year: _____
    Fifth year: _____

Estimate the cash flow for the business for the first five years:
    First year: _____
    Second year: _____
    Third year: _____
    Fourth year: _____
    Fifth year: _____

From what sources are the necessary funds expected to be raised?
    Cash on hand: _____
    Personal funds: _____
    Family: _____
    Friends: _____
    Conventional bank financing: _____
    Finance companies: _____
    Equipment manufacturers: _____
    Leasing companies: _____
    Venture capital: _____
    U.S. Small Business Administration: _____
    Equity financing (*check with current Securities and Exchange rules on sales of shares*): _____

Preparing a Profit and Loss Statement

A Profit and Loss Statement is the key financial statement for presenting how your business is performing over a period of time. The Profit and Loss Statement illuminates both the amounts of money that your business has spent on expenses and the amounts of money that your business has taken in over a specific period of time. Along with the Balance Sheet, which is discussed later in this chapter, the Profit and Loss Statement should become an integral part of both your short- and long-range business planning.

This section will explain how to prepare an Estimated Profit and Loss Statement for use in your Business Plan. The Estimated Profit and Loss Statement can serve a valuable business planning service by allowing you to project estimated changes in your business over various time periods and examine what the results may be. Projections of various business plans can be examined in detail and decisions can then be made on the basis of clear pictures of future scenarios. Your estimates of your business profits and losses can take into account industry changes, economic factors, and personal business decisions. Your estimates are primarily for internal business planning purposes, although it may be useful to use an Estimated Profit and Loss Statement to convey your future Business Plans to others. As a trial exercise, you should prepare an Estimated Profit and Loss Statement using your best estimates before you even begin business. You may wish to prepare such pre-business statements for monthly, quarterly, and annual time periods. You may also desire to prepare Estimated Profit and Loss Statements for the first several years of your business's existence.

The Estimated Profit and Loss Statement differs from the other type of Profit and Loss Statements in that the figures that you will use are projections based on expected business income and expenses for a time period in the future. The value of this type of financial planning tool is to allow you to see how various scenarios will affect your business. You may prepare this form as either a monthly, quarterly, or annual projection. To prepare this form, use the data that you have collected for the above Business Financial Worksheet. For more information on Profit and Loss Statements, please see Chapter 12.

1. The first figure that you will need will be your Estimated Gross Sales Income. If your business is a pure service business, put your estimated income on the *Estimated Service Income Total* line. If your business income comes from part sales and part service, place the appropriate figures on the correct lines.

2. If your business will sell items from inventory, you will need to calculate your Estimated Cost of Goods Sold. In order to have the necessary figures to make this computation, you will need to prepare a projection of your inventory costs and how many items you expect to sell. Fill in the *Estimated Cost of Goods Sold* figure on the Estimated Profit and Loss Statement. If your business is a pure service business,

skip this line. Determine your Estimated Net Sales Income Total by subtracting your Estimated Cost of Goods Sold from your Estimated Gross Sales Income.

3. Calculate your Estimated Total Income for the period by adding your Estimated Net Sales Income Total and your Estimated Service Income Total and any Estimated Miscellaneous Income (for example: interest earned on a checking account).

4. Fill in the appropriate Estimated Expense account categories on the Estimated Profit and Loss Statement. If you have a large number of categories, you may need to prepare a second sheet. Based on your future projections, fill in the totals for each of your separate expense accounts. Add in any Estimated Miscellaneous Expenses.

5. Total all of your expenses and subtract your Estimated Total Expenses figure from your Estimated Total Income figure to determine your Estimated Pre-Tax Profit for the time period.

Estimated Profit and Loss Statement

For the period of:

ESTIMATED INCOME			
Income	Estimated Gross Sales Income		
	Less Estimated Cost of Goods Sold		
	Estimated Net Sales Income Total		
	Estimated Service Income Total		
	Estimated Miscellaneous Income Total		
	Estimated Total Income		

ESTIMATED EXPENSES		
Expenses	Advertising expenses	
	Auto expenses	
	Cleaning and maintenance expenses	
	Charitable contributions	
	Dues and publications	
	Office equipment expenses	
	Freight and shipping expenses	
	Business insurance expenses	
	Business interest expenses	
	Legal and accounting expenses	
	Business meals and lodging	
	Miscellaneous expenses	
	Postage expenses	
	Office rent/mortgage expenses	
	Repair expenses	
	Office supplies	
	Sales taxes	

Federal unemployment taxes	
State unemployment taxes	
Telephone/Internet expenses	
Utility expenses	
Wages and commissions	
Estimated General Expenses Total	
Estimated Miscellaneous Expenses	
Estimated Total Expenses	

Estimated Pre-Tax Profit (Income less Expenses)

Preparing a Balance Sheet

A Profit and Loss Statement provides a view of business operations over a particular period of time. It allows a look at the income and expenses and profits or losses of the business during the time period. In contrast, a Balance Sheet is designed to be a look at the financial position of a company on a specific date. It shows what the business owns and owes on a fixed date. Its purpose is to depict the financial strength of a company as shown by its assets and liabilities. It is merely a visual representation of the basic business financial equation: assets – liabilities = equity (or *net worth*). Essentially, the Balance Sheet shows what the company would be worth if all of the assets were sold and all the liabilities were paid off. A value is placed on each asset and on each liability. These figures are then balanced by adjusting the value of the owner's equity figure in the equation. Your Balance Sheet will total your current and fixed assets and your current and long-term liabilities. Even if your business is very new, you will need to prepare a Balance Sheet of where the business currently stands financially. Use the figures that you have gathered for the previous Business Financial Worksheet to complete your Current Balance Sheet. For further information on Balance Sheets, please refer to Chapter 12. Please follow the instructions below to prepare your Current Balance Sheet for your Business Financial Plan:

1. Your Current Assets consist of the following items:

    *   Cash in Bank (from your business bank account balance)
    *   Cash on Hand
    *   Accounts Receivable (if you have any yet)
    *   Inventory (if you have any yet)
    *   Prepaid Expenses (these may be rent, insurance, prepaid supplies, or similar items that have been paid for prior to their actual use)

2. Total all of your Current Assets on your Current Balance Sheet.

3. Your Fixed Assets consist of the following items, which should be valued at your actual cost:

    *   Equipment
    *   Autos and Trucks
    *   Buildings

4. Total your Fixed Assets (except land) on your Current Balance Sheet. Total all of the depreciation that you have previously deducted for all of your fixed assets (except land). Include in this figure any business deductions that you have taken for Section 179 write-offs on business equipment. *Note*: If you are just starting a business, you will not have any depreciation or Section 179 deductions as yet. En-

ter this total depreciation figure under "Less Depreciation" and subtract this figure from the figure for Total Fixed Assets (except land).

5. Enter the value for any land that your business owns. Land may not be depreciated. Add Total Fixed Assets (except land) amount, minus the (less depreciation) figure, and the value of the land. This is your Total Fixed Assets value.

6. Add any Miscellaneous Assets not yet included. These may consist of stocks, bonds, or other business investments. Total your Current, Fixed, and Miscellaneous Assets to arrive at your Total Assets figure.

7. Your Current Liabilities consist of the following items:

• Accounts Payable (if you have any yet)
• Miscellaneous Payable (include here the principal due on any short-term notes payable. Also include any interest on credit purchases, notes, or loans that has accrued but not been paid. Also list the current amounts due on any long-term liabilities. Finally, list any payroll or taxes that have accrued but not yet been paid)

8. Your Fixed Liabilities consist of Loans Payable (the principal of any long-term note, loan, or mortgage due). Any current amounts due should be listed as "Current Liabilities."

9. Total your Current and Fixed Liabilities to arrive at Total Liabilities.

10. Subtract your Total Liabilities from your Total Assets to arrive at your Owner's Equity. For a partnership, this figure represents the total of contributions by the partners plus earnings. Total Liabilities and Owner's Equity will always equal Total Assets.

Current Balance Sheet

As of:

ASSETS			
Current Assets	Cash in Bank		
	Cash on Hand		
	Accounts Receivable		
	Inventory		
	Prepaid Expenses		
	Total Current Assets		
Fixed Assets	Equipment (actual cost)		
	Autos and Trucks (actual cost)		
	Buildings (actual cost)		
	Total Fixed Assets (except land)		
	(less depreciation)		
	Net Total		
	Add Land (actual cost)		
	Total Fixed Assets		
	Total Miscellaneous Assets		
	Total Assets		
LIABILITIES			
Current Liabilities	Accounts Payable		
	Miscellaneous Payable		
	Total Current Liabilities		
Fixed Liabilities	Loans Payable (long-term)		
	Total Fixed Liabilities		
	Total Liabilities		
Owner's Equity	Net Worth or Capital Surplus + Stock Value		

CHAPTER 6
Operating a Sole Proprietorship

Having completed your Business Plan, including the Marketing and Financial Plans, you are ready to begin to understand, in detail, the type of business entity that you have chosen: the sole proprietorship. As noted in Chapter 1, there are numerous advantages to operating a business as a sole proprietorship, but there are also pitfalls. By understanding the actual operation of a sole proprietorship and the framework of laws within which sole proprietorships operate, it is easier to avoid the difficulties that come with the sole proprietorship form of business.

Sole proprietorships are the most common form of business operation. This is due, primarily, to the simplicity of this form of business. They are the easiest to set up. They are flexible. The taxation of sole proprietorships is relatively easy to understand. They allow the business to be under the complete control of the owner, and, unlike corporations or limited liability companies, they have very few paperwork requirements for compliance with state regulations.

Formation of a Sole Proprietorship

The formation of a sole proprietorship requires no special registration requirements in any state, beyond the registration of the use of a fictitious name for the business. Business name registration requirements will be discussed in Chapter 10. There may, of course, be particular registration requirements that apply to the particular business that the sole proprietorship may be engaged in, for example, the sale of firearms or the packaging of food products. Thus, the formation of a sole proprietorship is a relatively simple matter and is accomplished by the act of beginning to engage in a business. Each year thousands of individuals begin their sole proprietorship businesses with little or no preparation or planning. Although this type of business is simple to begin, it is also prone to failure for the same reason. Starting a business as a corporation, a limited liability company, or even a partnership requires more paperwork and planning, and thus allows the business owners a greater opportunity to make careful, well thought out decisions at the planning stages of the business. The step-by-step planning process in this book for starting a sole proprietorship will take you through a similar planning process and provide opportunities to foresee and avoid some of the potential problems that you may encounter as a sole proprietor.

Sole Proprietorship Property

There are a few general rules that govern sole proprietorship property. Property acquired by a sole proprietorship is the property of the owner of the sole proprietorship. Unlike a corporation, limited liability company, or partnership, the sole proprietorship is not, itself, a legal entity for the purpose of holding property. This means that the sole proprietorship is ignored for property purposes and the general laws relating to the ownership of property will apply. Thus, if a sole proprietor is married, the particular state laws that apply to the acquisition of property by a married person will apply. In many ways, this simplifies the issue of property ownership for the sole-owner business. It allows for easy transfer or sale of any business property by the sole owner. However, it also means that in order to obtain financing, the sole proprietor must be personally liable for any mortgages or debts incurred for the purchase of business property.

Sole Proprietorship Liability

In general, the owner of a sole proprietorship is personally liable for any loss or injury caused to any person in the course of the business. The owner of a sole proprietorship is also personally liable for any debts and obligations of the sole proprietorship. This issue is the major difference between operating a business as a sole proprietorship and operating as a corporation or limited liability company. In both corporations and limited liability companies, most states now allow one person to own and operate the company as a sole owner. However, as long as they comply with the extensive paperwork requirements of operating the corporation or limited liability company, the sole owners of those types of businesses do not place their personal assets at risk in the company's business. What this means is that if the sole owner of a corporation defaults on a loan that was made in the name of the corporation, only the assets of the corporation itself may be reached by the creditor in a court proceeding and judgement. If a sole proprietor defaults on a business loan, all of the personal assets (including the sole proprietor's own home) are at risk to collection and enforcement of a claim by a creditor.

This seemingly great disparity in liability is, in fact, not so great in the real world of business. Unless a corporation or limited liability company has sufficient other assets to offer as collateral for a business loan, virtually all financial institutions will require that the owners of a corporation or limited liability company personally obligate themselves to pay back the loan, thus putting their personal assets at risk in the same way as a sole proprietor. Regarding liability for injuries sustained by customers or employees, business liability insurance can provide security from the loss of personal assets for a sole proprietor. The actual day-to-day difference for a business caused by the personal liability of a sole proprietor is, in fact, minimal.

Sole Proprietorship Books And Records

Unlike corporations, partnerships, and limited liability companies, the owners of sole proprietorships are not required by state law to keep books and records. Although there are no state regulations relating to record-keeping, every sole proprietorship is required to keep sufficient records to comply with Federal tax requirements regarding business records. Taxation of sole proprietorships will be discussed in Chapter 15.

In general, the laws that relate to the affairs and conduct of an individual apply equally to the affairs and conduct of the owner of a sole proprietorship. Because the sole proprietorship form of business is not a legal entity itself, there is no effect from this type of business structure on the operation of laws relating to liability, property, taxation, or any other laws.

CHAPTER 7

Sole Proprietorship Paperwork

The business arena in America operates on a daily assortment of legal forms. There are more legal forms in use in American business than are used in the operations and governments of many foreign countries. The sole proprietorship is not immune to this flood of legal forms. While large corporations are able to obtain and pay expensive lawyers to deal with their legal problems and paperwork, most small businesses cannot afford such a course of action. The small business sole proprietorship must deal with a variety of legal documents, usually without the aid of an attorney.

Unfortunately, many businesspeople who are confronted with such forms do not understand the legal ramifications of the use of these forms. They simply sign them with the expectation that they are fairly standard documents, without any unusual legal provisions. They trust that the details of the particular document will fall within what is generally accepted within the industry or trade. In most cases, this may be true. In many situations, however, it is not. Our court system is clogged with cases in which two businesses are battling over what was really intended by the incomprehensible legal language in a certain legal document. Much of the confusion over company paperwork comes from two areas: First, there is a general lack of understanding among many in business regarding the framework of law. Second, many business documents are written in antiquated legal jargon that is difficult for even most lawyers to understand and nearly impossible for a layperson to comprehend.

The various legal documents that are used in this book are, however, written in plain English. Standard legal jargon, as used in most lawyer-prepared documents, is, for most people, totally incomprehensible. Despite the lofty arguments by attorneys regarding the need for such strained and difficult language, the vast majority of legalese is absolutely unnecessary. As with any form of communication, clarity, simplicity, and readability should be the goal in legal documents.

Unfortunately, in some specific instances, certain obscure legal terms are the only words that accurately and precisely describe some things in certain legal contexts. In those few cases, the unfamiliar legal term will be defined when first used. Generally, however, simple terms are used throughout this book. In most cases, masculine and feminine terms have been eliminated and the generic "it," "they," or "them" have been used instead. In the few situations in which this leads to awkward sentence construction, her/his or she/he may be used instead.

All of the legal documents contained in this book have been prepared in essentially the same manner by which attorneys create legal forms. Many people believe that lawyers prepare each legal document that they compose entirely from scratch. Nothing could be further from the truth. Invariably, lawyers begin their preparation of a legal document with a standardized legal form book. Every law library has multivolume sets of these encyclopedic texts that contain blank forms for virtually every conceivable legal situation. Armed with these pre-prepared legal forms, lawyers, in many cases, simply fill in the blanks and have their secretaries retype the form for the client. Of course, the client is generally unaware of this process. As lawyers begin to specialize in a certain area of legal expertise, they compile their own files containing such blank forms.

This book provides those businesspersons who wish to form a sole proprietorship with a set of forms that have been prepared with the problems and normal legal requirements of the typical small business in mind. They are intended to be used in those situations that are clearly described by their terms. Of course, while most document use will fall within the bounds of standard business practices, some legal circumstances will present nonstandard situations. The forms in this book are designed to be readily adaptable to most usual business situations. They may be carefully altered to conform to the particular transaction that confronts your business. However, if you are faced with a complex or tangled business situation, the advice of a competent lawyer is highly recommended. If you wish, you may also create forms for certain standard situations for your company and have your lawyer check them for compliance with any local legal circumstances.

The proper and cautious use of the forms provided in this book will allow the typical company to save considerable money on legal costs over the course of the life of the business, while enabling the business to comply with legal and governmental regulations. Perhaps more importantly, these forms will provide a method by which the businessperson can avoid costly misunderstandings about what exactly was intended in a particular situation. By using the forms provided to clearly document the proceedings of everyday company operations, disputes over what was really meant can be avoided. This protection will allow the business to avoid many potential lawsuits and operate more efficiently and in compliance with the law.

CHAPTER 8
Pre-Start-up Activities

The planning stage is vital to the success of any sole proprietorship. The structure of a new sole proprietorship must be carefully tailored to the specific needs of the business. By filling out a Pre-Start-up Worksheet, potential business owners will be able to have before them all of the basic data to use in preparing the necessary sole proprietorship paperwork. The process of preparing this worksheet will also help uncover any potential problems that the business may face. Please take the time to carefully and completely fill in all of the spaces. Following the worksheet, there is a Pre-Start-up checklist that provides a clear listing of all of the required actions necessary to begin a sole proprietorship business. Follow this checklist carefully as the sole proprietorship start-up process proceeds. Unfamiliar terms relating to business are explained in the glossary of this book. As the worksheet is filled in, please refer to the following explanations:

Sole proprietorship name: The selection of a name is often crucial to the success of a sole proprietorship. The name must not conflict with any existing company names, nor must it be deceptively similar to other names. Many states require or allow the registration of the use of a fictitious sole proprietorship name. Please refer to the discussion in Chapter 10 regarding business names and check the Appendix.

Owner: This listing should provide the name, address, and phone number of the proposed owner of the sole proprietorship.

Principal place of business: This must be the address of the actual physical location of the main business. It may not be a post office box. If the sole proprietorship is home-based, this address should be the home address.

Purpose of the sole proprietorship: Here you may note the specific business purpose of the sole proprietorship. In your Sole Proprietorship Plan, you will also note that your sole proprietorship has a general purpose of engaging in any and all lawful businesses in the state in which you operate.

State/local licenses required: Here you should note any specific requirements for licenses to operate your type of business. Most states require obtaining a tax ID number and a retail, wholesale, or sales tax license. A Federal tax ID number must be obtained by all sole proprietorships that will be employing any additional persons. Additionally, certain types of businesses will require health department approvals, state board licensing, or other forms of licenses: If necessary, check with a competent local attorney for details regarding the types of licenses required for your locality and business type.

Patents/copyrights/trademarks: If patents, copyrights, or trademarks will be part of the business of the sole proprietorship, they should be noted here.

State of sole proprietorship: In general, the sole proprietorship should be begun in the state in which it will conduct business.

Proposed date to begin sole proprietorship business: This should be the date on which you expect the sole proprietorship to begin its legal existence.

Initial investment: This figure is the total amount of money that will be invested in the business by the sole owner.

Initial indebtedness: If there is to be any initial indebtedness for the sole proprietorship, please list it here.

Proposed bank for sole proprietorship bank account: In advance of conducting sole proprietorship business, you should determine the bank that will handle the sole proprietorship accounts. Obtain from the bank the necessary bank paperwork, which will be signed by the owner.

Cost of setting up sole proprietorship: This cost should reflect the cost of obtaining professional assistance (legal or accounting); the cost of procuring the necessary supplies; and any other direct costs of the sole proprietorship process.

Fiscal year and accounting type: For accounting purposes, the fiscal year and accounting type (cash or accrual) of the sole proprietorship should be chosen in advance. Please consult with a competent accounting professional.

Insurance: Under this heading, consider the types of insurance that you will need, ranging from general casualty to various business liability policies. Also consider the need for the owner of the sole proprietorship to secure life and/or disability insurance.

Pre-Start-up Worksheet

Name/address/phone of owner

Name	Address	Phone
_____	_____	_____

Proposed name of the company

First choice: _____

Alternate choices: _____

_____

Location of Business

Address of principal place of business: _____

_____

Description of principal place of business: _____

_____

_____

Ownership of principal place of business (own or lease?): _____

_____

Other places of business: _____

_____

_____

Type of Business

Purpose of company: _____

_____

State/local licenses required: _____

Patents/copyrights/trademarks: _____

State of formation: _____

Proposed date to begin company business: _____

Initial investment total: $ _____
    Date when due: _____

Initial indebtedness: $ _____

Proposed bank for company bank account: _____

Cost of setting up company: _____

Fiscal year: _____

Accounting type (cash or accrual?): _____

Insurance needs: _____

Pre-Start-up Checklist

☐ Write state office for information regarding registration of business name (see Appendix)

☐ Complete Pre-Start-up Worksheet

☐ Prepare and file Statement of Intention to Conduct Business Under an Assumed or Fictitious Name (if required-check Appendix)

☐ Prepare Sole Proprietorship Plan

☐ Check state tax, employment, licensing, unemployment, and workers' compensation requirements

☐ Open company business bank account

☐ Check insurance requirements

☐ Prepare company record book (looseleaf binder)

☐ Prepare company accounting ledgers

☐ Prepare annual financial reports (in company record book)

☐ Maintain company tax records (filed with state and Federal authorities)

CHAPTER 9

Sole Proprietorship Plan

In this chapter you will prepare your Sole Proprietorship Plan. The Sole Proprietorship Plan provides the framework for the operation of the sole proprietorship business. Although not required by any state or local law, this plan will provide you with a record of your intentions and plans for your business. It mirrors documents that are prepared by partnerships, corporations, and limited liability companies. The purpose of this plan is different from the Business Plan that you prepared in Chapters 2-4. That plan was for the purpose of presenting your business plans to others for financing or other reasons. The plan in this chapter is to provide you, the owner of the sole proprietorship, with the details of how your business will be operated. Although the preparation of this plan may seem overly formal for a simple business, it will provide you with a written plan for how to set up your business in the most beneficial manner for its success. Have your completed Pre-Start-up Worksheet from Chapter 8 before you as you prepare your plan.

This chapter contains sample clauses for preparing your Sole Proprietorship Plan. Once you have chosen which of the clauses you will use and have filled in any required information, number the clauses that you have selected consecutively, and then retype the Sole Proprietorship Plan. If you are using a computer and word-processing program, simply select those clauses from the Forms-on-CD that you wish to use in your Sole Proprietorship Plan and print out a completed plan. A completed sample Sole Proprietorship Plan is included at the end of this chapter.

Sole Proprietorship Plan Checklist

- [ ] The name and address of the sole proprietor

- [ ] The main office of the sole proprietorship

- [ ] The purpose of the sole proprietorship

- [ ] Amount of initial capital and contributions to the sole proprietorship

- [ ] Accounting matters

  - [ ] Cash or accrual accounting

  - [ ] Calendar or other accounting periods

- [ ] Bank account

- [ ] Insurance

  - [ ] Life insurance

  - [ ] Disability insurance

  - [ ] Business liability insurance

- [ ] Additional provisions

Title and Introductory Matter

This Sole Proprietorship Plan is made on _____ , 20 ___ , by _____ , of _____ , City of _____ , State of _____ .

Sole Proprietorship Name

☐. Sole Proprietorship Name. The sole proprietorship shall be known as:
This name shall be property of the sole proprietorship.

Sole Proprietorship Office

☐. Sole Proprietorship Office. The sole proprietorship's principal place of business shall be:

Purpose of the Sole Proprietorship

☐. Purpose of the Sole Proprietorship. The purpose of this sole proprietorship is to:

In addition, the sole proprietorship may also engage in any lawful business under the laws of the State of _____ .

Start-up Capital

☐. Start-up Capital. The start-up capital will be a total of $ _____ .
The owner of the company agrees to dedicate the following property, services, or cash to the use of the company:

Property	Services	Cash

Accounting Matters

☐. Accounting Matters. The company will maintain accounting records on the (cash or accrual) basis and on a calendar year basis.

Bank Account

☐. Bank Account. The business will maintain a business checking bank account at:

Insurance

Choose any of the following:

☐. Insurance. The owner shall buy and maintain life insurance on his or her life in the amount of $ _____ .

☐. Insurance. The owner shall buy and maintain disability insurance in the amount of $ _____ .

Or:

☐. Insurance. The owner shall buy and maintain business liability insurance on the operations of the business in the amount of $ _____ .

Additional Provisions

☐. Additional Provisions. The following additional provisions are part of this Plan:

Signature Clause

Dated _____

_____
Owner Signature

_____
Printed Name of Owner

Sample Sole Proprietorship Plan

This Sole Proprietorship Plan is made on June 10, 2006, by Mary Celeste, of 123 Main Street, Centerville, Superior.

1. Business Office. The sole proprietorship's principal place of business shall be: 789 Dock Street, Douglas, Superior.

2. Purpose of Sole Proprietorship. The purpose of this sole proprietorship is to: engage in the business of operating a school of seamanship and yacht handling. In addition, the sole proprietorship may also engage in any lawful business under the laws of the State of Superior.

3. Start-up Capital. The start-up capital will be a total of $20,000.00. The owner of the sole proprietorship agrees to dedicate the following property or cash to this total amount:

Cash/property	Value
Cash	$10,000.00

4. Accounting Matters. The sole proprietorship will maintain accounting records that will be on the accrual basis and on a calendar year basis.

5. Bank Account. The sole proprietorship will maintain a business checking bank account at:

6. Insurance. The owner shall buy and maintain life insurance on his or her life in the amount of $50,000.00. The beneficiary shall be Andrea Doria. The owner shall buy and maintain disability insurance in the amount of $20,000.00. The beneficiary shall be Andrea Doria. The owner shall buy and maintain business liability insurance on the operations of the business in the amount of $100,000.

7. Additional Provisions. The following additional provisions are part of this Plan: None.

Dated June 10, 2006

Mary Celeste
Owner Signature

Mary Celeste
Printed Name of Owner

CHAPTER 10
Registration of Sole Proprietorship Name

The choice of a name for a business is an important aspect in the success of the business. Many business owners choose business names that contain their own names, for example: Mary and Bill's Restaurant or Smith and Jones Furniture Refinishing Company. As long as the owners' own names are the main designation of the business name, no registration of the name is generally required. If, however, the owner of a sole proprietorship chooses a name that is fictitious, many states require some type of registration of the assumed name. Examples of fictitious names might be The Landing Restaurant or Imperial Furniture Refinishing Company: names that do not identify the owners of the businesses. The main rationale for such fictitious name registration is to provide a public record of who owns businesses; owners that cannot be identified solely by the business name. This allows for a central registry of some kind, should a third party need to file a lawsuit or claim of some kind against the unidentified owner.

Some states do not require registration but simply allow business owners to register their business names as a method to prevent infringement of others upon the use of a particular name, in the manner of registering the trademark or tradename of a business. The Appendix of this book provides a listing of each state's business name registration requirements. Note that some states require registration with state authorities, often the Secretary of State, while other states provide for registration in the county in which the business intends to do business.

In all states, there are either statutory rules or judge-decided case law that prevent a business from adopting a name that is deceptive to the public. Thus, for example, a business cannot imply that it is owned or operated by a licensed practitioner in a state-regulated profession if such is not, in fact, the case. Nor may a business adopt a name that is deceptively similar to the name of another business. In many states, there is a method by which to check a registry of business names that are in use. This allows potential conflicts with other business names to be resolved prior to the adoption of a name. In addition, some states provide for the reservation of a business name even before the actual operation of the business has commenced.

Finally, some states require the publication of a statement in local newspapers that provides a notice to the public that a certain business will be operating in a community under an assumed or fictitious name. This allows the public to be notified of the names and addresses of the actual owners of the business. Please carefully check the listing for your state in the Appendix for the requirements that you will need to follow in the registration of your business name. Following is a standard form for registering a business name. Although this form should suffice in most locales, your own state or local authorities may proscribe a mandatory form for such registration. Please check with your particular registration authorities.

Statement of Intention to Conduct Business Under an Assumed or Fictitious Name

The undersigned party does hereby state his/her intention to carry on the business of _____ , at the business location of _____ , in the City of _____ , in the State of _____ , under the assumed or fictitious name of:

_____

The owner's name, home address, and percentage of ownership of the above-named business are as follows:

Name	*Address*	*Percentage of Ownership*
_____	_____	100 percent

Signed on _____ , 20 _____

_____
Business Owner Signature

_____
Business Owner Printed Name

CHAPTER 11

Employee Documents

The legal forms in this chapter cover a variety of situations that arise in the area of employment. From hiring an employee to subcontracting work on a job, written documents that outline each person's responsibilities and duties are important for keeping an employment situation on an even keel. The employment contract contained in this chapter may be used and adapted for virtually any employment situation. Of course, it is perfectly legal to hire an employee without a contract at all. In many businesses, this is common practice. However, as job skills and salaries rise and employees are allowed access to sensitive and confidential business information, written employment contracts are often a prudent business practice. An independent contractor may also be hired to perform a particular task. As opposed to an employee, this type of worker is defined as one who maintains his or her own independent business, uses his or her own tools, and does not work under the direct supervision of the person who has hired him or her. A contract for hiring an independent contractor is provided in this chapter.

General Employment Contract: This form may be used for any situation in which an employee is hired for a specific job. The issues addressed by this contract are as follows:

- That the employee will perform a certain job and any incidental further duties
- That the employee will be hired for a certain period and for a certain salary
- That the employee will be given certain job benefits (for example: sick pay, vacations, etc.)
- That the employee agrees to abide by the employer's rules and regulations
- That the employee agrees to sign agreements regarding confidentiality and inventions
- That the employee agrees to submit any employment disputes to mediation and arbitration

The information necessary to complete this form is as follows:

- The names and addresses of the employer and employee
- A complete description of the job
- The date the job is to begin and the length of time that the job will last
- The amount of compensation and benefits for the employee (salary, sick pay, vacation, bonuses, and retirement and insurance benefits)
- Any additional documents to be signed

- Any additional terms
- The state whose laws will govern the contract
- Signatures of employer and employee

Independent Contractor Agreement: This form should be used when hiring an independent contractor. It provides a standard form for the hiring out of specific work to be performed within a set time period for a particular payment. It also provides a method for authorizing extra work under the contract. Finally, this document provides that the contractor agrees to *indemnify* (reimburse or compensate) the owner against any claims or liabilities arising from the performance of the work. To complete this form, fill in a detailed description of the work; dates by which certain portions of the job are to be completed; the pay for the job; the terms and dates of payment; and the state whose laws will govern the contract.

Contractor/Subcontractor Agreement: This form is intended to be used by an independent contractor to hire a subcontractor to perform certain work on a job that the contractor has agreed to perform. It provides for the "farming out" of specific work to be performed by the subcontractor within a set time period for a particular payment. It also provides a method for authorizing extra work under the contract. Finally, this document provides that the subcontractor agrees to indemnify the contractor against any claims or liabilities arising from the performance of the work. To complete this form, fill in a detailed description of the work; dates by which portions of the job are to be completed; the pay for the job; the terms and dates of payment; and the state whose laws will govern the contract.

General Employment Contract

This contract is made on _____ , 20 _____ , between
_____ , employer, of
_____ , City of _____ ,
State of _____ , and _____ ,
employee, of _____ , City of _____
_____ , State of _____ .

For valuable consideration, the employer and employee agree as follows:

1. The employee agrees to perform the following duties and job description:

   The employee also agrees to perform further duties incidental to the general job description. This is considered a full-time position.

2. The employee will begin work on _____ , 20 _____ . This position shall continue for a period of _____ .

3. The employee will be paid the following:

   Weekly salary: $ _____

   The employee will also be given the following benefits:

   Sick pay: $ _____
   Vacations: $ _____
   Bonuses: $ _____
   Retirement benefits: $ _____
   Insurance benefits: $ _____

4. The employee agrees to abide by all rules and regulations of the employer at all times while employed.

5. This contract may be terminated by:

   (a) Breach of this contract by the employee
   (b) The expiration of this contract without renewal
   (c) Death of the employee
   (d) Incapacitation of the employee for over _____ days in any one (1) year

6. The employee agrees to sign the following additional documents as a condition to obtaining employment:

7. Any dispute between the employer and employee related to this contract will be settled by voluntary mediation. If mediation is unsuccessful, the dispute will be settled by binding arbitration using an arbitrator of the American Arbitration Association.

8. Any additional terms of this contract:

9. No modification of this contract will be effective unless it is in writing and is signed by both the employer and employee. This contract binds and benefits both parties and any successors. Time is of the essence of this contract. This document is the entire agreement between the parties. This contract is governed by the laws of the State of
_____ .

Dated: _____ , 20 _____

_____
Signature of Employer

_____
Printed Name of Employer

_____
Signature of Employee

_____
Printed Name of Employee

Independent Contractor Agreement

This agreement is made on _____ , 20 _____ , between
_____ , owner, of
_____ , City of _____ ,
State of _____ , and _____ ,
contractor, of _____ , City of
_____ , State of _____ .

For valuable consideration, the owner and contractor agree as follows:

1. The contractor agrees to furnish all of the labor and materials to do the following work for the owner as an independent contractor:

2. The contractor agrees that the following portions of the total work will be completed by the dates specified:

   Work:

   Dates: _____

3. The contractor agrees to perform this work in a workmanlike manner according to standard practices. If any plans or specifications are part of this job, they are attached to and are part of this agreement.

4. The owner agrees to pay the contractor as full payment $ _____ , for doing the work outlined above. This price will be paid to the contractor on satisfactory completion of the work in the following manner and on the following dates:

   Work:

   Dates: _____

5. The contractor and the owner may agree to extra services and work, but any such extras must be set out and agreed to in writing by both the contractor and the owner.

6. The contractor agrees to indemnify and hold the owner harmless from any claims or liability arising from the contractor's work under this agreement.

7. No modification of this agreement will be effective unless it is in writing and is signed by both parties. This agreement binds and benefits both parties and any successors. Time is of the essence of this agreement. This document, including any attachments, is the entire agreement between the parties. This agreement is governed by the laws of the State of _____ .

Dated: _____ , 20 _____

_____
Signature of Owner

_____
Printed Name of Owner

_____
Signature of Contractor

_____
Printed Name of Contractor

Contractor/Subcontractor Agreement

This agreement is made on _____ , 20 _____ , between
_____ , contractor, of
_____ , City of _____ ,
State of _____ , and _____ ,
subcontractor, of _____ , City of
_____ , State of _____ .

1. The subcontractor, as an independent contractor, agrees to furnish all of the labor and materials to do the following portions of the work specified in the agreement between the contractor and the owner dated _____ , 20 _____ .

2. The subcontractor agrees that the following portions of the total work will be completed by the dates specified:

   Work:

   Dates: _____

3. The subcontractor agrees to perform this work in a workmanlike manner according to standard practices. If any plans or specifications are part of this job, they are attached to and are part of this agreement.

4. The contractor agrees to pay the subcontractor as full payment $ _____ , for doing the work outlined above. This price will be paid to the subcontractor on satisfactory completion of the work in the following manner and on the following dates:

   Work:

   Dates: _____

5. The contractor and subcontractor may agree to extra services and work, but any such extras must be set out and agreed to in writing by both the contractor and the subcontractor.

6. The subcontractor agrees to indemnify and hold the contractor harmless from any claims or liability arising from the subcontractor's work under this agreement.

7. No modification of this agreement will be effective unless it is in writing and is signed by both parties. This agreement binds and benefits both parties and any successors. Time is of the essence of this agreement. This document, including any attachments, is the entire agreement between the parties. This agreement is governed by the laws of the State of _____ .

Dated: _____ , 20 _____

_____
Signature of Contractor

_____
Printed Name of Contractor

_____
Signature of Subcontractor

_____
Printed Name of Subcontractor

CHAPTER 12

Business Financial Recordkeeping

Each year, thousands of small businesses fail because their owners have lost control of their finances. Many of these failures are brought on by the inability of the business owners to understand the complex accounting processes and systems that have become relatively standard in modern business. Accounting and bookkeeping have, in most businesses, been removed from the direct control and, therefore, understanding of the business owners themselves. If business owners cannot understand the financial situation of their own businesses, they have little chance of succeeding.

Keeping accurate and clear business financial records can, for many business owners, be the most difficult part of running a business. For most business owners, understanding those records is, at best, a struggle. And yet maintaining a set of clear and understandable financial records is perhaps the single most important factor that separates successful businesses from those that fail. The purpose of the next few chapters is to provide the small business owner with a clear understanding of how to develop a concise and easily-understood financial recordkeeping system, keep the books for a business, and, perhaps most importantly, actually understand those records.

Modern business practices have tended to complicate many areas of business when, in many cases, simplification is what most business owners need. In law, in management, and in accounting, many important business functions have been obscured from their owners by intricate systems and complex terminology. Business owners must then turn the handling of these affairs over to specialized professionals in a particular field. The result, in many cases, is that business owners lose crucial understanding of those portions of their business. With this loss of understanding comes the eventual and almost inevitable loss of control.

This is particularly true for small business owners and their financial records. It is absolutely vital that emerging small business owners intimately understand their financial position. Daily decisions must be made that can make or break a fledgling business. If the financial records of a small business are delegated to an outside accountant or bookkeeper, it is often difficult, if not impossible, for a novice business owner to understand the current financial position of the business on a day-to-day basis. Critical business decisions are then made on the basis of incomplete or often unknown financial information.

The basic aspects of the accounting outlined in this book have been used successfully by millions of businesses in the past. The system presented in this book is designed to be set up and initially used by the business owners themselves. This will insure that the system is both thoroughly understood by the owner and provides the type of information that the owner actually wants. As a business grows and becomes more complex, and a business owner becomes more comfortable with financial recordkeeping, other more sophisticated and complex accounting systems may become appropriate. There are numerous computer-based accounting programs on the market, such as QuickBooks, that can provide the framework for a company accounting system. However, in order to understand and use any of the computer accounting systems, it is necessary to first have an understanding of the basics of financial recordkeeping.

Understanding Financial Records

The purpose of any business financial recordkeeping system is to provide a clear vision of the relative health of the business, both on a day-to-day basis and periodically. Business owners themselves need to know whether they are making a profit, why they are making a profit, which parts of the business are profitable, and which are not. This information is only available if the business owner has a clear and straight-forward recordkeeping system. Business owners also need to be able to produce accurate financial statements for income tax purposes, for loan proposals, and for the purpose of selling the business. Clear, understandable, and accurate business records are vital to the success of any small business. In order to design a good recordkeeping system for a particular business, an understanding of certain fundamental ideas of accounting is necessary. For those unfamiliar with the terms and concepts of accounting, grasping these basic ideas may be the most difficult part of accounting, even simplified accounting.

First, let's get some of the terminology clarified. *Accounting* is the design of the recordkeeping system that a business uses and the preparation and interpretation of reports based on the information that is gathered and put into the system. *Bookkeeping* is the actual inputting of the financial information into the recordkeeping system. The purpose of any business recordkeeping system is to allow the business owner to easily understand and use the information gathered. Certain accounting principles and terms have been adopted as standard over the years to make it easier to understand a wide range of business transactions. In order to understand what a recordkeeping system is trying to accomplish, it is necessary to define some of the standard ways of looking at a business. There are two standard reports that are the main sources of business financial information: the *balance sheet* and the *profit-and-loss statement*.

The Balance Sheet

The purpose of the balance sheet is to look at what the business owns and owes on a specific date. By seeing what a business owns and owes, anyone looking at a balance sheet can tell the relative financial position of the business at that point in time. If the business owns more than it owes, it is in good shape financially. On the other hand, if it owes more than it owns, the business may be in trouble. The balance sheet is the universal financial document used to view this aspect of a business. It provides this information by laying out the value of the assets and the liabilities of a business. One of the most critical financial tasks that a small business owner must confront is keeping track of what the business owns and owes. Before the business buys or sells anything or makes a profit or loss, the business must have some assets.

The *assets* of a business are anything that the business owns. These can be cash on hand or in a bank account; personal property, like office equipment, vehicles, tools, or supplies; inventory, or material that will be sold to customers; real estate, buildings, and land; and money that is owed to the business. Money that is owed to a business is called its *accounts receivable*, basically the money that the business hopes to eventually receive. The total of all of these things that a business owns are the business's assets.

The *liabilities* of a business are anything that the business owes to others. These consist of long-term debts, such as a mortgage on real estate or a long-term loan. Liabilities also consist of any short-term debts, such as money owed for supplies or taxes. Money that a business owes to others is called its *accounts payable*, basically the money that the business hopes to eventually pay. In addition to money owed to others, the *equity* of a business is also considered a liability. The equity of a business is the value of the ownership of the business. It is the value that would be left over if all of the debts of the business were paid off. If the business is a partnership or a sole proprietorship, the business equity is referred to as the *net worth* of the business. If the business is a corporation, the owner's equity is called the *capital surplus* or *retained capital*. All of the debts of a business and its equity are together referred to as the business's liabilities.

The basic relationship between assets and liabilities is shown in a simple equation:

Assets = Liabilities

This simple equation is the basis of business accounting. When the books of a business are said to *balance*, it is this equation that is in balance: the assets of a business must equal the liabilities of a business. Since the liabilities of a business consist of both equity and debts, the equation can be expanded to read:

Assets = Debts + Equity

Rearranging the equation can provide a simple explanation of how to arrive at the value of a business to the owner, or its equity:

$$Equity = Assets - Debts$$

A basic tenet of recordkeeping is that both sides of this financial equation must always be equal. The formal statement of the assets and liabilities of a specific business on a specific date is called a *balance sheet*. A balance sheet is usually prepared on the last day of a month, quarter, or year. A balance sheet simply lists the amounts of the business's assets and liabilities in a standardized format.

On a balance sheet, the assets of a business are generally broken down into two groups: *current assets* and *fixed assets*. Current assets consist of cash, accounts receivable (remember, money that the business intends to receive; basically, bills owed to the business), and inventory. Current assets are generally considered anything that could be converted into cash within one year. Fixed assets are more permanent-type assets and include vehicles, equipment, machinery, land, and buildings owned by the business.

The liabilities of a business are broken down into three groups: *current liabilities, long-term liabilities*, and *owner's equity*. Current liabilities are short-term debts, generally those that a business must pay off within one year. This includes accounts payable (remember, money that the business intends to pay; basically, bills the business owes), and taxes that are due. Long-term liabilities are long-term debts such as mortgages or long-term business loans. Owner's equity is whatever is left after debts are deducted from assets. Thus, the owner's equity is what the owner would have left after all of the debts of the business were paid off. Owner's equity is the figure that is adjusted to make the equation of assets and liabilities balance.

Let's look at a simple example: a basic sales business.

Smith's Gourmet Foods has the following assets: Smith has $500.00 in a bank account, is owed $70.00 by customers who pay for their food monthly, has $200.00 worth of food supplies, and owns food preparation equipment worth $1,300.00.

These are the assets of Smith's Gourmet Foods and they are shown on a balance sheet as follows:

Cash	$	500.00
+ Accounts owed to it	$	70.00
+ Inventory	$	200.00
+ Equipment	$	1,300.00
= Total assets	$	2,070.00

Smith also has the following debts: $100.00 owed to the supplier of the food, $200.00 owed to the person from whom she bought the food equipment, and $100.00 owed to the state for sales taxes that have been collected on food sales. Thus, the debts of Smith's Gourmet Foods are shown as follows:

	Accounts it owes	$	100.00
+	Loans it owes	$	200.00
+	Taxes it owes	$	100.00
=	Total debts	$	400.00

To find what Smith's equity in this business is, we need to subtract the amount of the debts from the amount of the assets. Remember: assets – debts = equity. Thus, the owner's equity in Smith's Gourmet Foods is as follows:

	Total assets	$ 2,070.00
–	Total debts	$ 400.00
=	Owner's equity	$ 1,670.00

That's it. The business of Smith's Gourmet Foods has a net worth of $1,670.00. If Smith paid off all of the debts of the business, there would be $1,670.00 left. This basic method is used to determine the net worth of businesses worldwide, from the smallest to the largest: assets = debts + equity, or assets – debts = equity. Remember, both sides of the equation always have to be equal.

The Profit and Loss Statement

The other main business report is the *profit and loss statement*. This report is a summary of the income and expenses of the business during a certain period. Profit and loss statements are sometimes referred to as *income statements* or *operating statements*. You may choose to prepare a profit and loss statement monthly, quarterly, or annually, depending on your particular needs. You will, at a minimum, need to have an annual profit and loss statement in order to streamline your tax return preparation.

A profit and loss statement, however, provides much more than assistance in easing your tax preparation burdens. It allows you to clearly view the performance of your business over a particular time period. As you begin to collect a series of profit and loss statements, you will be able to conduct various analyses of your business. For example, you will be able to compare monthly performances over a single year to determine which month was the best or worst for your business. Quarterly results will also be able to be contrasted. The comparison of several annual expense and revenue figures will allow you to judge the growth or shrinkage of your business over time. Numerous other comparisons are possible, depending on your particular business. How have sales been influenced by advertising expenses? Are production costs higher this quarter than last? Do seasons have an impact on sales? Are certain expenses becoming a burden on the business? The profit and loss statement is one of the key financial statements for the analysis of your business.

Generally, *income* for a business is any money that it has received or will receive during a certain period. *Expenses* are any money that it has paid or will pay out during a certain period. Simply put, if the business has more income than expenses during a certain period, it has made a profit. If it has more expenses than income, then the business has a loss for that period of time.

Income can be broken down into two basic types: service income and sales income. The difference between the two types of income lies in the need to consider inventory costs. *Service income* is income derived from performing a service for someone (cutting hair, for example). *Sales income* is revenue derived from selling a product of some type. With service income, the profit can be determined simply by deducting the expenses that are associated with making the income. With sales income, however, in addition to deducting the expenses of making the income, the cost of the product that was sold must also be taken into account. This is done through inventory costs. Thus, for sales income, the income from selling a product is actually the sales income minus the cost of the product to the seller. This inventory cost is referred to as the *cost of goods sold*.

A profit and loss statement begins with a sale. Back to the food business as an example: Smith had the following transactions during the month of July: $250.00 worth of food was sold, the wholesale cost of the food that was sold was $50.00, the cost of napkins, condiments, other supplies, and rent amounted to $100.00, and interest payments on the equipment loan were $50.00. Thus, Smith's profit and loss statement would be prepared as follows:

Gross sales income	$ 250.00
− Cost of food	$ 50.00
= Net sales income	$ 200.00
Operating expenses	$ 100.00
+ Interest payments	$ 50.00
= Net expenses	$ 150.00

Thus, for the month of July, Smith's business performed as follows:

Net sales income	$ 200.00
− Net expenses	$ 150.00
= Net profit	$ 50.00

Again, this simple setup reflects the basics of profit and loss statements for all types of businesses, no matter what their size. For a pure service business, with no inventory of any type sold to customers: income – expenses = net profit. For a sales-type business or a sales/service combined business: income – cost of goods sold – expenses = profit.

These two types of summary reports—the balance sheet and the profit and loss statement—are the basic tools for understanding the financial health of any business. The figures on them can be used for many purposes to understand the operations of a business. The balance sheet shows what proportion of a business's assets are actually owned by the business owner and what proportion is owned or owed to someone else.

Looking at Smith's balance sheet, we can see that the owner's equity is $1,670.00 of assets of $2,070.00. Thus, we can see that the owner has more than 80 percent ownership of the business, a very healthy situation. There are numerous ways to analyze the figures on these two financial statements. Understanding what these figures mean and how they represent the health of a business are keys to keeping control of the finances of any business.

Accounting Methods

There are a few more items that must be understood regarding financial recordkeeping. First is the method for recording the records. There are two basic methods for measuring transactions: the *cash method* and the *accrual method*. Cash-method accounting is a system into which income is recorded when it is received and expenses are recorded when they are paid. With cash accounting, there is no effective method to accurately reflect inventory costs. Thus, Internal Revenue Service regulations require that the cash method of accounting may only be used by those few businesses that are solely service businesses and do not sell any materials to their customers at all, even a few spare parts. If a business sells any type of product or material whatsoever, it must use the accrual method of accounting. (An exception to this general rule is allowed for any corporation or partnership with annual gross receipts of under $5 million.)

The accrual method of accounting counts income and expenses when they are due to the business. Income is recorded when the business has a right to receive the income. In other words, accounts receivable (bills owed to the business) are considered as income that has already been received by the business. Expenses are considered and recorded when they are due, even if they are not yet paid. In other words, accounts payable (bills owed by the business) are considered expenses to the business when they are received, not when they are actually paid. The vast majority of businesses will wish to use the accrual method of accounting. A business must choose to keep its records either on the accrual basis or on the cash basis. Once this decision is made, approval from the IRS must be obtained before the method can be changed. After you select the type of accounting you will use, please consult a tax professional if a change in the system must be made.

Accounting Systems

In addition, there are two basic types of recordkeeping systems: *single-entry* and *double-entry*. Both types are able to be used to keep accurate records, although the double-entry system has more ways available to double-check calculations. Double-entry recordkeeping is, however, much more difficult to master, in that each and every transaction must be entered in two separate places in the records. The system that is used in this book is a modified form of single-entry accounting. The benefits of ease of use of a single-entry system far outweigh the disadvantages of this system. The IRS recommends single-entry records for beginning small businesses, and states that this type of system can be "relatively simple...used effectively...and is adequate for income tax purposes." Many accountants will disagree with this and insist that only double-entry accounting is acceptable. For the small business owner who wishes to understand his or her own company's finances, the advantages of single-entry accounting far outweigh the disadvantages.

Accounting Periods

A final item to consider is the accounting period for your business. A business is allowed to choose between a *fiscal-year* accounting period and a *calendar-year* period. A fiscal year consists of 12 consecutive months that do not end on December 31st. A calendar year consists of 12 consecutive months that do end on December 31st. There are complex rules relating to the choice of fiscal-year accounting. Partnerships and S-corporations may generally choose to report on a fiscal-year basis only if there is a valid business purpose that supports the use of a fiscal year. This generally complicates the reporting of income and should be avoided unless there is an important reason to choose a fiscal-year accounting period. If a fiscal-year period is considered necessary, please consult a tax or accounting professional as there are complicated rules to comply with.

For the majority of small businesses, the choice of a calendar-year period is perfectly adequate and, in most cases, will simplify the tax reporting and accounting recordkeeping. In the year in which a business is either started or ended, the business year for reporting may not be a full year. Thus, even for those who choose to use a calendar year, the first year may actually start on a date other than January 1st.

The simplified small business accounting system that is explained in this book is a modified single-entry accounting system. It is presented as a system for accrual-basis accounting for small businesses. The records are designed to be used on a calendar-year basis. Within these basic parameters, the system can be individually tailored to meet the needs of most small businesses.

The backbone of the recordkeeping system is the Chart of Accounts for your business. A chart of accounts will list each of the income, expense, asset, or debt categories that you wish to keep track of. Every business transaction that you make and every financial record that you create will fit into one of these four main categories. Your transactions will either be money coming in (income) or money going out (expenses). Your records will also track things the business owns (assets) or things the business owes (debts). The chart of accounts that you create in the next chapter will allow you to itemize and track each of these four broad categories in detail.

Following is a checklist for setting up your business financial recordkeeping using this book:

Financial Recordkeeping Checklist

- ☐ Set up your business chart of accounts

- ☐ Open a business checking account

- ☐ Prepare a check register

- ☐ Set up a business petty cash fund

- ☐ Prepare a petty cash register

- ☐ Set up asset accounts

- ☐ Prepare current asset account records

- ☐ Prepare fixed asset account records

- ☐ Set up expense account records

- ☐ Set up income account records

- ☐ Set up a payroll system

- ☐ Prepare payroll time sheets

- ☐ Prepare payroll depository records

- ☐ Determine proper tax forms for use in business

CHAPTER 13

Business Accounts

The financial recordkeeping system that you will set up using this book is designed to be adaptable to any type of business. Whether your business is a service business, a manufacturing business, a retail business, a wholesale distributorship, or a combination of any of these, you will be able to easily adapt this simplified system to work with your particular situation. A key to designing the most useful recordkeeping system for your particular needs is to examine your type of business in depth. After a close examination of the particular needs and operations of your type of business, you will need to set up an array of specific accounts to handle your financial records. This set of general accounts is called a Chart of Accounts.

A Chart of Accounts will list all of the various categories of financial transactions that you will need to track. There will be an account for each general type of expense that you want to keep track of. You will also have a separate account for each type of income your business will receive. Accounts will also be set up for your business assets and liabilities. Setting up an account for each of these categories consists of the simple task of deciding which items you will need to categorize, selecting a name for the account, and assigning a number to the account.

Before you can set up your accounts, you need to understand the reason for setting up these separate accounts. It is possible, although definitely not recommended, to run a business and merely keep track of your income and expenses without any itemization at all. However, you would be unable to analyze how the business is performing beyond a simple check to see if you have any money left after paying the expenses. You would also be unable to properly fill in the necessary information for business income tax returns. A major reason for setting up separate accounts for many business expense and income transactions is to separate and itemize the amounts spent in each category so that this information is available at tax time. This insures that a business is taking all of its allowable business deductions. The main reason, however, to set up individual accounts is to allow the business owner to have a clear view of the financial health of the business. With separate accounts for each type of transaction, a business owner can analyze the proportional costs and revenues of each aspect of the business. Is advertising costing more than labor expenses? Is the income derived from sale items worth the discount of the sale? Only by using the figures obtained from separate itemized accounts can these questions be answered.

In the following sections, you will select and number the various accounts for use in your business Chart of Accounts. You will select various income accounts, expense accounts, asset accounts, and liability accounts. You will also assign a number to each account. For ease of use, you should assign a particular number value to all accounts of one type. For example, all income accounts may be assigned #10 to 29. Sales income may be Account #11; service income may be Account #12, interest income may be Account #13. Similarly, expenses may be assigned #30 to 79. Balance Sheet accounts for assets and liabilities may be #80 to 99. Be sure to leave enough numbers for future expansion of your list of accounts. There will normally be far more expense accounts than any other type of account.

If you have income or expenses from many sources, you may wish to use a three-digit number to identify each separate category. For example, if your business consists of renting out residential houses and you have 10 properties, you may wish to set up a separate income and expense account for each property. You may wish to assign Accounts #110 to 119 to income from all properties. Thus, for example, you could then assign rental income from Property #1 to Account #111, rental income from Property #2 to Account #112, rental income from Property #3 to Account #113, and so on. Similarly, expenses can be broken down into separate accounts for individual properties. All advertising expenses could be Accounts #510 to 519; thus, advertising expenses for Property #1 could then be assigned Account #511, advertising expenses for Property #2 would be assigned Account #512, etc.

How your individual Chart of Accounts will be organized will be specific to your particular business. If you have a simple business with all income coming from one source, you will probably desire a two-digit number from, for example, 10 to 29, assigned to that income account. On the other hand, a more complex business with many sources of income and many different types of expenses may wish to use a system of three-digit numbers. Take some time to analyze your specific business to decide how you wish to set up your accounts. Ask yourself what type of information you will want to extract from your financial records. Do you need more details of your income sources? Then you should set up several income accounts for each type and possibly even each source of your income. Would you like more specific information on your expenses? Then you would most likely wish to set up clear and detailed expense accounts for each type of expense that you must pay.

Be aware that you may wish to alter your Chart of Accounts as your business grows. You may find that you have set up too many accounts and unnecessarily complicated your recordkeeping tasks. You might wish to set up more accounts once you see how your Balance Sheets and Profit and Loss Statements look. You can change, add, or delete accounts at any time. Remember, however, that any transactions that have been recorded in an account must be transferred to any new account or accounts that take the place of the old account.

Income Accounts

These are accounts that are used to track the various sources of your company's income. There may be only a few sources of income for your business or you may wish to track your income in more detail. The information which you collect in your income accounts will be used to prepare your Profit and Loss Statements periodically. Recall that a Profit and Loss Statement is also referred to as an Income and Expense Statement.

On the Chart of Accounts that is used in this book, income is separated into several categories. You can choose the income account categories which best suit your type of business. If your business is a service business, you may wish to set up accounts for labor income and for materials income. Or you may wish to set up income accounts in more detail, for example: sales income, markup income, income from separate properties, or income from separate sources in your business, etc. Nonsales income, such as bank account interest income or income on the sale of business equipment, should be placed in separate individual income accounts. You may also wish to set up separate income accounts for income from different ongoing projects or income from separate portions of your business.

Following is a list of various general income accounts. Decide how much detail you will want in your financial records regarding income and then choose the appropriate accounts. You may wish to name and create different accounts than are listed here. After you have chosen your income accounts, assign a number to each account.

Income Chart of Accounts

Account #	Account Name and Description
	Income from sale of goods
	Income from services
	Income from labor charges
	Income from sales discounts
	Income from interest revenue
	Income from consulting
	Miscellaneous income

Expense Accounts

These are the accounts that you will use to keep track of your expenses. Each separate category of expense should have its own account. Many of the types of accounts are dictated by the types of expenses which should be itemized for tax purposes. You will generally have separate accounts for advertising costs, utility expenses, rent, phone costs, etc. One or more separate accounts should also be set up to keep track of inventory expenses. These should be kept separate from other expense accounts as they must be itemized for tax purposes.

Following is a list of various general expense accounts. Please analyze your business and determine which accounts would be best suited to select for your particular situation. You will then number these accounts, as you did the income accounts. The categories presented are general categories that match most Internal Revenue Service tax forms. You may, of course, set up separate accounts that are not listed to suit your particular needs. Try not to set up too many accounts or you will have a hard time trying to remember all of them. Also note that you may add or delete accounts as you need them. If you delete an account, however, you must shift any transactions that you have recorded in that account to a new account.

Expense Chart of Accounts

Account #	Account Name and Description
	Advertising expenses
	Auto expenses
	Cleaning and maintenance expenses
	Charitable contributions
	Dues and publications
	Office equipment expenses
	Freight and shipping expenses
	Business insurance expenses
	Business interest expenses
	Legal expenses
	Business meals and lodging
	Miscellaneous expenses
	Postage expenses
	Office rent expenses
	Repair expenses
	Office supplies
	Sales taxes paid
	Federal unemployment taxes paid
	State unemployment taxes paid
	Telephone expenses
	Utility expenses
	Wages and commissions

Asset and Liability Accounts

Asset and liability accounts are collectively referred to as *Balance Sheet Chart of Accounts*. This is because the information collected on them is used to prepare your business Balance Sheets. You will set up current and fixed asset accounts and current and long-term liability accounts. Types of current asset accounts are cash, short-term notes receivable, accounts receivable, inventory, and prepaid expenses. Fixed assets may include equipment, vehicles, buildings, land, long-term notes receivable, and long-term loans receivable.

Types of current liability accounts are *short-term notes payable* (money due within one year), *short-term loans payable* (money due on a loan within one year), unpaid taxes, and unpaid wages. Long-term liability accounts may be *long-term notes payable* (money due more than one year in the future) or *long-term loans payable* (money due on a loan more than one year in the future). Finally, you will need an owner's equity account to tally the ownership value of your business.

Choose the asset and liability accounts that best suit your business and assign appropriate numbers to each account.

Balance Sheet Chart of Accounts

Account #	Account Name and Description
	Accounts receivable (current asset)
	Bank checking account (current asset)
	Bank savings account (current asset)
	Cash on hand (current asset)
	Notes receivable (current asset, if short-term)
	Loans receivable (current asset, if short-term)
	Inventory (current asset)
	Land (fixed asset)
	Buildings (fixed asset)
	Vehicles (fixed asset)
	Equipment (fixed asset)
	Machinery (fixed asset)
	Accounts payable (current debt)
	Notes payable (current, if due within 1 year)
	Loans payable (current, if due within 1 year)
	Notes payable (long-term debt, if over 1 year)
	Loans payable (long-term debt, if over 1 year)
	Mortgage payable (long-term debt, if over 1 year)
	Retained capital

Chart of Accounts

After you have selected and numbered each of your accounts, you should prepare your Chart of Accounts. Simply type the number and name of each account in a numerical list. You will refer to this chart often as you prepare your financial records. Following is a sample completed Chart of Accounts. This sample chart is set up to reflect the business operations of our sample company, Smith's Gourmet Foods. This is a company that prepares and packages food products and delivers the products directly to consumers in their homes. The chart reflects that the income will primarily come from one source: direct customer payments for the products that are sold. The expense accounts are chosen to cover most of the standard types of business expenses that a small business will encounter. The Balance Sheet accounts reflect that the business will have as assets only a bank account, some accounts receivable, inventory, and some equipment. The only liabilities that this business will have, at least initially, will be a loan for equipment and accounts payable. Although this sample Chart of Accounts is fairly brief, it covers all of the basic accounts that the business will need as it begins. There is sufficient room in the numbering system chosen to add additional accounts as the business expands.

Sample Chart of Accounts

Account #	Account Name and Description
11	Income from sale of goods
12	Miscellaneous income
31	Advertising expenses
32	Auto expenses
33	Cleaning and maintenance expenses
34	Office equipment expenses
35	Business insurance expenses
36	Business meals and lodging
37	Miscellaneous expenses
38	Postage expenses
39	Repair expenses
40	Office supplies
41	Sales taxes paid
42	Telephone expenses
43	Office rent expense
51	Cash on hand (current asset)
52	Accounts receivable (current asset)
53	Bank checking account (current asset)
54	Inventory (current asset)
61	Equipment (fixed asset)
71	Accounts payable (current debt)
81	Loans payable (long-term debt)
91	Retained capital

Tracking Business Assets

After setting up a Chart of Accounts the next financial recordkeeping task for a business will consist of preparing a method to keep track of the assets of the business. Recall that the assets of a business are everything that is owned by the business and are either current assets that can be converted to cash within a year or fixed assets that are more long-term in nature. Each of these two main categories of assets will be discussed separately.

Current Assets

Following is a list of typical current assets for a business:

- Business bank checking account
- Business bank savings account
- Cash (petty cash fund and cash on hand)
- Accounts receivable (money owed to the company)
- Inventory

A company may have other types of current assets such as notes or loans receivable, but the five listed above are the basic ones for most small businesses. In complex double-entry accounting systems, the current asset account balances are constantly being changed. In a double-entry system, each time an item of inventory is sold, for example, the account balance for the inventory account must be adjusted to reflect the sale. In single-entry systems, all asset and liability accounts are updated only when the business owner wishes to prepare a Balance Sheet. This may be done monthly, quarterly, or annually. At a minimum, this updating must take place at the end of the year in order to have the necessary figures available for tax purposes.

Current Asset Account

The main form for tracking your current business assets will be a Current Asset Account sheet. A copy of this form follows this discussion. On this form, you will periodically track the value of the current asset that you are following, except for your inventory. (For inventory, you will use specialized inventory records.) You should prepare a separate Current Asset Account sheet for each asset. For example, if your current assets consist of a business checking account, cash on hand, and accounts receivable, you will have three separate Current Asset Accounts, one for each category of asset. These forms are very simple to use. Follow the instructions below:

1. Simply fill in the account number for the Current Asset Account for which you are setting up the form. You will get this number from your Chart of Accounts. Fill in also a description of the account. For example: Account #53—Business Banking Account.

2. You must then decide how often you will be preparing a Balance Sheet and updating your Balance Sheet account balances. If you wish to keep close track of your finances, you may wish to do this on a monthly basis. For many businesses, a quarterly Balance Sheet may be sufficient. All businesses, no matter how small, must prepare a Balance Sheet at least annually at the end of the year. Decide how often you wish to update the balances and enter the time period in the space provided.

3. Next, enter the date that you open the account. Under description, enter "Opening Balance." In the "Balance" column, enter the opening value. The amount to enter for an opening balance will be as follows:

    *   For a bank account, this will be the opening balance of the account
    *   For cash on hand, this will be the opening balance of the petty cash fund and cash on hand for sales, such as the cash used in a cash register
    *   For accounts receivable, this will be the total amount due from all accounts

4. After you have entered the balances on the appropriate Current Asset Account sheet, you will transfer the balances to your Balance Sheet.

Current Asset Account

Account #:

Account Name:

Period:

Date	Description of Asset	Balance	

Inventory

Any business that sells an item of merchandise to a customer must have a system in place to keep track of inventory. *Inventory* is considered any merchandise or materials that are held for sale during the normal course of your business. Inventory costs include the costs of the merchandise or products themselves and the costs of the materials and paid labor that go into creating a finished product. Inventory does not include the costs of the equipment or machinery that you need to create the finished product.

There are several reasons you will need a system of inventory control. First, if you are stocking parts or supplies to sell, you will need to keep track of what you have ordered, what is in stock, and when you will need to reorder. You will also need to keep track of the cost of your inventory for tax purposes. The amount of money that you spend on your inventory is not fully deductible in the year spent as a business deduction. The only portion of your inventory cost that will reduce your gross profit for tax purposes is the actual cost of the goods that you have sold during the tax year.

The basic method for keeping track of inventory costs for tax purposes is to determine the cost of goods sold. First, you will need to know how much inventory is on hand at the beginning of the year. To this amount, you add the cost of any additional inventory you purchased during the year. Finally, you determine how much inventory is left at the end of the year. The difference is essentially the cost (to you) of the inventory that you sold during the year. This amount is referred to as the *cost of goods sold*. Every year at tax time, you will need to figure the cost of goods sold. Additionally, you may need to determine your cost of goods sold monthly or quarterly for various business purposes.

Using our sample company, Smith's Gourmet Foods, we will start the owner's first year in business with an inventory of $0.00. When her business begins, there is no inventory. During the first year, she purchases $17,500.00 worth of products that are for selling to customers. At the end of the year, she counts all of the items that are left in her possession and determines her cost for these items. The cost of the items left unsold at the end of the year is $3,700.00.

The calculation of the cost of goods sold for the first year in business is as follows:

	Inventory at beginning of first year	$ 00.00
+	Cost of inventory added during year	$ 17,500.00
=	Cost of inventory	$ 17,500.00
−	Inventory at end of first year	$ 3,700.00
=	Cost of Goods Sold for first year	$ 13,800.00

For the second year in business, the figure for the inventory at the beginning of the year is the value of the inventory at the end of the previous year. Thus, if Smith's Gourmet Foods added $25,000.00 additional inventory during the second year of operation and the value of the inventory at the end of the second year was $4,800.00, the cost-of-goods-sold calculations for the second year would be as follows:

	Inventory at beginning of second year	$ 3,700.00
+	Cost of inventory added during year	$ 25,000.00
=	Cost of inventory	$ 28,700.00
−	Inventory at end of second year	$ 4,800.00
=	Cost of goods sold for second year	$ 23,900.00

Thus, for the second year in operation the cost of goods sold would be $23,900.00. This amount would be deducted from the gross revenues that Smith's Gourmet Foods took in for the year to determine the gross profit for the second year in business.

Physical Inventory Report

This form should be used to record the results of an actual physical counting of the inventory at the end of the year and at whatever other times during the year you decide to take a physical inventory. If you decide that you will need to track your inventory monthly or quarterly, you may need to prepare this form for those time periods. To prepare this form, take the following steps:

1. The form should be dated and signed by the person doing the inventory.

2. The quantity and description of each item of inventory should be listed, along with an item number if applicable.

3. The cost (to you) of each item should be then listed under "Unit Price." A total per item cost is then calculated by multiplying the quantity of units by the unit price. This total per item cost should be listed in the far right-hand column. You will need to extract this per item unit price from your Periodic or Perpetual Inventory Records (explained next).

4. The total inventory cost should be figured by adding all of the figures in the far right-hand column.

Physical Inventory Report

Date: Taken by:

Quantity	Description	Item #	Unit Price		Total	
				TOTAL		

Periodic Inventory Record

This is the form that you will use to keep continual track of your inventory if you have a relatively small inventory. You will use the Periodic Inventory Record for the purpose of keeping track of the costs of your inventory and of any orders of additional inventory. You will refer to this record when you need to order additional inventory, determine when an order should be received, and determine the cost of your inventory items at the end of the year or at other times if desired. If you have an extensive inventory, you will need to consult an accounting professional to assist you in setting up a perpetual-type inventory system. Or you may be able to set up a complex inventory system using commercial accounting software that is available.

1. Prepare a separate Periodic Inventory Record for each item of inventory. Identify the type of item that is being tracked by description and by item number, if applicable. You may also wish to list the supplier of the item.

2. The first entry on the Periodic Inventory Record should be the initial purchase of inventory. On the right-hand side of the record, list the following items:

   - Date purchased
   - Quantity purchased
   - Price per item
   - Total price paid
   - *Note*: Shipping charges should not be included in the prices entered. Only the actual costs of the goods should be listed.

3. When you are running low on a particular item and place an order, on the left-hand side of the record enter the following information:

   - Date of the order
   - The order number
   - The quantity ordered
   - The date the order is due to arrive

4. When the order arrives, enter the actual details about the order on the right-hand side of the page. This will allow you to keep track of your order of inventory items and also allow you to keep track of the cost of your items of inventory.

Periodic Inventory Record

Item: Item #:
Supplier:

INVENTORY ORDERED

Date	Order #	Quantity	Due

INVENTORY RECEIVED

Date	Quantity	Price	Total

Cost of Goods Sold Report

The final record for inventory control is the Cost of Goods Sold Report. It is on this report that you will determine the actual cost to your business of the goods that were sold during a particular time period. There are numerous methods to determine the value of your inventory at the end of a time period. The three most important are the specific identification method, the first-in first-out (FIFO) method, and the last-in first-out (LIFO) method. Specific identification is the easiest to use if you have only a few items of inventory, or one-of-a-kind type merchandise. With this method, you actually keep track of each specific item of inventory. You keep track of when you obtained the item, its cost, and when you sold the specific item. With the FIFO method, you keep track only of general quantities of your inventory. Your inventory costs are calculated as though the oldest inventory merchandise was sold first. The first items that you purchased are the first items that you sell. With the LIFO method, the cost values are calculated as though you sold your most-recently purchased inventory first. It is important to note that you do not necessarily have to actually sell your first item first to use the FIFO method and that you don't have to actually sell your last item first to use the LIFO method of calculation.

Although there may be significant advantages in some cases to using the LIFO method, it is also a far more complicated system than the FIFO. The specific identification method allows you to simply track each item of inventory and deduct the actual cost of the goods that you sold during the year. The FIFO method allows you to value your inventory on hand at the end of a time period based on the cost of your most recent purchases.

1. At the end of your chosen time period (monthly, quarterly, or annually), take an actual physical inventory count on your Physical Inventory Report.

2. Using the most recent purchases as listed on your Periodic Inventory Record, determine the unit price of the items left in your inventory and enter this in the Unit Price column on your Physical Inventory Report.

3. Once all of your items of inventory have been checked, counted, and a unit price determined, simply total each item and then total the value of the entire inventory. If you are conducting your final annual inventory, this figure is your inventory value at year's end.

4. On the Cost of Goods Sold Report, enter this number on the line titled "Inventory Value at End of Period." If this is your first year in business, enter "zero" as the Inventory Value at Beginning of Period. For later periods, the Inventory Value at Beginning of Period will be the Inventory Value at End of Period from the previous time period.

5. Using your Periodic Inventory Records, total the amount of orders during the period that are listed in the "Inventory Received" column. This total will be entered on the "Inventory Added During Period" line. Now simply perform the calculations. You will use the figures on this report at tax time to prepare your taxes.

Note: This type of inventory calculation is not intended for manufacturing companies that manufacture finished goods from raw materials or for those with gross annual receipts more than $10 million. For those types of companies, an additional calculation is necessary because of uniform capitalization rules. This tax rule requires that manufacturing inventory values include the overhead associated with the manufacturing process. Please consult an accounting professional if your business falls into this category.

Cost of Goods Sold Report

Period Ending:

Inventory Value at Beginning of Period
+ Inventory Added during Period
= Total Inventory Value
− Inventory Value at End of Period
= Cost of Goods Sold

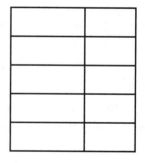

Beginning Inventory Value for Next Period
(Take from Inventory Value at End of This Period)

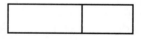

Fixed Assets

The final category of assets that you will need to track are your *fixed assets*. Fixed assets are the more permanent assets of your business, generally the assets that are not for sale to customers. The main categories of these fixed assets are:

- Buildings
- Land
- Machinery
- Tools
- Furniture and Equipment
- Vehicles

There are many more types of fixed assets, such as patents, copyrights, and goodwill. However, the six listed above are the basic ones for most small businesses. If your business includes other types of fixed assets, please consult an accounting professional. For those with basic fixed assets, you will need to keep track of the actual total costs to you to acquire them. These costs include sales taxes, transportation charges, installation costs, etc. The total cost of a fixed asset to you is referred to as the asset's *cost basis*. With a major exception explained below, the costs of fixed assets are, generally, not immediately deductible as a business expense. Rather, except for land, their costs are deductible proportionately over a period of time. This proportionate deduction is referred to as *depreciation*. Since these assets generally wear out over time (except for land), each year you are allowed to deduct a portion of the initial cost as a legitimate business expense. Each type of fixed asset is given a specific time period for dividing up the cost into proportional amounts. This time period is called the *recovery period* of the asset. Depreciation is a very complex subject and one whose rules change nearly every year. The full details of depreciation are beyond the scope of this book. What follows is only a general outline of depreciation rules. It will allow you to begin to set up your fixed asset records. However, you will need to consult either an accounting or tax professional or consult specific tax preparation manuals for details on how your specific assets should be depreciated.

The major exception to depreciation rules is that, under the rules of Internal Revenue Service Code Section 179, every year a total of $112,000.00 (beginning in the tax year 2005, this amount will be adjusted annually for inflation) of your fixed asset costs can be immediately used as a business deduction. This means that if your total purchases of equipment, tools, vehicles, etc., during a year amounted to less than $112,000.00, you can deduct all of the costs as current expenses. If your total fixed asset costs are more than $112,000.00, you can still deduct the first $112,000.00 in costs and then depreciate the remaining costs over time. Here are some basic rules relating to depreciation:

1. The depreciation rules that were in effect at the time of the purchase of the asset will be the rules that apply to that particular asset.

2. The actual cost to you of the asset is the cost basis that you use to compute your depreciation amount each year.

3. Used assets that you purchase for use in your business can be depreciated in the same manner as new assets.

4. Assets that you owned prior to going into business and that you will use in your business can be depreciated. The cost basis will be the lower of their actual market value when you begin to use them in your business or their actual cost to you. For example, you start a carpentry business and use your personal power saw in the business. It cost $150.00 new, but is now worth about $90.00. You can depreciate $90.00 (or deduct this amount as an expense if the total of your fixed asset deductions is less than $112,000.00).

5. You may depreciate proportionately those assets that you use partially for business and partially for personal use. In the above example, if you use your saw 70 percent of the time in your business and 30 percent for personal use, you may deduct or depreciate 70 percent of $90.00, which is $63.00.

The tax depreciation rules set up several categories of asset types for the purpose of deciding how long a period you must use to depreciate the asset. Cars, trucks, computer equipment, copiers, and similar equipment are referred to as five-year property. Most machinery, heavy equipment, and office furniture are referred to as seven-year property. This means that for these types of property the actual costs are spread out and depreciated over five or seven years—that is, the costs are deducted over a period of five or seven years.

There are also several different ways to compute how much of the cost can be depreciated each year. There are three basic methods: straight-line, MACRS, and ACRS. Straight-line depreciation spreads the deductible amount equally over the recovery period. Thus for the power saw that is worth $90.00 and is used 70 percent of the time in a business, the cost basis that can be depreciated is $63.00. This asset has a recovery period of seven years. Spreading the $63.00 over the seven-year period allows you to deduct a total of $9.00 per year as depreciation of the saw. After the first year, the saw will be valued on your books at $54.00. Thus, after seven years, the value of the saw on your books will be zero. It will have been fully depreciated. You will have finally been allowed to fully deduct its cost as a business expense. Of course, if you have fixed asset costs of less than $112,000.00 for the year you put the saw in service, you will be allowed to claim the entire $63.00 deduction that first year. See the glossary for an explanation of MACRS and ACRS depreciations.

Other methods of depreciation have more complicated rules that must be applied. For full details, please refer to a tax preparation manual or consult a tax or accounting professional.

Following are listed various types of property that are depreciable or deductible. Consult this list to determine which of your business purchases may be depreciated and which of them may be written off as an immediately deductible expense. Recall that up to $112,000.00 of depreciable assets may be immediately deductible as a special Section 179 deduction. Of course, also remember that tax laws are always subject to change.

DEDUCTIBLE EXPENSES

Advertising
Bad debts
Bank charges
Books and periodicals
Car and truck expenses:
    Gas, repairs, licenses,
      insurance, maintenance
Commissions to salespersons
Independent contractor costs
Donations
Dues to professional groups
Educational expenses
Entertainment of clients
Freight costs
Improvements worth less than
    $100
Insurance
Interest costs
Laundry and cleaning
Licenses for business

Legal and professional fees
Maintenance
Office equipment worth less than
    $100
Office furniture worth less than $100
Office supplies
Pension plans
Postage
Printing costs
Property taxes
Rent
Repairs
Refunds, returns, and allowances
Sales taxes collected
Sales taxes paid on purchases
Telephone
Tools worth less than $100
Uniforms
Utilities
Wages paid

DEPRECIABLE PROPERTY

Business buildings (not land)
Office furniture worth over $100
Office equipment worth over $100

Business machinery
Tools worth over $100
Vehicles used in business

Fixed Asset Account

Recall that fixed assets are business purchases that are depreciable, unless you elect to deduct fixed asset expenses up to $112,000.00 per year. For recordkeeping purposes, you will prepare a Fixed Asset Account record for each fixed asset that you have if you have acquired more than $112,000.00 in a calendar year. If you have acquired less than $112,000.00 worth in a year, you may put all of your fixed asset records on one Fixed Asset Account record.

To prepare your Fixed Asset Account record, follow these instructions:

1. List the date on which you acquired the property. If the property was formerly personal property, list the date on which you converted it to business property.

2. Then list the property by description. Enter the actual cost of the property. If the property is used, enter the lower amount of the cost of the property or the actual market value of the property. If the property is part business and part personal, enter the value of the business portion of the property.

3. If you will have more than $112,000.00 worth of depreciable business property during the year, you will additionally need to enter information in the next three columns on the record. First, you will need to enter the recovery period for each asset. For most property other than buildings, this will be either five or seven years. Please consult a tax manual or tax professional.

4. You will need to enter the method of depreciation. Again, check a tax manual or tax professional.

5. Finally, you will need to determine the amount of the deduction for the first year (*Hint:* consult a tax manual or tax professional).

6. Once you have set up a method for each fixed asset, each year you will determine the additional deduction and update the balance. You will then use that figure on your business tax return and in the preparation of your Balance Sheet.

Fixed Asset Account

Date	Item	Cost		Years	Method	Annual	Balance	

Tracking Business Debts

Business debts are also referred to as *business liabilities*. However, technically, business liabilities also include the value of the owner's equity in the business. Business debts can be divided into two general categories. First are *current debts*, those that will normally be paid within one year. The second general category is *long-term debts*. These are generally debts that will not be paid off within one year. Current debts for most small businesses consist primarily of accounts payable and taxes that are due during the year. For small businesses, the taxes that are due during a year fall into three main categories: estimated income tax payments, payment of collected sales taxes, and payroll taxes. Since the collection and payment of sales taxes are handled differently in virtually every state, you will need to contact your state's department of revenue or similar body to determine the specific necessary recordkeeping requirements for that business debt. Payroll taxes will be explained in the next chapter and estimated taxes will be dealt with in Chapter 15.

That leaves us only with accounts payable to track as a current debt. You will have only one simple form to use to keep track of this important category. *Accounts payable* are the current bills that your business owes. They may be for equipment or supplies that you have purchased on credit or for items that you have ordered on account. Regardless of the source of the debt, you will need a clear system to record the debt and keep track of how much you still owe on the debt.

Long-term debts are, generally, debts based on business loans for equipment, inventory, business-owned vehicles, or business property. In the accounting system outlined in this book, you will only keep track of the current principal and interest for these debts. For long-term debts of your business, you will fill in the Long-Term Debt Record, that is explained later in this chapter. You will find an Accounts Payable Record on the following form. You will enter any bills or short-term debts that you do not pay immediately on this record. If you pay the bill off upon receipt of the bill, you need not enter the amount on this record. Your records for expenses will take care of the necessary documentation for those particular debts. If your business has many accounts payable that must be tracked, it may be a good idea to prepare an individual Accounts Payable Record for each account.

Accounts Payable Record

Follow these instructions to prepare and fill in this particular form:

1. For those debts that you do not pay off immediately, you will need to record the following information in the left-hand column of the record:

   - The date the debt was incurred
   - To whom you owe the money
   - Payment terms (for instance: due within 30, 60, or 90 days)
   - The amount of the debt

2. In the right-hand column of the Accounts Payable Record, you will record the following information:

   - The date of any payments
   - To whom the payments were made
   - The amount of any payments made

3. By periodically totaling the left- and right-hand columns, you will be able to take a look at the total amount of your unpaid accounts payable. You may wish to do this weekly, monthly, or quarterly. You will also need this figure for your total unpaid accounts payable for the preparation of your Balance Sheet.

4. When you have totaled your accounts payable at the end of your chosen periodic interval, you should start a new record and carry the unpaid accounts over to it. Using this simple record, you will be able to check your accounts payable at a glance and also have enough information available to use in preparing a Balance Sheet for your business.

Accounts Payable Record

Period from: to:

UNPAID ACCOUNTS				
Date	Due to	Terms	Amount	
		TOTAL		

PAYMENTS			
Date	Paid to	Amount	
	TOTAL		

Total Unpaid Accounts

− Total Payments

= Total Accounts Payable

Long-Term Debt Record

If your business has any outstanding loans that will not be paid off within one year, you will prepare a Long-Term Debt Record for each loan. You will track the principal and interest paid on each long-term debt of your business. This information will enable you to have long-term debt figures for use in preparing your Balance Sheet and interest-paid figures for use in preparing your Profit and Loss Statements. On the following page, you will find a Long-Term Debt Record to be used for this purpose. In order to fill in this record, follow these directions:

1. You will need to enter the following information for each company to whom a loan is outstanding:

    - Company name
    - Address
    - Contact person
    - Phone number
    - Loan account number
    - Loan interest rate
    - Original principal amount of the loan
    - Term of the loan

2. You will need a loan payment book or amortization schedule in order to obtain the necessary information regarding the portions of each of your payments that are principal and interest. As you make a payment, enter the following information:

    - Date of payment
    - Total payment made
    - Amount of principal paid
    - Amount of interest paid
    - Balance due (the previous balance minus principal)

3. Total the balance due after each payment. Using this method of tracking accounts payable will allow you to always have a running total of your long-term liability for each long-term debt.

4. To prepare a Balance Sheet entry for long-term debts, you will simply need to total all of the various account balances for all of your long-term debts.

5. You should also periodically total all of the columns on your Long-Term Debt Record. You will need the totals of the interest paid for your Annual Expense Summaries.

Long-Term Debt Record

Company:
Address:
Contact Person
Loan Account #:
Original Loan Amount:

Phone:
Loan Interest Rate:
Term:

Date	Payment		Principal		Interest		Balance	
TOTALS								

Tracking Business Expenses

The expenses of a business are all of the transactions of the business where money is paid out of the business, with one general exception. Money paid out of the business to pay off the principal of a loan is not considered an expense of a business. Because of the tax deductibility of the cost of most business expenses, it is crucial for a business to keep careful records of what has been spent to operate the business. But even beyond the need for detailed expense records for tax purposes, a small business needs a clear system that will allow a quick examination of where money is being spent. The tracking of business expenses will allow you to quickly see where your money is flowing.

In order to track your business expenses, you will use a Weekly Expense Record and a Monthly Expense Summary. You may also need to use a number of additional specialized forms if your business needs dictate their use. There is also an Annual Expense Summary for totaling your expense payments.

On your Weekly Expense Record, you will record all of your business expenses in chronological order. The expense transactions will generally come from three main sources: your business bank account check register, your monthly business credit card statements, and your petty cash register. You will transfer all of the expenses from these three sources to the main expense record. This will provide you with a central listing of all of the expenditures for your business.

From this record, you will transfer your expenses to a Monthly Expense Summary. On the Monthly Expense Summary, you will enter a line for each expense type that you have listed on your business Chart of Accounts. You will then go through your Weekly Expense Records for each month and total the expenses for each account. You will enter this total in the column for the specific type of expense.

Finally, on a monthly basis, you will transfer the totals for your various expense categories to the Annual Expense Summary record. On this record, you collect and record the total monthly expenses. With these figures, you will be able to easily total your expense amounts to ascertain your quarterly and annual expenses.

By recording your business expenses in this manner, you should have little difficulty being able to keep track of the money flowing out of your business on a daily, weekly, monthly, quarterly, and annual basis. You will have all of the information that you will need to easily provide the necessary expenditure figures for preparing a Profit and Loss Statement. Remember that you must tailor the forms to fit your particular business.

Weekly Expense Record

1. Fill in the date or dates that the form will cover where indicated at the top.

2. Beginning with your bank account check register, transfer the following information from the register to the Weekly Expense Record:

   • The date of the transaction
   • The check number
   • To whom the amount was paid
   • The expense account number (from your Chart of Accounts)
   • The amount of the transaction

3. Next, transfer the following information from your records that you have kept regarding your petty cash to the expense record:

   • The date of the transaction
   • In the "Check #" column, put "PC" indicating it was a petty cash expense
   • To whom the amount was paid
   • The expense account number (off your Chart of Accounts)
   • The amount of the transaction
   • *Note*: Do not list the checks that you make out to "Petty Cash" as an expense

4. For credit card transactions, follow these rules:

   • Do not list payment to a credit card company as an expense
   • List the monthly amount on the credit card bill for interest as an interest expense
   • Individually, list each business purchase on the credit card as a separate expense item, assigning an account number to each separate business charge. Make a notation for the date, to whom the expense was paid, and the amount. In the "Check #" column, provide the type of credit card, for example, "V" for Visa
   • Do not list any personal charge items as business expenses
   • If a charged item is used partially for business and partially for personal reasons, list only that portion that is used for business reasons as a business expense

5. At the end of the period, total the Amount column. You will use this weekly total expense amount to cross-check your later calculations.

6. It is a good idea to keep all of your various business expense receipts for at least three years after the tax period to which they relate. You may wish to buy envelopes for each weekly period, label each appropriately, and file your weekly business expense receipts in them. This will make it easy to find each specific receipt, if necessary.

Weekly Expense Record

Week of:

Date	Check #	To Whom Paid	Account #	Amount	
			TOTALS		

Monthly Expense Summary

Using this record, you will compile and transfer the total expense amount for each expense category. In this way, you will be able to keep a monthly total of all of the expenses, broken down by category of expense. To fill in this form, do the following:

1. Indicate the month that the Monthly Expense Summary will cover where shown.

2. In the first column on the left-hand side, list all of your expense account names and numbers from your business Chart of Accounts.

3. In the next column, using your Weekly Expense Records, transfer the amounts for each expense. If you have more than four expense amounts for any account, use a second Monthly Expense Summary to record additional amounts.

4. In the Total column, list the total expenses in each category for the month.

5. At the bottom of the page, total the amount for all of the categories for the month. Don't forget to include any amounts from any additional records in your totals.

6. To double-check your transfers and your calculations, total all of your Weekly Expense Record total amounts. This figure should equal your Monthly Expense Summary total for that month. If there is a discrepancy, check each of your figures until you discover the error.

Monthly Expense Summary

Month of:

Account Name/#	Amount		Amount		Amount		Amount		Total	
								TOTAL		

Annual Expense Summary

1. Fill in the year. Fill in your account numbers from your Chart of Accounts across the top row. If you have more than nine expense accounts, use a second and third page, if necessary.

2. On a monthly basis, carry the totals from all of the rows on your Monthly Expense Summaries to the appropriate column of the Annual Expense Summary.

3. At the end of each quarter, total all of the monthly entries to arrive at your quarterly totals for each category.

4. To double-check your monthly calculations, total your categories across each month and put this total in the final column. Compare this total with the total on your Monthly Expense Records. If there is a discrepancy, check each of your figures until you discover the error. Don't forget to include your extra records if you have more than nine expense accounts to list.

5. To double-check your quarterly calculations, total your monthly totals in the final quarterly column. This figure should equal the total of the quarterly category totals across the quarterly row. If there is a discrepancy, check each of your figures until you discover the error.

6. Finally, total each of your quarterly amounts to arrive at the annual totals. To cross-check your calculations, total the quarterly totals in the final column. This figure should equal the total for all of the annual totals in each category across the Annual Total row. If there is a discrepancy, check each of your figures until you discover the error.

Annual Expense Summary

Year of:

Account # ⇨																	Total
January																	
February																	
March																	
1st Quarter																	
April																	
May																	
June																	
2nd Quarter																	
July																	
August																	
September																	
3rd Quarter																	
October																	
November																	
December																	
4th Quarter																	
Annual TOTAL																	

Tracking Business Income

The careful tracking of your business income is one of the most important accounting activities you will perform. It is essential for your business that you know intimately where your income comes from. Failure to accurately track income and cash is one of the most frequent causes of business failure. You must have in place a clear and easily understood system to track your business income. There are three separate features of tracking business income that must be incorporated into your accounting system. You will need a system in place to handle cash, a system to track all of your sales and service income, and a system to handle credit sales.

The first system you will need is a clear method for handling cash on a weekly basis. This is true no matter how large or small your business may be and regardless of how much or how little cash is actually handled. You must have a clear record of how much cash is on hand and how much cash is taken in during a particular time period. You will also need to have a method to tally this cash flow on a monthly basis. For these purposes, two forms are provided: a Weekly Cash Report and a Monthly Cash Report Summary.

The second feature of your business income tracking system should be a method to track your actual income from sales or services. This differs from your cash tracking. With these records you will track taxable and nontaxable income whether the income is in the form of cash, check, credit card payment, or payment on an account. Please note that when *nontaxable income* is referred to, it means only that income which is not subject to any state or local sales tax (generally, this will be income from the performance of a service). These records will also track your intake of sales taxes, if applicable. For this segment of your income tracking, you will have a Weekly Income Record. You will also track your income on income summaries that will provide you with monthly, quarterly, and annual reports of your taxable income, nontaxable income, and sales tax collection.

The third feature of your business income tracking consists of a method to track and bill credit sales. With this portion of income tracking, you will list and track all of your sales to customers that are made on account or on credit. The accounts that owe you money are referred to as your *accounts receivable*. These are the accounts from whom you hope to receive payment. The tracking of these credit sales will take place on a Monthly Credit Sales Record. You will also use a Credit Sales Aging Report to see how your customers are doing over time. The actual billing of these credit sales will require you to prepare and incorporate an invoice, statement, and past due statement, all of which are explained at the end of this chapter.

Tracking Cash

Most businesses will have to handle cash in some form. Here we are not talking about the use of petty cash. *Petty cash* is the cash that a business has on hand for the payment of minor expenses that may crop up and for which the use of a business check is not convenient. The cash handling discussed in this section is the daily handling of cash used to take money in from customers or clients and the use of a cash drawer or some equivalent. You must have some method to accurately account for the cash used in your business in this regard.

Weekly Cash Report

1. You must decide how much cash you will need to begin each period with sufficient cash to meet your needs and make change for cash sales. Usually $100.00 should be sufficient for most needs. Choose a figure and begin each period with that amount in your cash drawer. Excess cash that has been collected should be deposited in your business bank account. Each period, fill in the date and the cash on hand on your Weekly Cash Report.

2. As you take in cash and checks throughout the period, record each item of cash taken in, checks taken in, and any instances of cash paid out. *Cash out* does not mean change that has been made, but rather cash paid out for business purposes (for example, a refund).

3. Your business may have so much daily cash flow that it will be burdensome to record each item of cash flow on your sheet. In that case, you will need a cash register of some type. Simply total the cash register at the end of the day and record the total cash in, checks in, and cash out in the appropriate places on the Weekly Cash Report.

4. At the end of each period, total your Cash In and Checks In. Add these two amounts to your Cash on Hand at the beginning of the period. This equals your Total Receipts for the period. Subtract any Cash Out from this amount for the Balance on Hand. Make a bank deposit for all of the checks and for all of the cash in excess of the amount that you will need to begin the next period. Subtract the Bank Deposit from the Balance. This figure should equal your actual cash on hand at the end of the period.

5. In the space for deposits, note the following: a deposit number, if applicable; the date of the deposit; the deposit amount; and the name and signature of the person who made the deposit. Don't forget to also record your deposit in your business bank account check register.

Weekly Cash Report

Week of: _____   Cash on Hand Beginning: _____

Week	CASH IN			CHECKS IN			CASH OUT		
	Name	Amount		Name	Amount		Name	Amount	
1									
2									
3									
4									
5									
6									
7									
8									
9									
10									
11									
12									
TOTAL									

Deposit #:	
Deposit Date:	
Deposit Amount:	
Deposited by:	
Signed:	

Total Cash in		
+ Total Checks in		
+ Cash on Hand Beginning		
= Total Receipts		
– Total Cash Out		
= Balance on Hand		
– Bank Deposit		
= Cash on Hand Ending		

Monthly Cash Report Summary

This form will be used to keep a monthly record of your Weekly Cash Reports. It serves as a monthly listing of your cash flow and of your business bank account deposits. You will, of course, also record your bank deposits in your business bank account check register. To use this form, follow these instructions:

1. On a weekly basis, collect your Weekly Cash Reports. From each Report, record the following information on the monthly summary:

   • Cash on hand at the beginning of the period
   • Cash taken in
   • Checks taken in
   • Cash paid out
   • The amount of the weekly bank deposit
   • Cash on hand at the end of the period and after the bank deposit

2. You can total the Deposit column as a cross-check against your bank account check register record of deposits.

Monthly Cash Report Summary

Month:

Date	On Hand		Cash in		Checks in		Cash out		Deposit		On Hand	
1												
2												
3												
4												
5												
6												
7												
8												
9												
10												
11												
12												
13												
14												
15												
16												
17												
18												
19												
20												
21												
22												
23												
24												
25												
26												
27												
28												
29												
30												
31												

Tracking Income

The second feature of your business income tracking system should be a method to keep track of your actual income. This portion of the system will provide you with a list of all taxable and nontaxable income and of any sales taxes collected, if applicable. For sales tax information, please contact your state's sales tax revenue collection agency. If your state has a sales tax on the product or service that you provide, you will need accurate records to determine your total taxable and nontaxable income and the amount of sales tax that is due. For this purpose and for the purpose of tracking all of your income for your own business analysis, you should prepare a Weekly Income Record. The information from these reports will then be used to prepare Monthly and Annual Income Summaries.

Weekly Income Record

1. You will need to contact your state taxing agency for information on how to determine if a sale or the provision of a service is taxable or nontaxable. You will also need to determine the appropriate rates for sales tax collection.

2. For each item, record the following information:

   - Invoice number
   - Taxable income amount
   - Sales tax amount
   - Nontaxable income amount
   - Total income (Taxable, sales tax, and nontaxable amounts combined)

3. On a weekly basis, total the amounts in each column to determine the totals for the particular time period. These figures will be carried over to the Monthly and Annual Income Summaries, that will be explained next.

Weekly Income Record

Week of:

Invoice #	Taxable Income		Sales Tax		Nontaxable Income		Total Income	
Weekly TOTAL								

Monthly Income Summary

1. Fill in the appropriate month.

2. Using your Weekly Income Records, record the following information for each week:

   • Invoice number
   • Total taxable income amount
   • Total sales tax amount
   • Total nontaxable income amount
   • Total income (taxable, sales tax, and nontaxable amounts combined)

3. On a monthly basis, total the amounts in each column to determine the totals for the particular month. These figures will be carried over to the Annual Income Summary, that will be explained next.

Monthly Income Summary

Month of:

Invoice #	Taxable Income		Sales Tax		Nontaxable Income		Total Income	
Monthly TOTAL								

Annual Income Summary

1. On a monthly basis, carry the totals from all of the columns on your Monthly Income Summary to the appropriate columns of the Annual Income Summary.

2. At the end of each quarter, total all of the monthly entries to arrive at your quarterly totals for each category.

3. To double-check your monthly calculations, total your categories across each month and put this total in the final column. Compare this total with the total on your Monthly Income Summaries. If there is a discrepancy, check each of your figures until you discover the error.

4. To double-check your quarterly calculations, total your monthly totals in the final column. This figure should equal the total of the quarterly category totals across the quarterly row. If there is a discrepancy, check each of your figures until you discover the error.

5. Finally, total your quarterly amounts to arrive at the annual totals. To cross-check your calculations, total the quarterly totals in the final column. This figure should equal the total for all of the annual totals across the Annual Total row. If there is a discrepancy, check each of your figures until you discover the error.

Annual Income Summary

Year of:

Date	Taxable Income		Sales Tax		Nontaxable Income		Total Income	
January								
February								
March								
1st Quarter								
April								
May								
June								
2nd Quarter								
July								
August								
September								
3rd Quarter								
October								
November								
December								
4th Quarter								
Annual TOTAL								

Tracking Credit Sales

The final component of your business income tracking system will be a logical method to track your credit sales. You will use a Monthly Credit Sales Record to track the actual sales on credit, and Credit Sales Aging Report to track the payment on these sales. In addition, several forms are provided for the billing of these credit sales: an Invoice, Statement, Past Due Statement, and Credit Memo.

Monthly Credit Sales Record

1. Fill in the appropriate date or time period.

2. For each sale that is made on credit, fill in the following information from the customer Invoice (see Invoice instructions later in this chapter):

   - Invoice number
   - Date of the sale
   - Customer name
   - Total sale amount

3. The final column is for recording the date that the credit sale has been paid in full.

4. The information from your Monthly Credit Sales Record will also be used to prepare your Credit Sales Aging Report on a monthly basis.

Monthly Credit Sales Record

Month of:

Invoice #	Sale Date	Customer	Sale Total		Date Paid

Credit Sales Aging Report

This report is used to track the current status of your credit sales or accounts receivables. Through the use of this form you will be able to track whether or not the people or companies that owe you money are falling behind on their payments. With this information, you will be able to determine how to handle these accounts: sending past due notices, halting sales to them, turning them over to a collection agency, etc. To use this form, do the following:

1. Decide on which day of the month you would like to perform your credit sales aging calculations.

2. For each credit sales account, enter the name of the account from your Monthly Credit Sales Record.

3. In the "Total" column, enter the total current amount that is owed to you. If this figure is based on credit sales during the current month, enter this figure again in the "Current" column. Do this for each credit account.

4. Each month you will prepare a new Credit Sales Aging Report on a new sheet. On the same date in the next month, determine how much of the originally owed balance has been paid off. Enter the amount of the unpaid balance from the previous month in the "30–60 days" column. Enter any new credit sales for the month under the "Current" column. The figure in the "Total" column should be the total of all of the columns to the right of the "Total" column.

5. Each month, determine how much was paid on the account, deduct that amount from the oldest amount due, and shift the amounts due over one column to the right. Add any new credit sales to the "Current" column and put the total of the amounts in the "Total" column.

6. After entering the information for each month, total each of the columns across the "Total" line at the bottom of the report. The "Total" column is 100 percent of the amount due. Calculate the percentage for each of the other columns to determine how much of your accounts receivable are 30, 60, 90, or more than 90 days overdue.

Credit Sales Aging Report

Account Name	Total		Current		30–60 Days		60–90 Days		90 Days +	
TOTALS										
PERCENT	100%									

Invoices and Statements

For credit sales, you will need to provide each customer with a current Invoice. You will also need to send a Statement if the balance is not paid within the first 30 days. In addition, you will need to send a Past Due Statement if the balance becomes overdue. Finally, a Credit Memo form is provided to record instances when a customer is given credit for a returned item. You will need to produce two copies of each of these forms: one for your records and one for the customer.

Invoice

The invoice is your key credit sales document. To prepare and track invoices, follow these directions:

1. Make a number of copies of the Invoice form. You can insert your business card in the upper-left corner before copying. Number each form consecutively. Make a photocopy of the form when the form is sent out to the customer or print two copies if using the Forms-on-CD.

2. For each order, fill in the following information:

    - Date
    - Invoice number
    - Name and address of who will be billed for the order
    - Name and address where the order will be shipped
    - Item number of the product or service sold
    - Quantity ordered
    - Description of the item
    - Per unit price of the item
    - Total amount billed (quantity times per unit price)

3. Subtotal all of the items where shown. Add any sales taxes and shipping costs and total the balance.

4. Record the pertinent information from the Invoice on the Monthly Credit Sales Record.

5. Record the pertinent information from the Invoice on the Monthly Income Summary.

6. Send one copy of the Invoice to the customer with the order and file the other copy in a file for your invoices.

Invoice

Date:

Invoice No.:

Bill to:

Ship to:

Item #	Qty.	Description	Price Each		Total	
			Subtotal			
			Tax			
			Shipping			
			BALANCE			

Statement and Past Due Statement

Statements are used to send your credit customers a notice of the amount that is currently due. Statements are generally sent at 30-day intervals, beginning either 30 days after the Invoice is sent, at the beginning of the next month, or at the next cycle for sending statements. Follow these instructions for preparing your statements:

1. You should decide on a statement billing cycle. Generally, this is a specific date each month (for example: the 1st, 10th, or 15th of each month).

2. Make a copy of the Statement form using your business card in the upper-left corner. Fill in the date and the account name and address in the "Account" box.

3. In the body of the form, enter information from any Invoice that is still unpaid as of the date you are completing the Statement. You should enter the following items for each unpaid Invoice:

   - The date of the Invoice
   - A description of the Invoice (including Invoice number)
   - Any payments received since the last statement or since the sale
   - The amount still owed on that Invoice

4. When all of the invoice information for all the customer's invoices has been entered, total the "Amount Due" column and enter the balance at the bottom. The information on the Statement can then be used to enter information on your Credit Sales Aging Report.

5. The Past Due Statement is simply a version of the basic Statement that includes a notice that the account is past due. This Past Due Statement should be sent when the account becomes overdue. Fill it out in the same manner used for statements.

Statement

Date:

Account:

Date	Description	Payment		Amount Due	

Please pay this BALANCE

Past Due Statement

Date:

Account:

This account is now past due. Please pay upon receipt to avoid collection costs

Date	Description	Payment		Amount Due	

Please pay this BALANCE

Credit Memo

The final form for tracking your business income is the Credit Memo. This form is used to provide you and your customer with a written record of any credit given for goods that have been returned by the customer. You will need to set a policy regarding when such credit will be given (for example, for only a certain time period after the sale, for defects, or for other limitations). To use the Credit Memo, follow these instructions:

1. Fill in the date, the number of the original Invoice, and the customer's name and address in the "Credit" box.

2. Fill in the following information in the body of the Credit Memo:

    - Item number of item returned
    - Quantity of items returned
    - Description of item returned
    - Per unit price of item returned
    - Total amount of credit (quantity x per unit price)

3. Subtotal the credit for all items. Add any appropriate sales tax credit and total those amounts for the credit. This is the amount that will be credited or refunded to the customer.

4. In the lower left corner of the form, indicate the reason for the return, any necessary approval, and the date of the approval.

5. Handle the Credit Memo like a negative Invoice. Record the amount of credit as a negative on the Weekly Income Record.

6. Record the pertinent information from the Credit Memo as a negative amount on the appropriate Monthly Credit Sales Record, if the Credit Memo applies to a previous sale on credit that was recorded on a Monthly Credit Sales Record.

Credit Memo

Date:

Invoice #:

Credit to:

GOODS RETURNED

Item #	Qty.	Description	Price Each		Total	

Reason for return:

Approved by:

Date:

Subtotal

Tax

CREDIT

CHAPTER 14
Business Payroll

One of the most difficult and complex accounting functions that small businesses face is their payroll. Because of the various state and Federal taxes that must be applied and the myriad government forms that must be prepared, the handling of a business payroll often causes accounting nightmares. Even if there is only one employee, there is a potential for problems.

First, let's examine the basics. If your business is a corporation, all pay must be handled as payroll, even if you are the only employee. The corporation is a separate entity and the corporation itself will be the employer. You and any other people that you hire will be the employees. A business payroll entails a great deal of paperwork and has numerous government tax filing deadlines. You will be required to make payroll tax deposits, file various quarterly payroll tax returns, and make additional end-of-the-year reports.

Initially, you must take certain steps to set up your payroll and official status as an employer. The following information contains the instructions only for meeting Federal requirements. Please check with your particular state and local governments for information regarding any additional payroll tax, state unemployment insurance, or workers' compensation requirements.

Setting up Your Payroll

1. The first step in becoming an employer is to file Internal Revenue Service Form SS-4: *Application for Employer Identification Number*. This will officially register your business with the Federal government as an employer. This form and instructions are included on the Forms-on-CD.

2. Next, each employee must fill in an IRS Form W-4: *Employee's Withholding Allowance Certificate*. This will provide you with the necessary information regarding withholding allowances to enable you to prepare your payroll.

3. You must then determine the gross salary or wage that each employee will earn. For each employee, complete an Employee Payroll Record and prepare a Quarterly Payroll Time Sheet as explained later in this chapter.

4. You will then need to consult the tables in IRS Circular E: *Employer's Tax Guide*. From the tables in this publication, you will be able to determine the proper deductions for each employee for each pay period. If your employees are paid on an hourly basis and the number of hours worked is different each pay period, you will have to perform these calculations for each pay period.

5. Before you pay your employee, you should open a separate business bank account for handling your business payroll tax deductions and payments. This will allow you to immediately deposit all taxes due into this separate account and help prevent the lack of sufficient money available when the taxes are due.

6. Next you will pay your employee and record the deduction information on the Employee Payroll Record.

7. When you have completed paying all of your employees for the pay period, you will write a separate check for the total amount of all of your employees' deductions and any employer's share of taxes. You will then deposit this check into your business payroll tax bank account that you set up following the instructions above.

8. At the end of every month, you will need to transfer the information regarding employee deductions to your Payroll Depository Record and Annual Payroll Summary. Copies of these forms and instructions are included later in this chapter. You will then calculate your employer share of Social Security and Medicare taxes. Each month (or quarter if your tax liability is more than $2,500.00 per quarter), you will need to deposit the correct amount of taxes due to the Federal government. This is done either by making a monthly payment to your bank for the taxes due using IRS Form 8109: *Federal Tax Deposit Coupon* or by making the payment on a quarterly basis when you file IRS Form 941: *Employer's Quarterly Federal Tax Return*. Copies of these forms are contained on the Forms-on-CD.

9. On a quarterly or annual basis, you will also need to make a tax payment for Federal Unemployment Tax, using IRS Form 940: *Employer's Annual Federal Unemployment (FUTA) Tax Return*. This tax is solely the responsibility of the employer and is not deducted from the employee's pay. Also on a quarterly basis, you will need to file IRS Form 941: *Employer's Quarterly Federal Tax Return*. If you have made monthly deposits of your taxes due, there will be no quarterly taxes to pay, but you will still need to file these forms quarterly.

10. Finally, to complete your payroll, at the end of the year you must do the following:

- Prepare IRS Form W-2: *Wage and Tax Statement* for each employee
- File IRS Form W-3: *Transmittal of Wage and Tax Statements*

Remember that your state and local tax authorities will generally have additional requirements and taxes that will need to be paid. In many jurisdictions, these requirements are tailored after the Federal requirements and the procedures and due dates are similar.

Quarterly Payroll Time Sheet

On the following page is a Quarterly Payroll Time Sheet. If your employees are paid an hourly wage, you will prepare a sheet like this for each employee for each quarter during the year. On this sheet you will keep track of the following information:

- Number of hours worked (daily, weekly, and quarterly)
- Number of regular and overtime hours worked

The information from this Quarterly Payroll Time Sheet will be transferred to your individual Employee Payroll Record in order to calculate the employee's paycheck amounts. This is explained following the Quarterly Payroll Time Sheet.

Quarterly Payroll Time Sheet

Employee:

Week of	Sun	Mon	Tue	Wed	Thu	Fri	Sat	Reg	OT	Total
Quarterly TOTAL										

Employee Payroll Record

You will use this form to track each employee's payroll information.

1. For each employee, fill in the following information at the top of the form:

   - Name and address of employee
   - Employee's Social Security number
   - Number of exemptions claimed by employee on Form W-4
   - Regular and overtime wage rates
   - Pay period (ie., weekly, biweekly, monthly, etc.)
   - Date check is written
   - Payroll check number

2. For each pay period, fill in the number of regular and overtime ("OT") hours worked by the employee from his or her Quarterly Payroll Time Sheet. Multiply this amount by the employee's wage rate to determine the *gross pay*. For example: 40 hours at the regular wage of $8.00/hour = $320.00; plus five hours at the overtime wage rate of $12.00/hour = $60.00. Gross pay for the period is $320.00 + $60.00 = $380.00.

3. Determine the Federal withholding tax deduction for the pay amount by consulting the withholding tax tables in IRS Circular E: *Employer's Tax Guide*. Enter this figure on the form in the "Fed. W/H" column.

4. Determine the employee's share of Social Security and Medicare deductions. As of 2000, the employee's Social Security share rate is 6.2 percent and the employee's Medicare share rate is 1.45 percent. Multiply these rates times the employee's gross wages and enter the figures in the appropriate places; the "S/S Ded." and "Medic. Ded." columns. For example: for $380.00, the Social Security deduction would be $380.00 x .062 = $23.56 and the Medicare deduction would be $380.00 x .0145 = $5.51.

5. Determine any state taxes and enter in the appropriate column.

6. Subtract all of the deductions from the employee's gross wages to determine the employee's *net pay*. Enter this figure in the final column and prepare the employee's paycheck using the deduction information from this sheet. Also prepare a check to your payroll tax bank account for a total of the Federal withholding amount and two times the Social Security and Medicare amounts. This includes your employer share of these taxes. The employer's share of Social Security and Medicare taxes is equal to the employee's share.

Employee Payroll Record

Employee:
Address:

Social Security #:
Number of Exemptions:
Rate of Pay: Overtime Rate:
Pay Period:

Date	Check #	Pay Period	Reg. Hours	OT Hours	Gross Pay	Fed. W/H	S/S Ded.	Medic. Ded.	State Taxes	Net Pay
Pay Period TOTAL										

Payroll Depository Record

You will be required to deposit taxes with the IRS on a monthly or quarterly basis (unless your total employment taxes totaled more than $50,000.00 for the previous year, in which case you should obviously consult an accountant). If your employment taxes total less than $2,500.00 per quarter, you may pay your payroll tax liability when you quarterly file your Federal Form 941: *Employer's Quarterly Federal Tax Return*. If your payroll tax liability is more than $2,500.00 per quarter, you must deposit your payroll taxes on a monthly basis with a bank using IRS Form 8109: *Federal Tax Deposit Coupon*. Copies of these two Federal forms are contained on the Forms-on-CD. To track your payroll tax liability, use the Payroll Depository Record which follows these instructions:

1. On a monthly basis, total each column on all of your Employee Payroll Records. This will give you a figure for each employee's Federal withholding, Social Security, and Medicare taxes for the month.

2. Total all of the Federal withholding taxes for all employees for the month and enter this figure in the appropriate column on the Payroll Depository Record.

3. Total Social Security and Medicare taxes for all of your employees for the entire month and enter this figure in the appropriate columns on the Payroll Depository Record. Note that "SS/EE" refers to Social Security/Employee's Share and that "MC/EE" refers to Medicare/Employee's Share.

4. Enter identical amounts in the SS/ER and MC/ER columns as you have entered in the SS/EE and MC/EE columns. "ER" refers to the employer's share. The employer's share of Social Security and Medicare is the same as the employee's share, but is not deducted from the employee's pay.

5. Total all of the deductions for the month. This is the amount of your total monthly Federal payroll tax liability. If necessary, write a check to your local bank for this amount and deposit it using IRS Form 8109: *Federal Tax Deposit Coupon*.

6. If you must file only quarterly, total all three of your monthly amounts on a quarterly basis and pay this amount when you file your IRS Form 941: *Employer's Quarterly Federal Tax Return*. On a yearly basis, total all of the quarterly columns to arrive at your total annual Federal payroll tax liability.

Payroll Depository Record

Month	Fed. W/H		SS/EE		SS/ER		MC/EE		MC/ER		Total	
January												
February												
March												
1st Quarter												

1st Quarter Total Number of Employees: Total Wages Paid:

Month	Fed. W/H		SS/EE		SS/ER		MC/EE		MC/ER		Total	
April												
May												
June												
2nd Quarter												

2nd Quarter Total Number of Employees: Total Wages Paid:

Month	Fed. W/H		SS/EE		SS/ER		MC/EE		MC/ER		Total	
July												
August												
September												
3rd Quarter												

3rd Quarter Total Number of Employees: Total Wages Paid:

Month	Fed. W/H		SS/EE		SS/ER		MC/EE		MC/ER		Total	
October												
November												
December												
4th Quarter												

4th Quarter Total Number of Employees: Total Wages Paid:

Yearly TOTAL												

Yearly Total Number of Employees: Total Wages Paid:

Annual Payroll Summary

The final payroll form is used to total all of the payroll amounts for all employees on a monthly, quarterly, and annual basis. Much of the information on this form is similar to the information that you compiled for the Payroll Depository Record. However, the purpose of this form is to provide you with a record of all of your payroll costs, including the payroll deduction costs. This form will be useful for both tax and planning purposes as you examine your business profitability on a quarterly and annual basis. Follow these directions to prepare this form:

1. For each month, total all of your employees' gross and net pay amounts from their individual Employee Payroll Records and transfer these totals to this form.

2. For each month, transfer the amounts for Federal withholding from the Payroll Depository Record to this form.

3   For each month, total both columns on your Payroll Depository Record for SS/EE ("Social Security/Employee") and SS/ER ("Social Security/Employer") and transfer this total to the "S/S Taxes" column on this summary. Total the MC/EE ("Medicare/ Employee") and MC/ER ("Medicare/Employer") columns also and enter the total in the "Medicare Taxes" column on this form.

4. On a quarterly basis, total the columns to determine your quarterly payroll costs. Annually, total the quarterly amounts to determine your annual costs.

Annual Payroll Summary

	Gross Pay		Federal W/H		S/S Taxes		Medicare Taxes		State Taxes		Net Pay	
January												
February												
March												
1st Quarter Total												
April												
May												
June												
2nd Quarter Total												
July												
August												
September												
3rd Quarter Total												
October												
November												
December												
4th Quarter Total												
Yearly TOTAL												

Payroll Checklist

☐ File IRS Form SS-4: *Application for Employer Identification Number* and obtain Federal Employer Identification Number (FEIN)

☐ Obtain IRS Form W-4: *Employee's Withholding Allowance Certificate* for each employee

☐ Set up Quarterly Payroll Time Sheets and Employee Payroll Records for employees

☐ Open separate business payroll tax bank account

☐ Consult IRS Circular E: *Employer's Tax Guide* and use tables to determine withholding tax amounts

☐ Obtain information on any applicable state or local taxes

☐ List Federal withholding, Social Security, Medicare, and any state or local deductions on Employee Payroll Record

☐ Pay employees and deposit appropriate taxes in payroll tax bank account

☐ Fill in Payroll Depository Record and Annual Payroll Summary

☐ Pay payroll taxes

> ☐ Monthly, using IRS Form 8109: *Federal Tax Deposit Coupon*, if your payroll tax liability is more than $2,500 per quarter

> ☐ Quarterly, using IRS Form 941: *Employer's Quarterly Federal Tax Return*, if your payroll tax liability is less than $2,500 per quarter

> ☐ Annually, file IRS Form 940: *Employer's Annual Federal Unemployment (FUTA) Tax Return*

☐ Annually, prepare and file IRS Form W-2: *Wage and Tax Statement* and IRS Form W-3: *Transmittal of Wage and Tax Statement* for each employee

CHAPTER 15

Taxation of Sole Proprietorship

The taxation of sole proprietorships is a relatively easy concept to understand. The sole proprietorship is not considered a separate entity for Federal tax purposes. Thus, all of the profits and losses of the business are simply personal and individual profits or losses of the sole owner. They are reported on IRS Schedule C: Profits or Losses of a Business or on IRS Schedule C-EZ: Net Profits of a Business and are included in the calculations for completing the owner's joint or single IRS Form 1040.

In this chapter, you will find an array of the Federal tax forms necessary for use in a sole proprietorship business. The financial records that you will compile using the forms in this book will make your tax preparation much easier, whether you handle this yourself or it is handled by a tax professional. A basic comprehension of the information required on Federal tax forms will help you understand why certain financial records are necessary. Understanding tax reporting will also assist you as you decide how to organize your business financial records.

Please note that many of the tax forms in this chapter will only apply to a sole proprietorship that actually hires employees. Simply because a sole proprietorship business is owned by one owner does not in any way restrict the sole owner from hiring employees or independent contractors to assist in the operation of the business. In fact, there have been sole proprietorships that have operated with many, many employees and at different locations and even in many states.

A checklist of tax forms is provided that details which IRS forms are necessary for this type of business. In addition, various schedules of tax filing are also provided to assist you in keeping your tax reporting timely. Finally, a sample of each form is presented at the end of this chapter and also on the Forms-on-CD.

Sole Proprietorship Tax Forms Checklist

☐ IRS Form 1040: *U.S. Individual Income Tax Return*.

☐ IRS Schedule C: *Profit or Loss From Business*. Must be filed with IRS Form 1040 by all sole proprietorships, unless Schedule IRS Schedule C-EZ is filed.

☐ IRS Schedule C-EZ: *Net Profit From Business*. May be filed if expenses are under $5,000 and other qualifications are met (See Schedule C-EZ).

☐ IRS Form 1040-SS: *Self-Employment Tax*. Required for any sole proprietor who shows $400 income from his or her business on IRS Schedule C or C-EZ.

☐ IRS Form 1040-ES: *Estimated Tax for Individuals*. Must be used by all sole proprietors who expect to make a profit requiring estimated taxes.

☐ IRS Form SS-4: *Application for Employer Identification Number*. Must be filed by all sole proprietors who will hire one or more employees.

☐ IRS Form W-2: *Wage and Tax Statement*. Must be filed by all sole proprietors who have one or more employees.

☐ IRS Form W-3: *Transmittal of Wage and Tax Statement*. Must be filed by all sole proprietors who have one or more employees.

☐ IRS Form W-4: *Employee's Withholding Allowance Certificate*. Must be provided to employees of sole proprietors. Not filed with the IRS.

☐ IRS Form 940: *Employer's Annual Federal Unemployment Tax Return (FUTA)*. Must be filed by all sole proprietors who have employees.

☐ IRS Form 941: *Employer's Quarterly Federal Tax Return*. Must be filed by all sole proprietors who have one or more employees.

☐ IRS Form 8109: *Federal Tax Deposit Coupon*. Used by all employers with quarterly employee tax liability over $2,500.00. (Obtain from IRS).

☐ IRS Form 8829: *Expenses for Business Use of Your Home*. Filed with annual IRS Form 1040, if necessary.

☐ Any required state and local income and sales tax forms.

Sole Proprietorship Monthly Tax Schedule

☐ If you have employees, and your payroll tax liability is over $2,500.00 quarterly, you must make monthly tax payments using IRS Form 8109.

☐ If required, file and pay any necessary state or local sales tax.

Sole Proprietorship Quarterly Tax Schedule

☐ Pay any required estimated taxes using vouchers from IRS Form 1040-ES.

☐ If you have employees, file IRS Form 941 and make any required payments of FICA and withholding taxes.

☐ If you have employees and your unpaid quarterly FUTA tax liability is over $500.00, make FUTA deposit using IRS Form 8109.

☐ If required, file and pay any necessary state or local sales tax.

Sole Proprietorship Annual Tax Schedule

☐ If you have employees, prepare IRS Forms W-2 and provide to employees by January 31, and file IRS Form W-3 and copies of all IRS Forms W-2 with IRS by January 31.

☐ If you have paid any independent contractors over $600 annually, prepare IRS Forms 1099 and provide to recipients by January 31; and file IRS Form 1096 and copies of all IRS Forms 1099 with IRS by January 31.

☐ Make required unemployment tax payment and file IRS Form 940

☐ File IRS Form 1040-SS with your annual IRS Form 1040.

☐ File IRS Schedule C and IRS Form 1040.

☐ File IRS Form 8829 with your annual IRS Form 1040, if necessary.

☐ If you are required, file and pay any necessary state or local sales, income, or unemployment taxes.

Form **SS-4**

(Rev. December 2001)

Department of the Treasury
Internal Revenue Service

Application for Employer Identification Number

(For use by employers, corporations, partnerships, trusts, estates, churches, government agencies, Indian tribal entities, certain individuals, and others.)

▶ See separate instructions for each line.   ▶ Keep a copy for your records.

EIN

OMB No. 1545-0003

Type or print clearly.

1   Legal name of entity (or individual) for whom the EIN is being requested

2   Trade name of business (if different from name on line 1)

3   Executor, trustee, "care of" name

4a   Mailing address (room, apt., suite no. and street, or P.O. box)

5a   Street address (if different) (Do not enter a P.O. box.)

4b   City, state, and ZIP code

5b   City, state, and ZIP code

6   County and state where principal business is located

7a   Name of principal officer, general partner, grantor, owner, or trustor

7b   SSN, ITIN, or EIN

8a   **Type of entity** (check only one box)

☐ Sole proprietor (SSN) _____

☐ Partnership

☐ Corporation (enter form number to be filed) ▶ _____

☐ Personal service corp.

☐ Church or church-controlled organization

☐ Other nonprofit organization (specify) ▶ _____

☐ Other (specify) ▶

☐ Estate (SSN of decedent) _____

☐ Plan administrator (SSN) _____

☐ Trust (SSN of grantor) _____

☐ National Guard   ☐ State/local government

☐ Farmers' cooperative   ☐ Federal government/military

☐ REMIC   ☐ Indian tribal governments/enterprises

Group Exemption Number (GEN) ▶ _____

8b   If a corporation, name the state or foreign country (if applicable) where incorporated

State

Foreign country

9   **Reason for applying** (check only one box)

☐ Started new business (specify type) ▶_____

☐ Hired employees (Check the box and see line 12.)

☐ Compliance with IRS withholding regulations

☐ Other (specify) ▶

☐ Banking purpose (specify purpose) ▶ _____

☐ Changed type of organization (specify new type) ▶ _____

☐ Purchased going business

☐ Created a trust (specify type) ▶ _____

☐ Created a pension plan (specify type) ▶ _____

10   Date business started or acquired (month, day, year)

11   Closing month of accounting year

12   First date wages or annuities were paid or will be paid (month, day, year). **Note:** *If applicant is a withholding agent, enter date income will first be paid to nonresident alien. (month, day, year)* . . . . ▶

13   Highest number of employees expected in the next 12 months. **Note:** *If the applicant does not expect to have any employees during the period, enter "-0-."* . . . . ▶

Agricultural	Household	Other

14   Check **one** box that best describes the principal activity of your business.

☐ Construction   ☐ Rental & leasing   ☐ Transportation & warehousing

☐ Real estate   ☐ Manufacturing   ☐ Finance & insurance

☐ Health care & social assistance   ☐ Wholesale–agent/broker

☐ Accommodation & food service   ☐ Wholesale–other   ☐ Retail

☐ Other (specify)

15   Indicate principal line of merchandise sold; specific construction work done; products produced; or services provided.

16a   Has the applicant ever applied for an employer identification number for this or any other business? . . . . ☐ Yes   ☐ No

Note: *If "Yes," please complete lines 16b and 16c.*

16b   If you checked "Yes" on line 16a, give applicant's legal name and trade name shown on prior application if different from line 1 or 2 above.

Legal name ▶   Trade name ▶

16c   Approximate date when, and city and state where, the application was filed. Enter previous employer identification number if known.

Approximate date when filed (mo., day, year) | City and state where filed | Previous EIN

Third Party Designee

Complete this section **only** if you want to authorize the named individual to receive the entity's EIN and answer questions about the completion of this form.

Designee's name

Designee's telephone number (include area code)
(   )

Address and ZIP code

Designee's fax number (include area code)
(   )

Under penalties of perjury, I declare that I have examined this application, and to the best of my knowledge and belief, it is true, correct, and complete.

Applicant's telephone number (include area code)
(   )

Name and title (type or print clearly) ▶

Signature ▶   Date ▶

Applicant's fax number (include area code)
(   )

For Privacy Act and Paperwork Reduction Act Notice, see separate instructions.   Cat. No. 16055N   Form **SS-4** (Rev. 12-2001)

Do I Need an EIN?

File Form SS-4 if the applicant entity does not already have an EIN but is required to show an EIN on any return, statement, or other document.[1] **See also the separate instructions for each line on Form SS-4.**

IF the applicant...	AND...	THEN...
Started a new business	Does not currently have (nor expect to have) employees	Complete lines 1, 2, 4a–6, 8a, and 9–16c.
Hired (or will hire) employees, including household employees	Does not already have an EIN	Complete lines 1, 2, 4a–6, 7a–b (if applicable), 8a, 8b (if applicable), and 9–16c.
Opened a bank account	Needs an EIN for banking purposes only	Complete lines 1–5b, 7a–b (if applicable), 8a, 9, and 16a–c.
Changed type of organization	Either the legal character of the organization or its ownership changed (e.g., you incorporate a sole proprietorship or form a partnership)[2]	Complete lines 1–16c (as applicable).
Purchased a going business[3]	Does not already have an EIN	Complete lines 1–16c (as applicable).
Created a trust	The trust is other than a grantor trust or an IRA trust[4]	Complete lines 1–16c (as applicable).
Created a pension plan as a plan administrator[5]	Needs an EIN for reporting purposes	Complete lines 1, 2, 4a–6, 8a, 9, and 16a–c.
Is a foreign person needing an EIN to comply with IRS withholding regulations	Needs an EIN to complete a Form W-8 (other than Form W-8ECI), avoid withholding on portfolio assets, or claim tax treaty benefits[6]	Complete lines 1–5b, 7a–b (SSN or ITIN optional), 8a–9, and 16a–c.
Is administering an estate	Needs an EIN to report estate income on Form 1041	Complete lines 1, 3, 4a–b, 8a, 9, and 16a–c.
Is a withholding agent for taxes on non-wage income paid to an alien (i.e., individual, corporation, or partnership, etc.)	Is an agent, broker, fiduciary, manager, tenant, or spouse who is required to file **Form 1042,** Annual Withholding Tax Return for U.S. Source Income of Foreign Persons	Complete lines 1, 2, 3 (if applicable), 4a–5b, 7a–b (if applicable), 8a, 9, and 16a–c.
Is a state or local agency	Serves as a tax reporting agent for public assistance recipients under Rev. Proc. 80-4, 1980-1 C.B. 581[7]	Complete lines 1, 2, 4a–5b, 8a, 9, and 16a–c.
Is a single-member LLC	Needs an EIN to file **Form 8832,** Classification Election, for filing employment tax returns, **or** for state reporting purposes[8]	Complete lines 1–16c (as applicable).
Is an S corporation	Needs an EIN to file **Form 2553,** Election by a Small Business Corporation[9]	Complete lines 1–16c (as applicable).

[1] For example, a sole proprietorship or self-employed farmer who establishes a qualified retirement plan, or is required to file excise, employment, alcohol, tobacco, or firearms returns, must have an EIN. **A partnership, corporation, REMIC (real estate mortgage investment conduit), nonprofit organization (church, club, etc.), or farmers' cooperative must use an EIN for any tax-related purpose even if the entity does not have employees.**

[2] However, **do not** apply for a new EIN if the existing entity only **(a)** changed its business name, **(b)** elected on Form 8832 to change the way it is taxed (or is covered by the default rules), or **(c)** terminated its partnership status because at least 50% of the total interests in partnership capital and profits were sold or exchanged within a 12-month period. (The EIN of the terminated partnership should continue to be used. See Regulations section 301.6109-1(d)(2)(iii).)

[3] Do not use the EIN of the prior business unless you became the "owner" of a corporation by acquiring its stock.

[4] However, IRA trusts that are required to file **Form 990-T,** Exempt Organization Business Income Tax Return, must have an EIN.

[5] A plan administrator is the person or group of persons specified as the administrator by the instrument under which the plan is operated.

[6] Entities applying to be a Qualified Intermediary (QI) need a QI-EIN even if they already have an EIN. **See Rev. Proc. 2000-12.**

[7] See also *Household employer* on page 4. (**Note:** State or local agencies may need an EIN for other reasons, e.g., hired employees.)

[8] Most LLCs **do not** need to file Form 8832. See **Limited liability company (LLC)** on page 4 for details on completing Form SS-4 for an LLC.

[9] An existing corporation that is electing or revoking S corporation status should use its previously-assigned EIN.

♻

How to Order Forms and Publications from IRS

 Call 1-800-TAX-FORM or 1-800-829-3676

Visit our web site at *www.irs.gov*

Other IRS Forms and Publications You May Need

- Form SS-4, Application for Employer Identification Number
- Form W-2, Wage and Tax Statement
- Form W-2c, Corrected Wage and Tax Statement
- Form W-3, Transmittal of Wage and Tax Statements
- Form W-3c, Transmittal of Corrected Wage and Tax Statements
- Form W-4, Employee's Withholding Allowance Certificate
- Form W-5, Earned Income Credit Advance Payment Certificate
- Form 940, Employer's Annual Federal Unemployment (FUTA) Tax Return
- Form 941, Employer's QUARTERLY Federal Tax Return
- Form 941c, Supporting Statement to Correct Information
- Form 943, Employer's Annual Federal Tax Return for Agricultural Employees
- Form 944, Employer's ANNUAL Federal Tax Return

- Form 945, Annual Return of Withheld Federal Income Tax
- Form 4070, Employee's Report of Tips to Employer

- Form 8027, Employer's Annual Information Return of Tip Income and Allocated Tips
- Instructions for Forms W-2 and W-3
- Instructions for Form 941
- Instructions for Form 944
- Notice 797, Possible Federal Tax Refund Due to the Earned Income Credit (EIC)
- Pub. 15 (Circular E), Employer's Tax Guide
- Pub. 15-A, Employer's Supplemental Tax Guide
- Pub. 15-B, Employer's Tax Guide to Fringe Benefits
- Pub. 51 (Circular A), Agricultural Employer's Tax Guide
- Pub. 596, Earned Income Credit
- Pub. 926, Household Employer's Tax Guide
- Pub. 947, Practice Before the IRS and Power of Attorney
- Schedule A (Form 940), Multi-State Employer and Credit Reduction Information
- Schedule B (Form 941), Report of Tax Liability for Semiweekly Schedule Depositors
- Schedule D (Form 941), Report of Discrepancies Caused by Acquisitions, Statutory Mergers, or Consolidations
- Schedule H (Form 1040), Household Employment Taxes

State Unemployment Tax Agencies

The following list of state unemployment tax agencies was provided to the IRS by the U.S. Department of Labor. For the most up-to-date contact information, visit the U.S. Department of Labor's website at *www.workforcesecurity.doleta.gov*.

State	Telephone	Web Address
Alabama	(334) 242-8467	www.dir.state.al.us
Alaska	(800) 448-3527	www.labor.state.ak.us
Arizona	(602) 248-9396	www.de.state.az.us
Arkansas	(501) 682-3253	www.state.ar.us/esd
California	(888) 745-3886	www.edd.cahwnet.gov
Colorado	(800) 480-8299	www.coworkforce.com
Connecticut	(860) 263-6550	www.ctdol.state.ct.us
Delaware	(302) 761-8484	www.delawareworks.com
District of Columbia	(202) 698-7550	www.dcnetworks.org
Florida	(800) 482-8293	www.floridajobs.org
Georgia	(404) 232-3301	www.dol.state.ga.us
Hawaii	(808) 586-8913	www.state.hi.us
Idaho	(800) 448-2977	www.labor.state.id.us
Illinois	(312) 793-1900	www.ides.state.il.us
Indiana	(317) 232-7436	www.in.gov/dwd
Iowa	(515) 281-5339	www.iowaworkforce.org
Kansas	(785) 296-5025	www.dol.ks.gov
Kentucky	(502) 564-6838	www.oet.ky.gov
Louisiana	(225) 342-2944	www.ldol.state.la.us
Maine	(207) 287-3176	www.state.me.us/labor
Maryland	(800) 492-5524	www.dllr.state.md.us
Massachusetts	(617) 626-5050	www.detma.org
Michigan	(313) 456-2180	www.michigan.gov/uia
Minnesota	(651) 296-6141	www.uimn.org
Mississippi	(601) 961-7755	www.mdes.ms.gov
Missouri	(573) 751-3340	www.dolir.mo.gov
Montana	(406) 444-6900	www.uid.dli.mt.gov
Nebraska	(402) 471-9935	www.dol.state.ne.us
Nevada	(775) 687-4545	www.detr.state.nv.us
New Hampshire	(603) 228-4033	www.nhes.state.nh.us
New Jersey	(609) 633-6400	www.state.nj.us
New Mexico	(505) 841-8582	www.dol.state.nm.us
New York	(800) 225-5829	www.labor.state.ny.us
North Carolina	(919) 733-7396	www.ncesc.com
North Dakota	(800) 472-2952	www.jobsnd.com
Ohio	(614) 466-2319	www.jfs.ohio.gov
Oklahoma	(405) 557-7170	www.oesc.state.ok.us
Oregon	(503) 947-1488, option 5	www.employment.oregon.gov
Pennsylvania	(717) 787-7679	www.dli.state.pa.us
Puerto Rico	(787) 754-5262	
Rhode Island	(401) 222-3696	www.uitax.ri.gov
South Carolina	(803) 737-3075	www.sces.org
South Dakota	(605) 626-2312	www.state.sd.us
Tennessee	(615) 741-2486	www.state.tn.us
Texas	(512) 463-2700	www.twc.state.tx.us
Utah	(801) 526-9400	www.jobs.utah.gov
Vermont	(802) 828-4252	www.labor.vermont.gov
Virginia	(804) 371-7159	www.VaEmploy.com
Virgin Islands	(340) 776-3700	www.vidol.gov
Washington	(360) 902-9360	www.wa.gov/esd
West Virginia	(304) 558-2675	www.workforcewv.org
Wisconsin	(608) 261-6700	www.dwd.state.wi.us
Wyoming	(307) 235-3217	http://wydoe.state.wy.us

Form 940

Department of the Treasury
Internal Revenue Service (99)

Employer's Annual Federal Unemployment (FUTA) Tax Return

OMB No. 1545-0028

2004

▶ See the separate Instructions for Form 940 for information on completing this form.

You must complete this section. ▶

Name (as distinguished from trade name)	Calendar year	T
		FF
Trade name, if any	Employer identification number (EIN)	FD
		FP
		I
Address (number and street)	City, state, and ZIP code	T

A Are you required to pay unemployment contributions to only one state? (If "No," skip questions B and C.) ☐ Yes ☐ No

B Did you pay all state unemployment contributions by January 31, 2005? ((1) If you deposited your total FUTA tax when due, check "Yes" if you paid all state unemployment contributions by February 10, 2005. (2) If a 0% experience rate is granted, check "Yes." (3) If "No," skip question C.) . . . . ☐ Yes ☐ No

C Were all wages that were taxable for FUTA tax also taxable for your state's unemployment tax? . . . . ☐ Yes ☐ No

D Did you pay all wages in a state other than New York? . . . . ☐ Yes ☐ No

If you answered "No" to any of these questions, you must file Form 940. If you answered "Yes" to all the questions, you may file Form 940-EZ, which is a simplified version of Form 940. (Successor employers, see **Special credit for successor employers** in the separate instructions.) You can get Form 940-EZ by calling 1-800-TAX-FORM (1-800-829-3676) or from the IRS website at **www.irs.gov.**

If you will not have to file returns in the future, check here (see **Who Must File** in the separate instructions) **and complete and sign the return** . . . . ▶ ☐

If this is an Amended Return, check here (see **Amended Returns** in the separate instructions) . . . . ▶ ☐

Part I   Computation of Taxable Wages

1	Total payments (including payments shown on lines 2 and 3) during the calendar year for services of employees	**1**	
2	Exempt payments. (Explain all exempt payments, attaching additional sheets if necessary.) ▶ ------------------------------------- ---	**2**	
3	Payments of more than $7,000 for services. Enter only amounts over the first $7,000 paid to each employee (see separate instructions). Do not include any exempt payments from line 2. The $7,000 amount is the federal wage base. Your state wage base may be different. **Do not use your state wage limitation**	**3**	
4	Add lines 2 and 3	**4**	
5	**Total taxable wages** (subtract line 4 from line 1) . . . . ▶	**5**	
6	Additional tax resulting from credit reduction for unpaid advances to the State of New York. Enter the wages included on line 5 for New York and multiply by .003. (See the separate Instructions for Form 940.) Enter the credit reduction amount here and in Part II, line 5: New York wages _____ x .003 = ... ▶	**6**	

Be sure to complete both sides of this form, and sign in the space provided on the back.

For Privacy Act and Paperwork Reduction Act Notice, see separate instructions.   ▼ **DETACH HERE** ▼   Cat. No. 11234O   Form **940** (2004)

- -

Form 940-V

Department of the Treasury
Internal Revenue Service

Payment Voucher

Use this voucher only when making a payment with your return.

OMB No. 1545-0028

2004

Complete boxes 1, 2, and 3. Do not send cash, and do not staple your payment to this voucher. Make your check or money order payable to the "United States Treasury." Be sure to enter your employer identification number (EIN), "Form 940," and "2004" on your payment.

1 Enter your employer identification number (EIN).	2 **Enter the amount of your payment.** ▶	Dollars	Cents
	3 Enter your business name (individual name for sole proprietors).		
	Enter your address.		
	Enter your city, state, and ZIP code.		

171

Name | Employer identification number (EIN)

Part II   Tax Due or Refund

1 Gross FUTA tax. (Multiply the wages from Part I, line 5, by .062) . . . . | **1**

2 Maximum credit. (Multiply the wages from Part I, line 5, by .054) . . | **2**

3 Computation of tentative credit (**Note:** *All taxpayers must complete the applicable columns.*)

(a) Name of state	(b) State reporting number(s) as shown on employer's state contribution returns	(c) Taxable payroll (as defined in state act)	(d) State experience rate period		(e) State ex- perience rate	(f) Contributions if rate had been 5.4% (col. (c) x .054)	(g) Contributions payable at experience rate (col. (c) x col. (e))	(h) Additional credit (col. (f) minus col.(g)) If 0 or less, enter -0-.	(i) Contributions paid to state by 940 due date
			From	To					

3a Totals . . . ▶

3b **Total tentative credit** (add line 3a, columns (h) and (i) only—for late payments, also see the instructions for Part II, line 4) . . . . ▶ | **3b**

4 **Credit:** Enter the smaller of the amount from Part II, line 2 or line 3b; or the amount from the worksheet on page 7 of the separate instructions . . . . | **4**

5 Enter the amount from Part I, line 6 . . . . | **5**

6 **Credit allowable** (subtract line 5 from line 4). If zero or less, enter "-0-" . . . . | **6**

7 **Total FUTA tax** (subtract line 6 from line 1). If the result is over $100, also complete Part III . . | **7**

8 Total FUTA tax deposited for the year, including any overpayment applied from a prior year . . | **8**

9 **Balance due** (subtract line 8 from line 7). Pay to the "United States Treasury." If you owe more than $100, see **Depositing FUTA Tax** on page 3 of the separate instructions . . . . . . ▶ | **9**

10 **Overpayment** (subtract line 7 from line 8). Check if it is to be: ☐ **Applied to next return** or ☐ **Refunded** . . . . ▶ | **10**

Part III   Record of Quarterly Federal Unemployment Tax Liability (Do not include state liability.) **Complete only if line 7 is over $100.** See page 7 of the separate instructions.

Quarter	First (Jan. 1–Mar. 31)	Second (Apr. 1–June 30)	Third (July 1–Sept. 30)	Fourth (Oct. 1–Dec. 31)	Total for year
Liability for quarter					

Third-Party Designee   Do you want to allow another person to discuss this return with the IRS (see separate instructions)? ☐ **Yes.** Complete the following.   ☐ **No**

Designee's name ▶   Phone no. ▶ (   )   Personal identification number (PIN) ▶ ☐☐☐☐☐

Under penalties of perjury, I declare that I have examined this return, including accompanying schedules and statements, and, to the best of my knowledge and belief, it is true, correct, and complete, and that no part of any payment made to a state unemployment fund claimed as a credit was, or is to be, deducted from the payments to employees.

Signature ▶   Title (Owner, etc.) ▶   Date ▶

Form **940** (2004)

172

Form **941 for 2005:** **Employer's Quarterly Federal Tax Return**

99011

(Rev. January 2005) Department of the Treasury — Internal Revenue Service

OMB No. 1545-0029

Employer identification number

Name (not your trade name)

Trade name (if any)

Address

Number   Street   Suite or room number

City   State   ZIP code

Report for this Quarter ...
(Check one.)

☐ **1:** January, February, March

☐ **2:** April, May, June

☐ **3:** July, August, September

☐ **4:** October, November, December

Read the separate instructions before you fill out this form. Please type or print within the boxes.

Part 1: Answer these questions for this quarter.

1 Number of employees who received wages, tips, or other compensation for the pay period including: *Mar. 12* (Quarter 1), *June 12* (Quarter 2), *Sept. 12* (Quarter 3), *Dec. 12* (Quarter 4)   **1**

2 Wages, tips, and other compensation **2**

3 Total income tax withheld from wages, tips, and other compensation **3**

4 If no wages, tips, and other compensation are subject to social security or Medicare tax . .   ☐ Check and go to line 6.

5 Taxable social security and Medicare wages and tips:

	Column 1		Column 2
5a Taxable social security wages		× .124 =	
5b Taxable social security tips		× .124 =	
5c Taxable Medicare wages & tips		× .029 =	

5d Total social security and Medicare taxes (*Column 2,* lines 5a + 5b + 5c = line 5d) . .   **5d**

6 Total taxes before adjustments (lines 3 + 5d = line 6) **6**

7 Tax adjustments (If your answer is a negative number, write it in brackets.):

7a Current quarter's fractions of cents . . . .

7b Current quarter's sick pay . . . .

7c Current quarter's adjustments for tips and group-term life insurance

7d Current year's income tax withholding (Attach Form 941c) . . .

7e Prior quarters' social security and Medicare taxes (Attach Form 941c)

7f Special additions to federal income tax (reserved use) . . . . .

7g Special additions to social security and Medicare (reserved use)

7h Total adjustments (Combine all amounts: lines 7a through 7g.) **7h**

8 Total taxes after adjustments (Combine lines 6 and 7h.) **8**

9 Advance earned income credit (EIC) payments made to employees **9**

10 Total taxes after adjustment for advance EIC (lines 8 – 9 = line 10) **10**

11 Total deposits for this quarter, including overpayment applied from a prior quarter . . .   **11**

12 Balance due (lines 10 – 11 = line 12) Make checks payable to the *United States Treasury* . .   **12**

13 Overpayment (If line 11 is more than line 10, write the difference here.)   Check one ☐ Apply to next return.
☐ Send a refund.

Next ➡

For Privacy Act and Paperwork Reduction Act Notice, see the back of the Payment Voucher.

Cat. No. 17001Z   Form **941** (Rev. 1-2005)

173

Name *(not your trade name)*   Employer identification number

Part 2: Tell us about your deposit schedule for this quarter.

If you are unsure about whether you are a monthly schedule depositor or a semiweekly schedule depositor, see *Pub. 15 (Circular E),* **section 11.**

14 [ ] [ ] Write the state abbreviation for the state where you made your deposits OR write "MU" if you made your deposits in *multiple* states.

15 Check one: [ ] **Line 10 is less than $2,500.** Go to Part 3.

[ ] **You were a monthly schedule depositor for the entire quarter. Fill out your tax liability for each month.** Then go to Part 3.

Tax liability: Month 1 [.   ]

Month 2 [.   ]

Month 3 [.   ]

Total [.   ] **Total must equal line 10.**

[ ] **You were a semiweekly schedule depositor for any part of this quarter.** Fill out *Schedule B (Form 941): Report of Tax Liability for Semiweekly Schedule Depositors,* and attach it to this form.

Part 3: Tell us about your business. If a question does NOT apply to your business, leave it blank.

16 **If your business has closed and you do not have to file returns in the future** . . . . [ ] Check here, and

enter the final date you paid wages [/   /   ] .

17 **If you are a seasonal employer and you do not have to file a return for every quarter of the year** . . [ ] Check here.

Part 4: May we contact your third-party designee?

Do you want to allow an employee, a paid tax preparer, or another person to discuss this return with the IRS? See the instructions for details.

[ ] Yes. Designee's name [   ]

Phone ( ) – [   ] Personal Identification Number (PIN) [ ] [ ] [ ] [ ] [ ]

[ ] No.

Part 5: Sign here

Under penalties of perjury, I declare that I have examined this return, including accompanying schedules and statements, and to the best of my knowledge and belief, it is true, correct, and complete.

X

Sign your name here [   ]

Print name and title [   ]

Date [/   /   ] Phone ( ) – [   ]

Part 6: For paid preparers only *(optional)*

Preparer's signature [   ]

Firm's name [   ]

Address [   ] EIN [   ]

[   ] ZIP code

Date [/   /   ] Phone ( ) – [   ] SSN/PTIN [   ]

[ ] Check if you are self-employed.

Page **2**   Form **941** (Rev. 1-2005)

a Control number	22222	OMB No. 1545-0008		

b Employer identification number (EIN)	**1** Wages, tips, other compensation	**2** Federal income tax withheld
c Employer's name, address, and ZIP code	**3** Social security wages	**4** Social security tax withheld
	5 Medicare wages and tips	**6** Medicare tax withheld
	7 Social security tips	**8** Allocated tips
d Employee's social security number	**9** Advance EIC payment	**10** Dependent care benefits

e Employee's first name and initial Last name	**11** Nonqualified plans	**12a** Code
	13 Statutory employee ☐ Retirement plan ☐ Third-party sick pay ☐	**12b** Code
	14 Other	**12c** Code
		12d Code
f Employee's address and ZIP code		

15 State Employer's state ID number	16 State wages, tips, etc.	17 State income tax	18 Local wages, tips, etc.	19 Local income tax	20 Locality name

Form **W-2** **Wage and Tax Statement**

2005

Department of the Treasury—Internal Revenue Service

Copy 1—For State, City, or Local Tax Department

a Control number	33333	For Official Use Only ▶ OMB No. 1545-0008		

b Kind of Payer	☐ 941 ☐ Military ☐ 943 ☐ CT-1 ☐ Hshld. emp. ☐ Medicare govt. emp. ☐ Third-party sick pay	1 Wages, tips, other compensation	2 Federal income tax withheld
		3 Social security wages	4 Social security tax withheld
c Total number of Forms W-2	d Establishment number	5 Medicare wages and tips	6 Medicare tax withheld
e Employer identification number (EIN)		7 Social security tips	8 Allocated tips
f Employer's name		9 Advance EIC payments	10 Dependent care benefits
		11 Nonqualified plans	12 Deferred compensation
		13 For third-party sick pay use only	
		14 Income tax withheld by payer of third-party sick pay	
g Employer's address and ZIP code			
h Other EIN used this year			
15 State Employer's state ID number		16 State wages, tips, etc.	17 State income tax
		18 Local wages, tips, etc.	19 Local income tax
Contact person		Telephone number ( )	For Official Use Only
Email address		Fax number ( )	

Under penalties of perjury, I declare that I have examined this return and accompanying documents, and, to the best of my knowledge and belief, they are true, correct, and complete.

Signature ▶   Title ▶   Date ▶

Form **W-3** Transmittal of Wage and Tax Statements   **2005**   Department of the Treasury
Internal Revenue Service

Send this entire page with the entire Copy A page of Form(s) W-2 to the Social Security Administration. Photocopies are not acceptable.

Do not send any payment (cash, checks, money orders, etc.) with Forms W-2 and W-3.

Reminder

Separate instructions. See the 2005 Instructions for Forms W-2 and W-3 for information on completing this form.

Purpose of Form

Use Form W-3 to transmit Copy A of Form(s) W-2, Wage and Tax Statement. Make a copy of Form W-3 and keep it with Copy D (For Employer) of Form(s) W-2 for your records. Use Form W-3 for the correct year. **File Form W-3 even if only one Form W-2 is being filed.** If you are filing Form(s) W-2 on magnetic media or electronically, **do not** file Form W-3.

When To File

File Form W-3 with Copy A of Form(s) W-2 by February 28, 2006.

Where To File

Send this entire page with the entire Copy A page of Form(s) W-2 to:

Social Security Administration
Data Operations Center
Wilkes-Barre, PA 18769-0001

Note. *If you use "Certified Mail" to file, change the ZIP code to "18769-0002." If you use an IRS-approved private delivery service, add "ATTN: W-2 Process, 1150 E. Mountain Dr." to the address and change the ZIP code to "18702-7997." See* **Publication 15** *(Circular E), Employer's Tax Guide, for a list of IRS-approved private delivery services.*

Do not send magnetic media to the address shown above.

Form W-4 (2005)

Purpose. Complete Form W-4 so that your employer can withhold the correct federal income tax from your pay. Because your tax situation may change, you may want to refigure your withholding each year.

Exemption from withholding. If you are exempt, complete only lines 1, 2, 3, 4, and 7 and sign the form to validate it. Your exemption for 2005 expires February 16, 2006. See Pub. 505, Tax Withholding and Estimated Tax.

Note. You cannot claim exemption from withholding if (a) your income exceeds $800 and includes more than $250 of unearned income (for example, interest and dividends) and (b) another person can claim you as a dependent on their tax return.

Basic instructions. If you are not exempt, complete the **Personal Allowances Worksheet** below. The worksheets on page 2 adjust your withholding allowances based on itemized deductions, certain credits, adjustments to income, or two-earner/two-job situations. Complete all worksheets that apply. However, you may claim fewer (or zero) allowances.

Head of household. Generally, you may claim head of household filing status on your tax return only if you are unmarried and pay more than 50% of the costs of keeping up a home for yourself and your dependent(s) or other qualifying individuals. See line **E** below.

Tax credits. You can take projected tax credits into account in figuring your allowable number of withholding allowances. Credits for child or dependent care expenses and the child tax credit may be claimed using the **Personal Allowances Worksheet** below. See Pub. 919, How Do I Adjust My Tax Withholding? for information on converting your other credits into withholding allowances.

Nonwage income. If you have a large amount of nonwage income, such as interest or dividends, consider making estimated tax payments using Form 1040-ES, Estimated Tax for Individuals. Otherwise, you may owe additional tax.

Two earners/two jobs. If you have a working spouse or more than one job, figure the total number of allowances you are entitled to claim on all jobs using worksheets from only one Form W-4. Your withholding usually will be most accurate when all allowances are claimed on the Form W-4 for the highest paying job and zero allowances are claimed on the others.

Nonresident alien. If you are a nonresident alien, see the Instructions for Form 8233 before completing this Form W-4.

Check your withholding. After your Form W-4 takes effect, use Pub. 919 to see how the dollar amount you are having withheld compares to your projected total tax for 2005. See Pub. 919, especially if your earnings exceed $125,000 (Single) or $175,000 (Married).

Recent name change? If your name on line 1 differs from that shown on your social security card, call 1-800-772-1213 to initiate a name change and obtain a social security card showing your correct name.

Personal Allowances Worksheet (Keep for your records.)

A	Enter "1" for **yourself** if no one else can claim you as a dependent	A _____
B	Enter "1" if: { • You are single and have only one job; or • You are married, have only one job, and your spouse does not work; or • Your wages from a second job or your spouse's wages (or the total of both) are $1,000 or less. } . .	B _____
C	Enter "1" for your **spouse**. But, you may choose to enter "-0-" if you are married and have either a working spouse or more than one job. (Entering "-0-" may help you avoid having too little tax withheld.)	C _____
D	Enter number of **dependents** (other than your spouse or yourself) you will claim on your tax return	D _____
E	Enter "1" if you will file as **head of household** on your tax return (see conditions under **Head of household** above) .	E _____
F	Enter "1" if you have at least $1,500 of **child or dependent care expenses** for which you plan to claim a credit . .	F _____
	(Note. Do **not** include child support payments. See **Pub. 503,** Child and Dependent Care Expenses, for details.)	
G	**Child Tax Credit** (including additional child tax credit): • If your total income will be less than $54,000 ($79,000 if married), enter "2" for each eligible child. • If your total income will be between $54,000 and $84,000 ($79,000 and $119,000 if married), enter "1" for each eligible child plus "1" **additional** if you have four or more eligible children.	G _____
H	Add lines A through G and enter total here. (**Note.** This may be different from the number of exemptions you claim on your tax return.) ▶	H _____
	For accuracy, complete all worksheets that apply. { • If you plan to **itemize or claim adjustments to income** and want to reduce your withholding, see the **Deductions and Adjustments Worksheet** on page 2. • If you have **more than one job** or are **married and you and your spouse both work** and the combined earnings from all jobs exceed $35,000 ($25,000 if married) see the **Two-Earner/Two-Job Worksheet** on page 2 to avoid having too little tax withheld. • If **neither** of the above situations applies, **stop here** and enter the number from line H on line 5 of Form W-4 below.	

- - - - - - - - - - - - - - - - - - - **Cut here and give Form W-4 to your employer. Keep the top part for your records.** - - - - - - - - - - - - - - - - - - -

Form **W-4**	**Employee's Withholding Allowance Certificate**	OMB No. 1545-0010
Department of the Treasury Internal Revenue Service	▶ Whether you are entitled to claim a certain number of allowances or exemption from withholding is subject to review by the IRS. Your employer may be required to send a copy of this form to the IRS.	2005

1 Type or print your first name and middle initial Last name		**2** Your social security number
Home address (number and street or rural route)	**3** ☐ Single ☐ Married ☐ Married, but withhold at higher Single rate. Note. If married, but legally separated, or spouse is a nonresident alien, check the "Single" box.	
City or town, state, and ZIP code	**4** If your last name differs from that shown on your social security card, check here. You must call 1-800-772-1213 for a new card. ▶ ☐	

5	Total number of allowances you are claiming (from line **H** above **or** from the applicable worksheet on page 2)	**5**
6	Additional amount, if any, you want withheld from each paycheck	**6** $
7	I claim exemption from withholding for 2005, and I certify that I meet **both** of the following conditions for exemption. • Last year I had a right to a refund of **all** federal income tax withheld because I had **no** tax liability **and** • This year I expect a refund of **all** federal income tax withheld because I expect to have **no** tax liability. If you meet both conditions, write "Exempt" here . . . . ▶	**7**

Under penalties of perjury, I declare that I have examined this certificate and to the best of my knowledge and belief, it is true, correct, and complete.

Employee's signature
(Form is not valid
unless you sign it.) ▶ _____   Date ▶ _____

8 Employer's name and address (Employer: Complete lines 8 and 10 only if sending to the IRS.)	**9** Office code (optional)	**10** Employer identification number (EIN)

For Privacy Act and Paperwork Reduction Act Notice, see page 2.   Cat. No. 10220Q   Form **W-4** (2005)

Deductions and Adjustments Worksheet

Note. Use this worksheet *only* if you plan to itemize deductions, claim certain credits, or claim adjustments to income on your 2005 tax return.

1	Enter an estimate of your 2005 itemized deductions. These include qualifying home mortgage interest, charitable contributions, state and local taxes, medical expenses in excess of 7.5% of your income, and miscellaneous deductions. (For 2005, you may have to reduce your itemized deductions if your income is over $145,950 ($72,975 if married filing separately). See *Worksheet 3* in Pub. 919 for details.) . . .	**1**	$
2	Enter: { $10,000 if married filing jointly or qualifying widow(er) / $ 7,300 if head of household / $ 5,000 if single or married filing separately }	**2**	$
3	**Subtract** line 2 from line 1. If line 2 is greater than line 1, enter "-0-"	**3**	$
4	Enter an estimate of your 2005 adjustments to income, including alimony, deductible IRA contributions, and student loan interest	**4**	$
5	**Add** lines 3 and 4 and enter the total. (Include any amount for credits from *Worksheet 7* in Pub. 919) .	**5**	$
6	Enter an estimate of your 2005 nonwage income (such as dividends or interest)	**6**	$
7	**Subtract** line 6 from line 5. Enter the result, but not less than "-0-"	**7**	$
8	**Divide** the amount on line 7 by $3,200 and enter the result here. Drop any fraction	**8**	
9	Enter the number from the **Personal Allowances Worksheet,** line H, page 1	**9**	
10	**Add** lines 8 and 9 and enter the total here. If you plan to use the **Two-Earner/Two-Job Worksheet,** also enter this total on line 1 below. Otherwise, **stop here** and enter this total on Form W-4, line 5, page 1 .	**10**	

Two-Earner/Two-Job Worksheet (See *Two earners/two jobs* on page 1.)

Note. Use this worksheet *only* if the instructions under line H on page 1 direct you here.

1	Enter the number from line H, page 1 (or from line 10 above if you used the **Deductions and Adjustments Worksheet**)	**1**	
2	Find the number in **Table 1** below that applies to the **LOWEST** paying job and enter it here	**2**	
3	If line 1 is **more than or equal to** line 2, subtract line 2 from line 1. Enter the result here (if zero, enter "-0-") and on Form W-4, line 5, page 1. **Do not** use the rest of this worksheet	**3**	

Note. If line 1 is *less than* line 2, enter "-0-" on Form W-4, line 5, page 1. Complete lines 4–9 below to calculate the additional withholding amount necessary to avoid a year-end tax bill.

4	Enter the number from line 2 of this worksheet	**4**	
5	Enter the number from line 1 of this worksheet	**5**	
6	**Subtract** line 5 from line 4	**6**	
7	Find the amount in **Table 2** below that applies to the **HIGHEST** paying job and enter it here	**7**	$
8	**Multiply** line 7 by line 6 and enter the result here. This is the additional annual withholding needed . .	**8**	$
9	Divide line 8 by the number of pay periods remaining in 2005. For example, divide by 26 if you are paid every two weeks and you complete this form in December 2004. Enter the result here and on Form W-4, line 6, page 1. This is the additional amount to be withheld from each paycheck	**9**	$

Table 1: Two-Earner/Two-Job Worksheet

Married Filing Jointly						All Others	
If wages from **HIGHEST** paying job are—	AND, wages from **LOWEST** paying job are—	Enter on line 2 above	If wages from **HIGHEST** paying job are—	AND, wages from **LOWEST** paying job are—	Enter on line 2 above	If wages from **LOWEST** paying job are—	Enter on line 2 above
$0 - $40,000	$0 - $4,000	0	$40,001 and over	30,001 - 36,000	6	$0 - $6,000	0
	4,001 - 8,000	1		36,001 - 45,000	7	6,001 - 12,000	1
	8,001 - 18,000	2		45,001 - 50,000	8	12,001 - 18,000	2
	18,001 and over	3		50,001 - 60,000	9	18,001 - 24,000	3
$40,001 and over	$0 - $4,000	0		60,001 - 65,000	10	24,001 - 31,000	4
	4,001 - 8,000	1		65,001 - 75,000	11	31,001 - 45,000	5
	8,001 - 18,000	2		75,001 - 90,000	12	45,001 - 60,000	6
	18,001 - 22,000	3		90,001 - 100,000	13	60,001 - 75,000	7
	22,001 - 25,000	4		100,001 - 115,000	14	75,001 - 80,000	8
	25,001 - 30,000	5		115,001 and over	15	80,001 - 100,000	9
						100,001 and over	10

Table 2: Two-Earner/Two-Job Worksheet

Married Filing Jointly		All Others	
If wages from **HIGHEST** paying job are—	Enter on line 7 above	If wages from **HIGHEST** paying job are—	Enter on line 7 above
$0 - $60,000	$480	$0 - $30,000	$480
60,001 - 110,000	800	30,001 - 70,000	800
110,001 - 160,000	900	70,001 - 140,000	900
160,001 - 280,000	1,060	140,001 - 320,000	1,060
280,001 and over	1,120	320,001 and over	1,120

Self-Employment Tax

► **Attach to Form 1040.** ► **See Instructions for Schedule SE (Form 1040).**

OMB No. 1545-0074

20**04**

Attachment
Sequence No. **17**

Name of person with **self-employment** income (as shown on Form 1040)	Social security number of person with **self-employment** income ►

Who Must File Schedule SE

You must file Schedule SE if:

- You had net earnings from self-employment from **other than** church employee income (line 4 of Short Schedule SE or line 4c of Long Schedule SE) of $400 or more **or**
- You had church employee income of $108.28 or more. Income from services you performed as a minister or a member of a religious order **is not** church employee income (see page SE-1).

Note. Even if you had a loss or a small amount of income from self-employment, it may be to your benefit to file Schedule SE and use either "optional method" in Part II of Long Schedule SE (see page SE-3).

Exception. If your only self-employment income was from earnings as a minister, member of a religious order, or Christian Science practitioner **and** you filed Form 4361 and received IRS approval not to be taxed on those earnings, **do not** file Schedule SE. Instead, write "Exempt–Form 4361" on Form 1040, line 57.

May I Use Short Schedule SE or Must I Use Long Schedule SE?

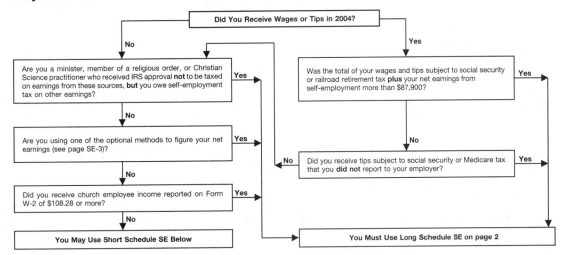

Section A—Short Schedule SE. Caution. Read above to see if you can use Short Schedule SE.

1	Net farm profit or (loss) from Schedule F, line 36, and farm partnerships, Schedule K-1 (Form 1065), box 14, code A	**1**
2	Net profit or (loss) from Schedule C, line 31; Schedule C-EZ, line 3; Schedule K-1 (Form 1065), box 14, code A (other than farming); and Schedule K-1 (Form 1065-B), box 9. Ministers and members of religious orders, see page SE-1 for amounts to report on this line. See page SE-2 for other income to report	**2**
3	Combine lines 1 and 2	**3**
4	**Net earnings from self-employment.** Multiply line 3 by 92.35% (.9235). If less than $400, **do not** file this schedule; you do not owe self-employment tax . . . . ►	**4**
5	**Self-employment tax.** If the amount on line 4 is: • $87,900 or less, multiply line 4 by 15.3% (.153). Enter the result here and on **Form 1040, line 57.** • More than $87,900, multiply line 4 by 2.9% (.029). Then, add $10,899.60 to the result. Enter the total here and on **Form 1040, line 57.**	**5**
6	**Deduction for one-half of self-employment tax.** Multiply line 5 by 50% (.5). Enter the result here and on **Form 1040, line 30**	**6**	

For Paperwork Reduction Act Notice, see Form 1040 instructions.   Cat. No. 11358Z   Schedule SE (Form 1040) 2004

181

Name of person with **self-employment** income (as shown on Form 1040)	Social security number of person with **self-employment** income ▶		

Section B—Long Schedule SE

Part I Self-Employment Tax

Note. If your only income subject to self-employment tax is **church employee income,** skip lines 1 through 4b. Enter -0- on line 4c and go to line 5a. Income from services you performed as a minister or a member of a religious order **is not** church employee income. See page SE-1.

A If you are a minister, member of a religious order, or Christian Science practitioner **and** you filed Form 4361, but you had $400 or more of **other** net earnings from self-employment, check here and continue with Part I . . . . . . ▶ ☐

1	Net farm profit or (loss) from Schedule F, line 36, and farm partnerships, Schedule K-1 (Form 1065), box 14, code A. **Note.** Skip this line if you use the farm optional method (see page SE-4)	**1**		
2	Net profit or (loss) from Schedule C, line 31; Schedule C-EZ, line 3; Schedule K-1 (Form 1065), box 14, code A (other than farming); and Schedule K-1 (Form 1065-B), box 9. Ministers and members of religious orders, see page SE-1 for amounts to report on this line. See page SE-2 for other income to report. **Note.** Skip this line if you use the nonfarm optional method (see page SE-4)	**2**		
3	Combine lines 1 and 2	**3**		
4a	If line 3 is more than zero, multiply line 3 by 92.35% (.9235). Otherwise, enter amount from line 3	**4a**		
b	If you elect one or both of the optional methods, enter the total of lines 15 and 17 here . . .	**4b**		
c	Combine lines 4a and 4b. If less than $400, **stop;** you do not owe self-employment tax. **Exception.** If less than $400 and you had **church employee income,** enter -0- and continue. . . . . ▶	**4c**		
5a	Enter your **church employee income** from Form W-2. See page SE-1 for definition of church employee income **5a**			
b	Multiply line 5a by 92.35% (.9235). If less than $100, enter -0-	**5b**		
6	**Net earnings from self-employment.** Add lines 4c and 5b	**6**		
7	Maximum amount of combined wages and self-employment earnings subject to social security tax or the 6.2% portion of the 7.65% railroad retirement (tier 1) tax for 2004	**7**	87,900	00
8a	Total social security wages and tips (total of boxes 3 and 7 on Form(s) W-2) and railroad retirement (tier 1) compensation. If $87,900 or more, skip lines 8b through 10, and go to line 11 . . . . **8a**			
b	Unreported tips subject to social security tax (from Form 4137, line 9) **8b**			
c	Add lines 8a and 8b	**8c**		
9	Subtract line 8c from line 7. If zero or less, enter -0- here and on line 10 and go to line 11 . ▶	**9**		
10	Multiply the **smaller** of line 6 or line 9 by 12.4% (.124)	**10**		
11	Multiply line 6 by 2.9% (.029)	**11**		
12	**Self-employment tax.** Add lines 10 and 11. Enter here and on **Form 1040, line 57** . . .	**12**		
13	**Deduction for one-half of self-employment tax.** Multiply line 12 by 50% (.5). Enter the result here and on **Form 1040, line 30** **13**			

Part II Optional Methods To Figure Net Earnings (see page SE-3)

Farm Optional Method. You may use this method only if **(a)** your gross farm income[1] was not more than $2,400 **or (b)** your net farm profits[2] were less than $1,733.

14	Maximum income for optional methods	**14**	1,600	00
15	Enter the **smaller** of: two-thirds (⅔) of gross farm income[1] (not less than zero) **or** $1,600. Also include this amount on line 4b above	**15**		

Nonfarm Optional Method. You may use this method only if **(a)** your net nonfarm profits[3] were less than $1,733 and also less than 72.189% of your gross nonfarm income[4] **and (b)** you had net earnings from self-employment of at least $400 in 2 of the prior 3 years.

Caution. You may use this method no more than five times.

16	Subtract line 15 from line 14	**16**		
17	Enter the **smaller** of: two-thirds (⅔) of gross nonfarm income[4] (not less than zero) **or** the amount on line 16. Also include this amount on line 4b above	**17**		

[1] From Sch. F, line 11, and Sch. K-1 (Form 1065), box 14, code B.

[2] From Sch. F, line 36, and Sch. K-1 (Form 1065), box 14, code A.

[3] From Sch. C, line 31; Sch. C-EZ, line 3; Sch. K-1 (Form 1065), box 14, code A; and Sch. K-1 (Form 1065-B), box 9.

[4] From Sch. C, line 7; Sch. C-EZ, line 1; Sch. K-1 (Form 1065), box 14, code C; and Sch. K-1 (Form 1065-B), box 9.

Schedule SE (Form 1040) 2004

2004 Instructions for Schedule SE (Form 1040)

Self-Employment Tax

Use Schedule SE (Form 1040) to figure the tax due on net earnings from self-employment. The Social Security Administration uses the information from Schedule SE to figure your benefits under the social security program. This tax applies no matter how old you are and even if you are already getting social security or Medicare benefits.

Additional information. See Pub. 533.

Section references are to the Internal Revenue Code.

General Instructions

What's New

For 2004, the maximum amount of self-employment income subject to social security tax is $87,900.

Who Must File Schedule SE

You must file Schedule SE if:

• Your net earnings from self-employment (see page SE-2) from other than church employee income were $400 or more, or

• You had church employee income of $108.28 or more—see *Employees of Churches and Church Organizations* below.

Who Must Pay Self-Employment (SE) Tax?

Self-Employed Persons

You must pay SE tax if you had net earnings of $400 or more as a self-employed person. If you are in business for yourself or you are a farmer, you are self-employed.

You must also pay SE tax on your share of certain partnership income and your guaranteed payments. See *Partnership Income or Loss* on page SE-2.

Employees of Churches and Church Organizations

If you had church employee income of $108.28 or more, you must pay SE tax. Church employee income is wages you received as an employee (other than as a minister or member of a religious order) of a church or qualified church-controlled organization that has a certificate in effect electing an exemption from employer social security and Medicare taxes.

Ministers and Members of Religious Orders

In most cases, you must pay SE tax on salaries and other income for services you performed as a minister, a member of a religious order who has not taken a vow of poverty, or a Christian Science practitioner. But if you filed Form 4361 and received

IRS approval, you will be exempt from paying SE tax on those net earnings. If you had no other income subject to SE tax, enter "Exempt—Form 4361" on Form 1040, line 57. However, if you had other earnings of $400 or more subject to SE tax, see line A at the top of Long Schedule SE.

 If you have ever filed Form 2031 to elect social security coverage on your earnings as a minister, you cannot revoke that election.

If you must pay SE tax, include this income on either Short or Long Schedule SE, line 2. But do not report it on Long Schedule SE, line 5a; it is not considered church employee income. Also, include on line 2:

• The rental value of a home or an allowance for a home furnished to you (including payments for utilities), and

• The value of meals and lodging provided to you, your spouse, and your dependents for your employer's convenience.

However, do not include on line 2:

• Retirement benefits you received from a church plan after retirement, or

• The rental value of a home or an allowance for a home furnished to you (including payments for utilities) after retirement.

If you were a duly ordained minister who was an employee of a church and you must pay SE tax, the unreimbursed business expenses that you incurred as a church employee are allowed only as an itemized deduction for income tax purposes. Subtract the allowable amount from your SE earnings when figuring your SE tax.

If you were a U.S. citizen or resident alien serving outside the United States as a minister or member of a religious order and you must pay SE tax, you cannot reduce your net earnings by the foreign housing exclusion or deduction.

See Pub. 517 for details.

Members of Certain Religious Sects

If you have conscientious objections to social security insurance because of your membership in and belief in the teachings

of a religious sect recognized as being in existence at all times since December 31, 1950, and which has provided a reasonable level of living for its dependent members, you are exempt from SE tax if you received IRS approval by filing Form 4029. In this case, do not file Schedule SE. Instead, enter "Exempt—Form 4029" on Form 1040, line 57. See Pub. 517 for details.

U.S. Citizens Employed by Foreign Governments or International Organizations

You must pay SE tax on income you earned as a U.S. citizen employed by a foreign government (or, in certain cases, by a wholly owned instrumentality of a foreign government or an international organization under the International Organizations Immunities Act) for services performed in the United States, Puerto Rico, Guam, American Samoa, the Commonwealth of the Northern Mariana Islands (CNMI), or the Virgin Islands. Report income from this employment on either Short or Long Schedule SE, line 2. If you performed services elsewhere as an employee of a foreign government or an international organization, those earnings are exempt from SE tax.

U.S. Citizens or Resident Aliens Living Outside the United States

If you are a self-employed U.S. citizen or resident alien living outside the United States, in most cases you must pay SE tax. You cannot reduce your foreign earnings from self-employment by your foreign earned income exclusion.

Exception. The United States has social security agreements with many countries to eliminate dual taxes under two social security systems. Under these agreements, you must generally pay social security and Medicare taxes to only the country you live in.

The United States now has social security agreements with the following countries: Australia, Austria, Belgium, Canada, Chile, Finland, France, Germany, Greece, Ireland, Italy, Luxembourg, the Netherlands, Norway, Portugal, South Korea, Spain, Sweden, Switzerland, and the

SE-1

Cat. No. 24334P

183

United Kingdom. Additional agreements are expected in the future. If you have questions about international social security agreements, you can:

- Visit the Social Security Administration (SSA) website at *www.socialsecurity. gov/international,*
- Call the SSA Office of International Programs at (410) 965-4538 or (410) 965-0377 (long-distance charges may apply), or
- Write to Social Security Administration, Office of International Programs, P.O. Box 17741, Baltimore, MD 21235-7741.

If your self-employment income is exempt from SE tax, you should get a statement from the appropriate agency of the foreign country verifying that your self-employment income is subject to social security coverage in that country. If the foreign country will not issue the statement, contact the SSA at the address shown above. Do not complete Schedule SE. Instead, attach a copy of the statement to Form 1040 and enter "Exempt, see attached statement" on Form 1040, line 57.

More Than One Business

If you had two or more businesses, your net earnings from self-employment are the combined net earnings from all of your businesses. If you had a loss in one business, it reduces the income from another. Figure the combined SE tax on one Schedule SE.

Joint Returns

Show the name of the spouse with SE income on Schedule SE. If both spouses have SE income, each must file a separate Schedule SE. However, if one spouse qualifies to use Short Schedule SE and the other has to use Long Schedule SE, both can use the same form. One spouse should complete the front and the other the back.

Include the total profits or losses from all businesses on Form 1040, as appropriate. Enter the combined SE tax on Form 1040, line 57.

Community Income

In most cases, if any of the income from a business (including farming) is community income, all of the income from that business is SE earnings of the spouse who carried on the business. The facts in each case will determine which spouse carried on the business. If you and your spouse are partners in a partnership, see *Partnership Income or Loss* on this page.

If you and your spouse had community income and file separate returns, attach Schedule SE to the return of the spouse with the SE income. Also, attach Schedule(s) C, C-EZ, or F to the return of each spouse.

If you are the spouse who carried on the business, you must include on Schedule SE, line 3, the net profit or (loss) reported

on the other spouse's Schedule C, C-EZ, or F (except income not included in net earnings from self-employment as explained on page SE-3). Enter on the dotted line to the left of Schedule SE, line 3, "Community Income Taxed to Spouse" and the amount of any net profit or (loss) allocated to your spouse as community income. Combine that amount with the total of lines 1 and 2 and enter the result on line 3.

If you are not the spouse who carried on the business and you had no other income subject to SE tax, enter "Exempt Community Income" on Form 1040, line 57; do not file Schedule SE. However, if you had other earnings subject to SE tax of $400 or more, enter on the dotted line to the left of Schedule SE, line 3, "Exempt Community Income" and the amount of net profit or (loss) from Schedule C, C-EZ, or F allocated to you as community income. If that amount is a net profit, subtract it from the total of lines 1 and 2, and enter the result on line 3. If that amount is a loss, treat it as a positive amount, add it to the total of lines 1 and 2, and enter the result on line 3.

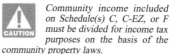 *Community income included on Schedule(s) C, C-EZ, or F must be divided for income tax purposes on the basis of the community property laws.*

Fiscal Year Filers

If your tax year is a fiscal year, use the tax rate and earnings base that apply at the time the fiscal year begins. Do not prorate the tax or earnings base for a fiscal year that overlaps the date of a rate or earnings base change.

Specific Instructions

Read the chart on page 1 of Schedule SE to see if you can use Section A, Short Schedule SE, or if you must use Section B, Long Schedule SE. For either section, you need to know what to include as net earnings from self-employment. Read the following instructions to see what to include as net earnings and how to fill in either Short or Long Schedule SE, lines 1 and 2. Enter all negative amounts in parentheses.

Net Earnings From Self-Employment

What Is Included in Net Earnings From Self-Employment?

In most cases, net earnings include your net profit from a farm or nonfarm business. If you were a partner in a partnership, see the following instructions.

Partnership Income or Loss

If you were a general or limited partner in a partnership, include on line 1 or line 2, whichever applies, the amount of net earnings from self-employment from Schedule K-1 (Form 1065), box 14, with code A, and Schedule K-1 (Form 1065-B), box 9. General partners should reduce this amount before entering it on Schedule SE by any section 179 expense deduction claimed, unreimbursed partnership expenses claimed, and depletion claimed on oil and gas properties. If you reduce the amount you enter on Schedule SE, attach an explanation.

If a partner died and the partnership continued, include in SE income the deceased's distributive share of the partnership's ordinary income or loss through the end of the month in which he or she died. See section 1402(f).

If you were married and both you and your spouse were partners in a partnership, each of you must pay SE tax on your own share of the partnership income. Each of you must file a Schedule SE and report the partnership income or loss on Schedule E (Form 1040), Part II, for income tax purposes.

SE income belongs to the person who is the member of the partnership and cannot be treated as SE income by the nonmember spouse even in community property states.

Share Farming

You are considered self-employed if you produced crops or livestock on someone else's land for a share of the crops or livestock produced (or a share of the proceeds from the sale of them). This applies even if you paid another person (an agent) to do the actual work or management for you. Report your net earnings for income tax purposes on Schedule F (Form 1040) and for SE tax purposes on Schedule SE. See Pub. 225 for details.

Other Income and Losses Included in Net Earnings From Self-Employment

1. Rental income from a farm if, as landlord, you materially participated in the production or management of the production of farm products on this land. This income is farm earnings. To determine whether you materially participated in farm management or production, do not consider the activities of any agent who acted for you. The material participation tests are explained in Pub. 225.

2. Cash or a payment-in-kind from the Department of Agriculture for participating in a land diversion program.

3. Payments for the use of rooms or other space when you also provided substantial services. Examples are hotel rooms, boarding houses, tourist camps or

homes, parking lots, warehouses, and storage garages.

4. Income from the retail sale of newspapers and magazines if you were age 18 or older and kept the profits.

5. Amounts received by current or former self-employed insurance agents and salespersons that are:

a. Paid after retirement but figured as a percentage of commissions received from the paying company before retirement,

b. Renewal commissions, or

c. Deferred commissions paid after retirement for sales made before retirement.

However, certain termination payments received by former insurance salespersons are not included in net earnings from self-employment (as explained in item 9 under *Income and Losses Not Included in Net Earnings From Self-Employment* on this page).

6. Income of certain crew members of fishing vessels with crews of normally fewer than 10 people. See Pub. 595 for details.

7. Fees as a state or local government employee if you were paid only on a fee basis and the job was not covered under a federal-state social security coverage agreement.

8. Interest received in the course of any trade or business, such as interest on notes or accounts receivable.

9. Fees and other payments received by you for services as a director of a corporation.

10. Recapture amounts under sections 179 and 280F that you included in gross income because the business use of the property dropped to 50% or less. Do not include amounts you recaptured on the disposition of property. See Form 4797.

11. Fees you received as a professional fiduciary. This may also apply to fees paid to you as a nonprofessional fiduciary if the fees relate to active participation in the operation of the estate's business, or the management of an estate that required extensive management activities over a long period of time.

12. Gain or loss from section 1256 contracts or related property by an options or commodities dealer in the normal course of dealing in or trading section 1256 contracts.

Income and Losses Not Included in Net Earnings From Self-Employment

1. Salaries, fees, etc., subject to social security or Medicare tax that you received for performing services as an employee, including services performed as a public official (except as a fee basis government employee as explained in item 7 under *Other Income and Losses Included in Net*

Earnings From Self-Employment) or as an employee or employee representative under the railroad retirement system.

2. Fees received for services performed as a notary public. If you had no other income subject to SE tax, enter "Exempt-Notary" on Form 1040, line 57. However, if you had other earnings of $400 or more subject to SE tax, enter "Exempt-Notary" and the amount of your net profit as a notary public from Schedule C or Schedule C-EZ on the dotted line to the left of Schedule SE, line 3. Subtract that amount from the total of lines 1 and 2 and enter the result on line 3.

3. Income you received as a retired partner under a written partnership plan that provides for lifelong periodic retirement payments if you had no other interest in the partnership and did not perform services for it during the year.

4. Income from real estate rentals if you did not receive the income in the course of a trade or business as a real estate dealer. Report this income on Schedule E.

5. Income from farm rentals (including rentals paid in crop shares) if, as landlord, you did not materially participate in the production or management of the production of farm products on the land. See Pub. 225 for details.

6. Dividends on shares of stock and interest on bonds, notes, etc., if you did not receive the income in the course of your trade or business as a dealer in stocks or securities.

7. Gain or loss from:

a. The sale or exchange of a capital asset;

b. The sale, exchange, involuntary conversion, or other disposition of property unless the property is stock in trade or other property that would be includible in inventory, or held primarily for sale to customers in the ordinary course of the business; or

c. Certain transactions in timber, coal, or domestic iron ore.

8. Net operating losses from other years.

9. Termination payments you received as a former insurance salesperson if all of the following conditions are met.

a. The payment was received from an insurance company because of services you performed as an insurance salesperson for the company.

b. The payment was received after termination of your agreement to perform services for the company.

c. You did not perform any services for the company after termination and before the end of the year in which you received the payment.

d. You entered into a covenant not to compete against the company for at least a 1-year period beginning on the date of termination.

e. The amount of the payment depended primarily on policies sold by or credited to your account during the last year of the agreement, or the extent to which those policies remain in force for some period after termination, or both.

f. The amount of the payment did not depend to any extent on length of service or overall earnings from services performed for the company (regardless of whether eligibility for the payment depended on length of service).

Statutory Employee Income

If you were required to check the box on Schedule C or C-EZ, line 1, because you were a statutory employee, do not include the net profit or (loss) from that Schedule C, line 31 (or the net profit from Schedule C-EZ, line 3), on Short or Long Schedule SE, line 2. But if you file Long Schedule SE, be sure to include statutory employee social security wages and tips from Form W-2 on line 8a.

Optional Methods

How Can the Optional Methods Help You?

Social security coverage. The optional methods may give you credit toward your social security coverage even though you have a loss or a small amount of income from self-employment.

Earned income credit (EIC). Using the optional methods may qualify you to claim the EIC or give you a larger credit if your net earnings from self-employment (determined without using the optional methods) are less than $1,600. Figure the EIC with and without using the optional methods to see if the optional methods will benefit you.

Additional child tax credit. Using the optional methods may qualify you to claim the additional child tax credit or give you a larger credit if your net earnings from self-employment (determined without using the optional methods) are less than $1,600. Figure the additional child tax credit with and without using the optional methods to see if the optional methods will benefit you.

Child and dependent care credit. The optional methods may help you qualify for this credit or give you a larger credit if your net earnings from self-employment (determined without using the optional methods) are less than $1,600. Figure this credit with and without using the optional methods to see if the optional methods will benefit you.

Self-employed health insurance deduction. The optional methods of computing net earnings from self-employment may be used to figure your self-employed health insurance deduction.

SE-3

185

Using the optional methods may give you the benefits described on page SE-3, but they may also increase your SE tax.

Farm Optional Method

You may use this method to figure your net earnings from farm self-employment if your gross farm income was $2,400 or less or your net farm profits were less than $1,733. Net farm profits is the total of the amounts from:

- Schedule F (Form 1040), line 36, and
- Schedule K-1 (Form 1065), box 14, with code A (from farm partnerships).

There is no limit on how many years you can use this method.

Under this method, you report on Part II, line 15, two-thirds of your gross farm income, up to $1,600, as your net earnings. This method can increase or decrease your net earnings from farm self-employment even if the farming business had a loss.

You can change the method after you file your return. That is, you can change from the regular to the optional method or from the optional to the regular method. To do this, file Form 1040X.

For a farm partnership, figure your share of gross income based on the partnership agreement. With guaranteed payments, your share of the partnership's gross income is your guaranteed payments plus your share of the gross income after it is reduced by all guaranteed payments made by the partnership. If you were a limited partner, include only guaranteed payments for services you actually rendered to or on behalf of the partnership.

Nonfarm Optional Method

You may be able to use this method to figure your net earnings from nonfarm self-employment if your net nonfarm profits were less than $1,733 and also less than 72.189% of your gross nonfarm income. Net nonfarm profits is the total of the amounts from:

- Schedule C (Form 1040), line 31,
- Schedule C-EZ (Form 1040), line 3,
- Schedule K-1 (Form 1065), box 14, with code A (from other than farm partnerships), and
- Schedule K-1 (Form 1065-B), box 9.

To use this method, you also must be regularly self-employed. You meet this requirement if your actual net earnings from self-employment were $400 or more in 2 of the 3 years preceding the year you use the nonfarm method. The net earnings of $400 or more could be from either farm or nonfarm earnings or both. The net earnings include your distributive share of partnership income or loss subject to SE tax. Use of the nonfarm optional method from nonfarm self-employment is limited to 5 years. The 5 years do not have to be consecutive.

Under this method, you report on Part II, line 17, two-thirds of your gross nonfarm income, up to $1,600, as your net earnings. But you cannot report less than your actual net earnings from nonfarm self-employment.

You can change the method after you file your return. That is, you can change from the regular to the optional method or from the optional to the regular method. To do so, file Form 1040X.

Figure your share of gross income from a nonfarm partnership in the same manner as a farm partnership. See *Farm Optional Method* on this page for details.

Using Both Optional Methods

If you can use both methods, you can report less than your total actual net earnings from farm and nonfarm self-employment, but you cannot report less than your actual net earnings from nonfarm self-employment alone.

If you use both methods to figure net earnings, you cannot report more than $1,600 of net earnings from self-employment.

SCHEDULE C
(Form 1040)

Department of the Treasury
Internal Revenue Service

Profit or Loss From Business
(Sole Proprietorship)
▶ Partnerships, joint ventures, etc., must file Form 1065 or 1065-B.
▶ Attach to Form 1040 or 1041. ▶ See Instructions for Schedule C (Form 1040).

OMB No. 1545-0074

2004

Attachment
Sequence No. **09**

Name of proprietor

Social security number (SSN)

A Principal business or profession, including product or service (see page C-2 of the instructions)

B Enter code from pages C-7, 8, & 9
▶

C Business name. If no separate business name, leave blank.

D Employer ID number (EIN), if any

E Business address (including suite or room no.) ▶
City, town or post office, state, and ZIP code

F Accounting method: **(1)** ☐ Cash **(2)** ☐ Accrual **(3)** ☐ Other (specify) ▶

G Did you "materially participate" in the operation of this business during 2004? If "No," see page C-3 for limit on losses ☐ Yes ☐ No

H If you started or acquired this business during 2004, check here . . . . ▶ ☐

Part I Income

1	Gross receipts or sales. **Caution.** If this income was reported to you on Form W-2 and the "Statutory employee" box on that form was checked, see page C-3 and check here . . . . . . ▶ ☐	**1**	
2	Returns and allowances	**2**	
3	Subtract line 2 from line 1	**3**	
4	Cost of goods sold (from line 42 on page 2)	**4**	
5	**Gross profit.** Subtract line 4 from line 3.	**5**	
6	Other income, including Federal and state gasoline or fuel tax credit or refund (see page C-3) . . .	**6**	
7	**Gross income.** Add lines 5 and 6 . . . . ▶	**7**	

Part II Expenses. Enter expenses for business use of your home **only** on line 30.

8	Advertising	**8**		19 Pension and profit-sharing plans	**19**	
9	Car and truck expenses (see page C-3).	**9**		20 Rent or lease (see page C-5):		
				a Vehicles, machinery, and equipment .	**20a**	
10	Commissions and fees . .	**10**		b Other business property. . .	**20b**	
11	Contract labor (see page C-4)	**11**		21 Repairs and maintenance . .	**21**	
12	Depletion	**12**		22 Supplies (not included in Part III) .	**22**	
13	Depreciation and section 179 expense deduction (not included in Part III) (see page C-4)	**13**		23 Taxes and licenses	**23**	
				24 Travel, meals, and entertainment:		
				a Travel	**24a**	
14	Employee benefit programs (other than on line 19). .	**14**		b Meals and entertainment		
15	Insurance (other than health) .	**15**		c Enter nondeduct-ible amount in-cluded on line 24b (see page C-5) .		
16	Interest:			d Subtract line 24c from line 24b .	**24d**	
a	Mortgage (paid to banks, etc.) .	**16a**		25 Utilities	**25**	
b	Other	**16b**		26 Wages (less employment credits) .	**26**	
17	Legal and professional services	**17**		27 Other expenses (from line 48 on page 2)	**27**	
18	Office expense	**18**				

28	**Total expenses** before expenses for business use of home. Add lines 8 through 27 in columns . . ▶	**28**	
29	Tentative profit (loss). Subtract line 28 from line 7	**29**	
30	Expenses for business use of your home. Attach **Form 8829**	**30**	
31	**Net profit or (loss).** Subtract line 30 from line 29. • If a profit, enter on **Form 1040, line 12,** and **also** on **Schedule SE, line 2** (statutory employees, see page C-6). Estates and trusts, enter on Form 1041, line 3. • If a loss, you **must** go to line 32.	**31**	
32	If you have a loss, check the box that describes your investment in this activity (see page C-6). • If you checked 32a, enter the loss on **Form 1040, line 12,** and **also** on **Schedule SE, line 2** (statutory employees, see page C-6). Estates and trusts, enter on Form 1041, line 3. • If you checked 32b, you **must** attach **Form 6198.**	**32a** ☐ All investment is at risk. **32b** ☐ Some investment is not at risk.	

For Paperwork Reduction Act Notice, see Form 1040 instructions. Cat. No. 11334P Schedule C (Form 1040) 2004

187

Part III   **Cost of Goods Sold** (see page C-6)

33   Method(s) used to
value closing inventory: **a** ☐ Cost   **b** ☐ Lower of cost or market   **c** ☐ Other (attach explanation)

34   Was there any change in determining quantities, costs, or valuations between opening and closing inventory? If
"Yes," attach explanation . . . . ☐ **Yes**   ☐ **No**

35 Inventory at beginning of year. If different from last year's closing inventory, attach explanation . .	**35**	
36 Purchases less cost of items withdrawn for personal use	**36**	
37 Cost of labor. Do not include any amounts paid to yourself	**37**	
38 Materials and supplies	**38**	
39 Other costs	**39**	
40 Add lines 35 through 39	**40**	
41 Inventory at end of year	**41**	
42 **Cost of goods sold.** Subtract line 41 from line 40. Enter the result here and on page 1, line 4 . .	**42**	

Part IV   **Information on Your Vehicle.** Complete this part **only** if you are claiming car or truck expenses on line 9 and are not required to file Form 4562 for this business. See the instructions for line 13 on page C-4 to find out if you must file Form 4562.

43   When did you place your vehicle in service for business purposes? (month, day, year) ▶ ..../........../.......... .

44   Of the total number of miles you drove your vehicle during 2004, enter the number of miles you used your vehicle for:

a Business ....   **b** Commuting ....   **c** Other ....

45   Do you (or your spouse) have another vehicle available for personal use?. . . . . ☐ **Yes**   ☐ **No**

46   Was your vehicle available for personal use during off-duty hours? . . . . ☐ **Yes**   ☐ **No**

47a   Do you have evidence to support your deduction? . . . . ☐ **Yes**   ☐ **No**

   b   If "Yes," is the evidence written? . . . . ☐ **Yes**   ☐ **No**

Part V   **Other Expenses.** List below business expenses not included on lines 8–26 or line 30.

....		
....		
....		
....		
....		
....		
....		
....		
48 **Total other expenses.** Enter here and on page 1, line 27	**48**	

2004 Instructions for Schedule C

Profit or Loss From Business

Use Schedule C (Form 1040) to report income or loss from a business you operated or a profession you practiced as a sole proprietor. Also, use Schedule C to report wages and expenses you had as a statutory employee. An activity qualifies as a business if your primary purpose for engaging in the activity is for income or profit and you are involved in the activity with continuity and regularity. For example, a sporadic activity or a hobby does not qualify as a business. To report income from a nonbusiness activity, see the instructions for Form 1040, line 21.

Small businesses and statutory employees with expenses of $5,000 or less may be able to file Schedule C-EZ instead of Schedule C. See Schedule C-EZ for details.

You may be subject to state and local taxes and other requirements such as business licenses and fees. Check with your state and local governments for more information.

Section references are to the Internal Revenue Code.

What's New

- The maximum amount of business expenses you can have and qualify to file Schedule C-EZ is increased from $2,500 to $5,000 for 2004. For other requirements you must meet, see Schedule C-EZ.

- You can use up to four vehicles simultaneously in your business and use the standard mileage rate. For details, see the instructions for line 9 beginning on page C-3.

- For certain business start-up costs paid or incurred after October 22, 2004, you can elect to deduct up to $5,000. This limit is reduced by the amount by which your start-up costs exceed $50,000. Also, the amortization period for certain business start-up costs paid or incurred after October 22, 2004, has been increased to 15 years. For details, see Pub. 535.

- You can elect to deduct costs of certain qualified film and television productions that begin after October 22, 2004. For details, see Pub. 535.

- You can elect to deduct certain forestation and reforestation costs paid or incurred after October 22, 2004, instead of amortizing them over 84 months. This election does not apply to estates and trusts. Also, the dollar limitation for amortization on certain forestation and reforestation costs paid or incurred after October 22, 2004, has been eliminated. For details, see Pub. 535.

General Instructions

Other Schedules and Forms You May Have To File

- Schedule A to deduct interest, taxes, and casualty losses not related to your business.

- Schedule E to report rental real estate and royalty income or (loss) that is not subject to self-employment tax.

- Schedule F to report profit or (loss) from farming.

- Schedule J to figure your tax by averaging your fishing income over the previous 3 years. Doing so may reduce your tax.

- Schedule SE to pay self-employment tax on income from any trade or business.

- Form 4562 to claim depreciation on assets placed in service in 2004, to claim amortization that began in 2004, to make an election under section 179 to expense certain property, or to report information on listed property.

- Form 4684 to report a casualty or theft gain or loss involving property used in your trade or business or income-producing property.

- Form 4797 to report sales, exchanges, and involuntary conversions (not from a casualty or theft) of trade or business property.

- Form 8271 if you are claiming or reporting on Schedule C or C-EZ any income, deduction, loss, credit, or other tax benefit from an interest purchased or otherwise acquired in a tax shelter required to be registered with the IRS.

- Form 8594 to report certain purchases or sales of groups of assets that constitute a trade or business.

- Form 8824 to report like-kind exchanges.

- Form 8829 to claim expenses for business use of your home.

Husband-wife business. If you and your spouse jointly own and operate a business and share in the profits and losses, you are partners in a partnership, whether or not you have a formal partnership agreement. Do not use Schedule C or C-EZ. Instead, file Form 1065. See Pub. 541 for more details.

Exception. If you and your spouse wholly own an unincorporated business as community property under the community property laws of a state, foreign country, or U.S. possession, you can treat the business either as a sole proprietorship or a partnership. The only states with community property laws are Arizona, California, Idaho, Louisiana, Nevada, New Mexico, Texas, Washington, and Wisconsin. A change in

your reporting position will be treated as a conversion of the entity.

Single-member limited liability company (LLC). Generally, a single-member domestic LLC is not treated as a separate entity for federal income tax purposes. If you are the sole member of a domestic LLC, file Schedule C or C-EZ (or Schedule E or F, if applicable). However, you can elect to treat a domestic LLC as a corporation. See Form 8832 for details on the election and the tax treatment of a foreign LLC.

Heavy highway vehicle use tax. If you use certain highway trucks, truck-trailers, tractor-trailers, or buses in your trade or business, you may have to pay a federal highway motor vehicle use tax. See the Instructions for Form 2290 to find out if you owe this tax.

Information returns. You may have to file information returns for wages paid to employees, certain payments of fees and other nonemployee compensation, interest, rents, royalties, real estate transactions, annuities, and pensions. You may also have to file an information return if you sold $5,000 or more of consumer products to a person on a buy-sell, deposit-commission, or other similar basis for resale. For details, see the 2004 General Instructions for Forms 1099, 1098, 5498, and W-2G.

If you received cash of more than $10,000 in one or more related transactions in your trade or business, you may have to file Form 8300. For details, see Pub. 1544.

Reportable Transaction Disclosure Statement

Use Form 8886 to disclose information for each reportable transaction in which you participated. Form 8886 must be filed for each tax year that your federal income tax liability is affected by your participation in the transaction. You may have to pay a penalty if you are required to file Form 8886 but do not do so. The following are reportable transactions.

- Any transaction that is the same as or substantially similar to tax avoidance transactions identified by the IRS.

- Any transaction offered under conditions of confidentiality for which you paid an advisor a minimum fee.

- Any transaction for which you have contractual protection against disallowance of the tax benefits.

- Any transaction resulting in a loss of at least $2 million in any single tax year or $4 million in any combination of tax years. (At least $50,000 for a single tax year if the loss arose from a foreign currency transaction defined in section 988(c)(1), whether or not the loss flows through from an S corporation or partnership.)

- Any transaction resulting in a book-tax difference of more than $10 million on a gross basis.

- Any transaction resulting in a tax credit of more than $250,000, if you held the asset generating the credit for 45 days or less.

See the Instructions for Form 8886 for more details and exceptions.

Additional Information

See Pub. 334 for more information for small businesses.

Specific Instructions

Filers of Form 1041. Do not complete the block labeled "Social security number (SSN)." Instead, enter your employer identification number (EIN) on line D.

Line A

Describe the business or professional activity that provided your principal source of income reported on line 1. If you owned more than one business, you must complete a separate Schedule C for each business. Give the general field or activity and the type of product or service. If your general field or activity is wholesale or retail trade, or services connected with production services (mining, construction, or manufacturing), also give the type of customer or client. For example, "wholesale sale of hardware to retailers" or "appraisal of real estate for lending institutions."

Line D

You need an employer identification number (EIN) only if you had a qualified retirement plan or were required to file an employment, excise, estate, trust, or alcohol, tobacco, and firearms tax return. If you need an EIN, see the Instructions for Form SS-4. If you do not have an EIN, leave line D blank. Do not enter your SSN.

Line E

Enter your business address. Show a street address instead of a box number. Include the suite or room number, if any. If you conducted the business from your home located at the address shown on Form 1040, page 1, you do not have to complete this line.

Line F

Generally, you can use the cash method, accrual method, or any other method permitted by the Internal Revenue Code. In all cases, the method used must clearly reflect income. Unless you are a qualifying taxpayer or a qualifying small business taxpayer, you must use the accrual method for sales and purchases of inventory items. See the Part III instructions on page C-6 for the definition of a qualifying taxpayer and a qualifying small business taxpayer. Special rules apply to long-term contracts. See section 460 for details.

If you use the cash method, show all items of taxable income actually or constructively received during the year (in cash, property, or services). Income is constructively received when it is credited to your account or set aside for you to use. Also, show amounts actually paid during the year for deductible expenses. However, if the payment of an expenditure creates an asset having a useful life that extends substantially beyond the close of the year, it may not be deductible or may be deductible only in part for the year of the payment. See Pub. 535.

If you use the accrual method, report income when you earn it and deduct expenses when you incur them even if you do not pay them during the tax year. Accrual-basis taxpayers are put on a cash basis for deducting business expenses owed to a related cash-basis taxpayer. Other rules determine the timing of deductions based on economic performance. See Pub. 538.

To change your accounting method, you generally must file Form 3115. You may also have to make an adjustment to prevent amounts of income or expense from being duplicated or omitted. This is called a section 481(a) adjustment.

Example. You change to the cash method of accounting and choose to account for inventoriable items in the same manner as materials and supplies that are not incidental. You accrued sales in 2003 for which you received payment in 2004. You must report those sales in both years as a result of changing your accounting method and must make a section 481(a) adjustment to prevent duplication of income.

A net negative section 481(a) adjustment is taken into account entirely in the year of the change. A net positive section 481(a) adjustment is generally taken into account over a period of 4 years. Include any net positive section 481(a) adjustments on line 6. If the net section 481(a) adjustment is negative, report it in Part V.

For details on figuring section 481(a) adjustments, see the Instructions for Form 3115, Rev. Proc. 2004-23, 2004-16 I.R.B. 785, available at *www.irs.gov/irb/2004-16_IRB/ar11.html*, and Rev. Proc. 2004-57, 2004-38 I.R.B. 498, available at *www.irs.gov/irb/2004-38_IRB/ar11.html*.

Line G

If your business activity was not a rental activity and you met any of the material participation tests below or the exception for oil and gas applies (explained on page C-3), check the "Yes" box. Otherwise, check the "No" box. If you check the "No" box, this business is a passive activity. If you have a loss from this business, see *Limit on losses* on page C-3. If you have a profit from this business activity but have current year losses from other passive activities or you have prior year unallowed passive activity losses, see the Instructions for Form 8582.

Material participation. Participation, for purposes of the seven material participation tests listed below, generally includes any work you did in connection with an activity if you owned an interest in the activity at the time you did the work. The capacity in which you did the work does not matter. However, work is not treated as participation if it is work that an owner would not customarily do in the same type of activity and one of your main reasons for doing the work was to avoid the disallowance of losses or credits from the activity under the passive activity rules.

Work you did as an investor in an activity is not treated as participation unless you were directly involved in the day-to-day management or operations of the activity. Work done as an investor includes:

- Studying and reviewing financial statements or reports on the activity,

- Preparing or compiling summaries or analyses of the finances or operations of the activity for your own use, and

- Monitoring the finances or operations of the activity in a nonmanagerial capacity.

Participation by your spouse during the tax year in an activity you own can be counted as your participation in the activity. This applies even if your spouse did not own an interest in the activity and whether or not you and your spouse file a joint return.

For purposes of the passive activity rules, you materially participated in the operation of this trade or business activity during 2004 if you met any of the following seven tests.

1. You participated in the activity for more than 500 hours during the tax year.

2. Your participation in the activity for the tax year was substantially all of the participation in the activity of all individuals (including individuals who did not own any interest in the activity) for the tax year.

3. You participated in the activity for more than 100 hours during the tax year, and you participated at least as much as any other person for the tax year. This includes individuals who did not own any interest in the activity.

4. The activity is a significant participation activity for the tax year, and you participated in all significant participation activities for more than 500 hours during the year. An activity is a "significant participation activity" if it involves the conduct of a trade or business, you participated in the activity for more than 100 hours dur-

ing the tax year, and you did not materially participate under any of the material participation tests (other than this test 4).

5. You materially participated in the activity for any 5 of the prior 10 tax years.

6. The activity is a personal service activity in which you materially participated for any 3 prior tax years. A personal service activity is an activity that involves performing personal services in the fields of health, law, engineering, architecture, accounting, actuarial science, performing arts, consulting, or any other trade or business in which capital is not a material income-producing factor.

7. Based on all the facts and circumstances, you participated in the activity on a regular, continuous, and substantial basis during the tax year. But you do not meet this test if you participated in the activity for 100 hours or less during the tax year. Your participation in managing the activity does not count in determining if you meet this test if any person (except you) (a) received compensation for performing management services in connection with the activity or (b) spent more hours during the tax year than you spent performing management services in connection with the activity (regardless of whether the person was compensated for the services).

Rental of personal property. A rental activity (such as long-term equipment leasing) is a passive activity even if you materially participated in the activity. However, if you met any of the five exceptions listed under *Rental Activities* in the Instructions for Form 8582, the rental of the property is not treated as a rental activity and the material participation rules above apply.

Exception for oil and gas. If you are filing Schedule C to report income and deductions from an oil or gas well in which you own a working interest directly or through an entity that does not limit your liability, check the "Yes" box. The activity of owning the working interest is not a passive activity regardless of your participation.

Limit on losses. If you checked the "No" box and you have a loss from this business, you may have to use Form 8582 to figure your allowable loss, if any, to enter on Schedule C, line 31. Generally, you can deduct losses from passive activities only to the extent of income from passive activities. For details, see Pub. 925.

Line H

If you started or acquired this business in 2004, check the box on line H. Also check the box if you are reopening or restarting this business after temporarily closing it, and you did not file a 2003 Schedule C or C-EZ for this business.

Part I. Income

Except as otherwise provided in the Internal Revenue Code, gross income includes income from whatever source derived. Gross income, however, does not include

extraterritorial income that is qualifying foreign trade income. Use Form 8873 to figure the extraterritorial income exclusion. Report it on Schedule C as explained in the Instructions for Form 8873.

Line 1

Enter gross receipts from your trade or business. Include amounts you received in your trade or business that were properly shown on Forms 1099-MISC. If the total amounts that were reported in box 7 of Forms 1099-MISC are more than the total you are reporting on line 1, attach a statement explaining the difference.

Statutory employees. If you received a Form W-2 and the "Statutory employee" box in box 13 of that form was checked, report your income and expenses related to that income on Schedule C or C-EZ. Enter your statutory employee income from box 1 of Form W-2 on line 1 of Schedule C or C-EZ and check the box on that line. Social security and Medicare tax should have been withheld from your earnings; therefore, you do not owe self-employment tax on these earnings. Statutory employees include full-time life insurance agents, certain agent or commission drivers and traveling salespersons, and certain homeworkers.

If you had both self-employment income and statutory employee income, you must file two Schedules C. You cannot use Schedule C-EZ or combine these amounts on a single Schedule C.

Installment sales. Generally, the installment method cannot be used to report income from the sale of (a) personal property regularly sold under the installment method, or (b) real property held for resale to customers. But the installment method can be used to report income from sales of certain residential lots and timeshares if you elect to pay interest on the tax due on that income after the year of sale. See section 453(l)(2)(B) for details. If you make this election, include the interest on Form 1040, line 62. Also, enter "453(l)(3)" and the amount of the interest on the dotted line to the left of line 62.

If you use the installment method, attach a schedule to your return. Show separately for 2004 and the 3 preceding years: gross sales, cost of goods sold, gross profit, percentage of gross profit to gross sales, amounts collected, and gross profit on amounts collected.

Line 6

Report on line 6 amounts from finance reserve income, scrap sales, bad debts you recovered, interest (such as on notes and accounts receivable), state gasoline or fuel tax refunds you got in 2004, credit for federal tax paid on gasoline or other fuels claimed on your 2003 Form 1040, prizes and awards related to your trade or business, and other kinds of miscellaneous business income. Include amounts you received in your trade or business as shown on Form 1099-PATR. Also, include any recapture of the deduction for clean-fuel

vehicles used in your business and clean-fuel vehicle refueling property. For details, see Pub. 535.

If the business use percentage of any listed property (defined in the instructions for line 13 on page C-4) decreased to 50% or less in 2004, report on this line any recapture of excess depreciation, including any section 179 expense deduction. Use Form 4797 to figure the recapture. Also, if the business use percentage drops to 50% or less on leased listed property (other than a vehicle), include on this line any inclusion amount. See Pub. 946 to figure the amount.

Part II. Expenses

Capitalizing costs of property. If you produced real or tangible personal property or acquired property for resale, certain expenses attributable to the property generally must be included in inventory costs or capitalized. In addition to direct costs, producers of inventory property generally must also include part of certain indirect costs in their inventory. Purchasers of personal property acquired for resale must include part of certain indirect costs in inventory only if the average annual gross receipts for the 3 prior tax years exceed $10 million. Also, you must capitalize part of the indirect costs that benefit real or tangible personal property constructed for use in a trade or business, or noninventory property produced for sale to customers. Reduce the amounts on lines 8 through 26 and Part V by amounts capitalized. For details, see Pub. 538.

Exception for certain producers. Producers who account for inventoriable items in the same manner as materials and supplies that are not incidental can currently deduct expenditures for direct labor and all indirect costs that would otherwise be included in inventory costs. See *Cost of Goods Sold* on page C-6 for more details.

Exception for creative property. If you are an artist, author, or photographer, you may be exempt from the capitalization rules. However, your personal efforts must have created (or reasonably be expected to create) the property. This exception does not apply to any expense related to printing, photographic plates, motion picture films, video tapes, or similar items. These expenses are subject to the capitalization rules. For details, see Pub. 538.

Line 9

You can deduct the actual expenses of running your car or truck or take the standard mileage rate. You must use actual expenses if you used your vehicle for hire (such as a taxicab) or you used more than four vehicles simultaneously in your business (such as in fleet operations). You cannot use actual expenses for a leased vehicle if you previously used the standard mileage rate for that vehicle.

You can take the standard mileage rate for 2004 only if you:

- Owned the vehicle and use the standard mileage rate for the first year you placed the vehicle in service, or

- Leased the vehicle and are using the standard mileage rate for the entire lease period (except the period, if any, before 1998).

If you deduct actual expenses:

- Include on line 9 the business portion of expenses for gasoline, oil, repairs, insurance, tires, license plates, etc., and

- Show depreciation on line 13 and rent or lease payments on line 20a.

If you take the standard mileage rate, multiply the number of business miles by 37.5 cents. Add to this amount your parking fees and tolls, and enter the total on line 9. Do not deduct depreciation, rent or lease payments, or your actual operating expenses.

For details, see Pub. 463.

Information on your vehicle. If you claim any car and truck expenses, you must provide certain information on the use of your vehicle by completing one of the following.

- Schedule C, Part IV, or Schedule C-EZ, Part III, if: (a) you are claiming the standard mileage rate, you lease your vehicle, or your vehicle is fully depreciated, and (b) you are not required to file Form 4562 for any other reason. If you used more than one vehicle during the year, attach your own schedule with the information requested in Schedule C, Part IV, or Schedule C-EZ, Part III, for each additional vehicle.

- Form 4562, Part V, if you are claiming depreciation on your vehicle or you are required to file Form 4562 for any other reason (see the instructions for line 13).

Line 11

Enter the total cost of contract labor for the tax year. Do not include contract labor deducted elsewhere on your return such as contract labor that you included in Part III. Also, do not include salaries and wages paid to your employees, instead see line 26.

Line 12

Enter your deduction for depletion on this line. If you have timber depletion, attach Form T. See Pub. 535 for details.

Line 13

Depreciation and section 179 expense deduction. Depreciation is the annual deduction allowed to recover the cost or other basis of business or investment property having a useful life substantially beyond the tax year. You can also depreciate improvements made to leased business property. However, stock in trade, inventories, and land are not depreciable. Depreciation starts when you first use the property in your business or for the production of income. It ends when you take the property out of service, deduct all your depreciable cost or other basis, or no longer use the property in your business or for the production of income. You can also elect under section 179 to expense part of the cost of certain property you bought in 2004 for use in your business. See the Instructions for Form 4562 to figure the amount to enter on line 13.

When to attach Form 4562. You must complete and attach Form 4562 only if:

- You are claiming depreciation on property placed in service during 2004;

- You are claiming depreciation on listed property (defined below), regardless of the date it was placed in service; or

- You are claiming a section 179 expense deduction.

If you acquired depreciable property for the first time in 2004, see Pub. 946.

Listed property generally includes, but is not limited to:

- Passenger automobiles weighing 6,000 pounds or less;

- Any other property used for transportation if the nature of the property lends itself to personal use, such as motorcycles, pickup trucks, etc.;

- Any property used for entertainment or recreational purposes (such as photographic, phonographic, communication, and video recording equipment);

- Cellular telephones or other similar telecommunications equipment; and

- Computers or peripheral equipment.

Exceptions. Listed property does not include photographic, phonographic, communication, or video equipment used exclusively in your trade or business or at your regular business establishment. It also does not include any computer or peripheral equipment used exclusively at a regular business establishment and owned or leased by the person operating the establishment. For purposes of these exceptions, a portion of your home is treated as a regular business establishment only if that portion meets the requirements under section 280A(c)(1) for deducting expenses for the business use of your home.

See the instructions for line 6 on page C-3 if the business use percentage of any listed property decreased to 50% or less in 2004.

Line 14

Deduct contributions to employee benefit programs that are not an incidental part of a pension or profit-sharing plan included on line 19. Examples are accident and health plans, group-term life insurance, and dependent care assistance programs. If you made contributions on your behalf as a self-employed person to a dependent care assistance program, complete Form 2441, Parts I and III, to figure your deductible contributions to that program.

Do not include on line 14 any contributions you made on your behalf as a self-employed person to an accident and health plan or for group-term life insurance. You may be able to deduct on Form 1040, line 31, the amount you paid for health insurance on behalf of yourself, your spouse, and dependents, even if you do not itemize your deductions. See the instructions for Form 1040, line 31, for details.

Line 15

Deduct premiums paid for business insurance on line 15. Deduct on line 14 amounts paid for employee accident and health insurance. Do not deduct amounts credited to a reserve for self-insurance or premiums paid for a policy that pays for your lost earnings due to sickness or disability. For details, see Pub. 535.

Lines 16a and 16b

Interest allocation rules. The tax treatment of interest expense differs depending on its type. For example, home mortgage interest and investment interest are treated differently. "Interest allocation" rules require you to allocate (classify) your interest expense so it is deducted (or capitalized) on the correct line of your return and receives the right tax treatment. These rules could affect how much interest you are allowed to deduct on Schedule C or C-EZ.

Generally, you allocate interest expense by tracing how the proceeds of the loan were used. See Pub. 535 for details.

If you paid interest on a debt secured by your main home and any of the proceeds from that debt were used in connection with your trade or business, see Pub. 535 to figure the amount that is deductible on Schedule C or C-EZ.

How to report. If you have a mortgage on real property used in your business (other than your main home), enter on line 16a the interest you paid for 2004 to banks or other financial institutions for which you received a Form 1098 (or similar statement). If you did not receive a Form 1098, enter the interest on line 16b.

If you paid more mortgage interest than is shown on Form 1098, see Pub. 535 to find out if you can deduct the additional interest. If you can, include the amount on line 16a. Attach a statement to your return explaining the difference and enter "See attached" in the margin next to line 16a.

If you and at least one other person (other than your spouse if you file a joint return) were liable for and paid interest on the mortgage and the other person received the Form 1098, include your share of the interest on line 16b. Attach a statement to your return showing the name and address of the person who received the Form 1098. In the margin next to line 16b, enter "See attached."

If you paid interest in 2004 that applies to future years, deduct only the part that applies to 2004.

Line 17

Include on this line fees for tax advice related to your business and for preparation of the tax forms related to your business.

C-4

192

Line 19

Enter your deduction for contributions to a pension, profit-sharing, or annuity plan, or plans for the benefit of your employees. If the plan included you as a self-employed person, enter contributions made as an employer on your behalf on Form 1040, line 32, not on Schedule C.

Generally, you must file the applicable form listed below if you maintain a pension, profit-sharing, or other funded-deferred compensation plan. The filing requirement is not affected by whether or not the plan qualified under the Internal Revenue Code, or whether or not you claim a deduction for the current tax year. There is a penalty for failure to timely file these forms.

Form 5500. File this form for a plan that is not a one-participant plan (see below).

Form 5500-EZ. File this form for a one-participant plan. A one-participant plan is a plan that only covers you (or you and your spouse).

For details, see Pub. 560.

Lines 20a and 20b

If you rented or leased vehicles, machinery, or equipment, enter on line 20a the business portion of your rental cost. But if you leased a vehicle for a term of 30 days or more, you may have to reduce your deduction by an amount called the inclusion amount. See Pub. 463 to figure your inclusion amount.

Enter on line 20b amounts paid to rent or lease other property, such as office space in a building.

Line 21

Deduct the cost of repairs and maintenance. Include labor, supplies, and other items that do not add to the value or increase the life of the property. Do not deduct the value of your own labor. Do not deduct amounts spent to restore or replace property; they must be capitalized.

Line 22

Generally, you can deduct the cost of supplies only to the extent you actually consumed and used them in your business during the tax year (unless you deducted them in a prior tax year). However, if you had incidental supplies on hand for which you kept no inventories or records of use, you can deduct the cost of supplies you actually purchased during the tax year, provided that method clearly reflects income.

Line 23

You can deduct the following taxes and licenses on this line.
- State and local sales taxes imposed on you as the seller of goods or services. If you collected this tax from the buyer, you must also include the amount collected in gross receipts or sales on line 1.
- Real estate and personal property taxes on business assets.
- Licenses and regulatory fees for your trade or business paid each year to state or local governments. But some licenses, such as liquor licenses, may have to be amortized. See Pub. 535 for details.
- Social security and Medicare taxes paid to match required withholding from your employees' wages. Also, federal unemployment tax paid. Reduce your deduction by the amount shown on Form 8846, line 4.
- Federal highway use tax.

Do not deduct the following on this line.
- Federal income taxes, including your self-employment tax. However, you can deduct one-half of your self-employment tax on Form 1040, line 30.
- Estate and gift taxes.
- Taxes assessed to pay for improvements, such as paving and sewers.
- Taxes on your home or personal use property.
- State and local sales taxes on property purchased for use in your business. Instead, treat these taxes as part of the cost of the property.
- State and local sales taxes imposed on the buyer that you were required to collect and pay over to state or local governments. These taxes are not included in gross receipts or sales nor are they a deductible expense. However, if the state or local government allowed you to retain any part of the sales tax you collected, you must include that amount as income on line 6.
- Other taxes and license fees not related to your business.

Line 24a

Enter your expenses for lodging and transportation connected with overnight travel for business while away from your tax home. Generally, your tax home is your main place of business regardless of where you maintain your family home. You cannot deduct expenses paid or incurred in connection with employment away from home if that period of employment exceeds 1 year. Also, you cannot deduct travel expenses for your spouse, your dependent, or any other individual unless that person is your employee, the travel is for a bona fide business purpose, and the expenses would otherwise be deductible by that person.

Do not include expenses for meals and entertainment on this line. Instead, see the instructions for lines 24b and 24c on this page.

Instead of keeping records of your actual incidental expenses, you can use an optional method for deducting incidental expenses only if you did not pay or incur meal expenses on a day you were traveling away from your tax home. The amount of the deduction is $3 a day. Incidental expenses include fees and tips given to porters, baggage carriers, bellhops, hotel maids, stewards or stewardesses and others on ships, and hotel servants in foreign countries. They do not include expenses for laundry, cleaning and pressing of clothing, lodging taxes, or the costs of telegrams or telephone calls. You cannot use this method on any day that you use the standard meal allowance (as explained in the instructions for lines 24b and 24c).

You cannot deduct expenses for attending a foreign convention unless it is directly related to your trade or business and it is as reasonable for the meeting to be held outside the North American area as within it. These rules apply to both employers and employees. Other rules apply to luxury water travel.

For details, see Pub. 463.

Lines 24b and 24c

On line 24b, enter your total business meal and entertainment expenses. Include meal expenses while traveling away from home for business. Instead of the actual cost of your meals while traveling away from home, you can use the standard meal allowance for your daily meals and incidental expenses. Under this method, you deduct a specified amount, depending on where you travel, instead of keeping records of your actual meal expenses. However, you must still keep records to prove the time, place, and business purpose of your travel.

The standard meal allowance is the federal M&IE rate. You can find these rates on the Internet at *www.policyworks.gov/perdiem.* For locations outside the continental United States, the applicable rates are published monthly. You can find these rates on the Internet at *www.state.gov.*

See Pub. 463 for details on how to figure your deduction using the standard meal allowance, including special rules for partial days of travel.

Business meal expenses are deductible only if they are (a) directly related to or associated with the active conduct of your trade or business, (b) not lavish or extravagant, and (c) incurred while you or your employee is present at the meal.

You cannot deduct any expense paid or incurred for a facility (such as a yacht or hunting lodge) used for any activity usually considered entertainment, amusement, or recreation.

Also, you cannot deduct membership dues for any club organized for business, pleasure, recreation, or other social purpose. This includes country clubs, golf and athletic clubs, airline and hotel clubs, and clubs operated to provide meals under conditions favorable to business discussion. But it does not include civic or public service organizations, professional organizations (such as bar and medical associations), business leagues, trade associations, chambers of commerce, boards of trade, and real estate boards, unless a principal purpose of the organization is to entertain, or provide entertainment facilities for, members or their guests.

There are exceptions to these rules as well as other rules that apply to sky-box rentals and tickets to entertainment events. See Pub. 463.

Generally, you can deduct only 50% of your business meal and entertainment expenses, including meals incurred while away from home on business. For individuals subject to the Department of Transportation (DOT) hours of service limits, that percentage is increased to 70% for business meals consumed during, or incident to, any period of duty for which those limits are in effect. Individuals subject to the DOT hours of service limits include the following persons:

- Certain air transportation workers (such as pilots, crew, dispatchers, mechanics, and control tower operators) who are under Federal Aviation Administration regulations.

- Interstate truck operators who are under DOT regulations.

- Certain merchant mariners who are under Coast Guard regulations.

However, you can fully deduct meals, incidentals, and entertainment furnished or reimbursed to an employee if you properly treat the expense as wages subject to withholding. You can also fully deduct meals, incidentals, and entertainment provided to a nonemployee to the extent the expenses are includible in the gross income of that person and reported on Form 1099-MISC. See Pub. 535 for details and other exceptions.

If you provide daycare in your home, see Pub. 587 for information on deducting the cost of meals and snacks you provide to your daycare recipients.

Figure how much of the amount on line 24b is not deductible and enter that amount on line 24c.

Line 25

Deduct only utility expenses for your trade or business.

Local telephone service. If you used your home phone for business, do not deduct the base rate (including taxes) of the first phone line into your residence. But you can deduct expenses for any additional costs you incurred for business that are more than the cost of the base rate for the first phone line. For example, if you had a second line, you can deduct the business percentage of the charges for that line, including the base rate charges.

Line 26

Enter the total salaries and wages for the tax year. Do not include salaries and wages deducted elsewhere on your return or amounts paid to yourself. Reduce your deduction by the amounts claimed on:

- Form 5884, Work Opportunity Credit, line 2;
- Form 8844, Empowerment Zone and Renewal Community Employment Credit, line 2;
- Form 8845, Indian Employment Credit, line 4;
- Form 8861, Welfare-to-Work Credit, line 2; and

- Form 8884, New York Liberty Zone Business Employee Credit, line 2.

If you provided taxable fringe benefits to your employees, such as personal use of a car, do not deduct as wages the amount applicable to depreciation and other expenses claimed elsewhere.

Line 30

Business use of your home. You may be able to deduct certain expenses for business use of your home, subject to limitations. You must attach Form 8829 if you claim this deduction. For details, see the Instructions for Form 8829 and Pub. 587.

Line 31

If you have a loss, the amount of loss you can deduct this year may be limited. Go to line 32 before entering your loss on line 31. If you answered "No" to Schedule C, Question G, also see the Instructions for Form 8582. Enter the net profit or deductible loss here. Combine this amount with any profit or loss from other businesses, and enter the total on Form 1040, line 12, and Schedule SE, line 2. Estates and trusts should enter the total on Form 1041, line 3.

If you have a net profit on line 31, this amount is earned income and may qualify you for the earned income credit. See the instructions for Form 1040, lines 65a and 65b, for details.

Statutory employees. Include your net profit or deductible loss from line 31 with other Schedule C amounts on Form 1040, line 12. However, do not report this amount on Schedule SE, line 2. If you are required to file Schedule SE because of other self-employment income, see the Instructions for Schedule SE.

Line 32

At-risk rules. Generally, if you have (a) a business loss and (b) amounts in the business for which you are not at risk, you will have to complete Form 6198 to figure your allowable loss. The at-risk rules generally limit the amount of loss (including loss on the disposition of assets) you can claim to the amount you could actually lose in the business.

Check box 32b if you have amounts for which you are not at risk in this business, such as the following.

- Nonrecourse loans used to finance the business, to acquire property used in the business, or to acquire the business that are not secured by your own property (other than property used in the business). However, there is an exception for certain nonrecourse financing borrowed by you in connection with holding real property.

- Cash, property, or borrowed amounts used in the business (or contributed to the business, or used to acquire the business) that are protected against loss by a guarantee, stop-loss agreement, or other similar

arrangement (excluding casualty insurance and insurance against tort liability).

- Amounts borrowed for use in the business from a person who has an interest in the business, other than as a creditor, or who is related under section 465(b)(3) to a person (other than you) having such an interest.

If all amounts are at risk in this business, check box 32a and enter your loss on line 31. But if you answered "No" to Question G, you may need to complete Form 8582 to figure your deductible loss. See the Instructions for Form 8582 for details.

If you checked box 32b, see Form 6198 to determine the amount of your deductible loss. But if you answered "No" to Question G, your loss may be further limited. See the Instructions for Form 8582. If your at-risk amount is zero or less, enter -0- on line 31. Be sure to attach Form 6198 to your return. If you checked box 32b and you do not attach Form 6198, the processing of your tax return may be delayed.

Any loss from this business not allowed for 2004 because of the at-risk rules is treated as a deduction allocable to the business in 2005. For details, see the Instructions for Form 6198 and Pub. 925.

Part III. Cost of Goods Sold

Generally, if you engaged in a trade or business in which the production, purchase, or sale of merchandise was an income-producing factor, you must take inventories into account at the beginning and end of your tax year.

However, if you are a qualifying taxpayer or a qualifying small business taxpayer, you can account for inventoriable items in the same manner as materials and supplies that are not incidental. To change your accounting method, see the instructions for line F on page C-2.

A qualifying taxpayer is a taxpayer (a) whose average annual gross receipts for the 3 prior tax years are $1 million or less, and (b) whose business is not a tax shelter (as defined in section 448(d)(3)).

A qualifying small business taxpayer is a taxpayer (a) whose average annual gross receipts for the 3 prior tax years are more than $1 million but not more than $10 million, (b) whose business is not a tax shelter (as defined in section 448(d)(3)), and (c) whose principal business activity is not an ineligible activity as explained in Rev. Proc. 2002-28. You can find Rev. Proc. 2002-28 on page 815 of Internal Revenue Bulletin 2002-18 at *www.irs.gov/pub/irs-irbs/irb02-18.pdf.*

Under this accounting method, inventory costs for raw materials purchased for use in producing finished goods and merchandise purchased for resale are deductible in the year the finished goods or merchandise are sold (but not before the year you paid for the raw materials or merchandise, if you are also using the cash method). Enter amounts paid for all raw materials and merchandise during 2004 on line 36. The amount you can deduct for 2004 is figured on line 42.

Additional information. For additional guidance on this method of accounting for inventoriable items, see Rev. Proc. 2001-10 if you are a qualifying taxpayer or Rev. Proc. 2002-28 if you are a qualifying small business taxpayer. You can find Rev. Proc. 2001-10 on page 272 of Internal Revenue Bulletin 2001-2 at *www.irs.gov/pub/ irs-irbs/irb01-02.pdf*, and Rev. Proc. 2002-28 on page 815 of Internal Revenue Bulletin 2002-18 at *www.irs.gov/pub/ irs-irbs/irb02-18.pdf*.

 Certain direct and indirect expenses may have to be capitalized or included in inventory. See the instructions for Part II beginning on page C-3.

Line 33

Your inventories can be valued at cost; cost or market value, whichever is lower; or any other method approved by the IRS. However, you are required to use cost if you are using the cash method of accounting.

Line 35

If you are changing your method of accounting beginning with 2004, refigure last year's closing inventory using your new method of accounting and enter the result on line 35. If there is a difference between last year's closing inventory and the refigured amount, attach an explanation and take it into account when figuring your section 481(a) adjustment. See the example on page C-2 for details.

Line 41

If you account for inventoriable items in the same manner as materials and supplies that are not incidental, enter on line 41 the portion of your raw materials and merchandise purchased for resale that are included on line 40 and were not sold during the year.

Part V. Other Expenses

Include all ordinary and necessary business expenses not deducted elsewhere on Schedule C. List the type and amount of each expense separately in the space provided. Enter the total on lines 48 and 27. Do not include the cost of business equipment or furniture, replacements or permanent improvements to property, or personal, living, and family expenses. Do not include charitable contributions. Also, you cannot deduct fines or penalties paid to a government for violating any law. For details on business expenses, see Pub. 535.

Amortization. Include amortization in this part. For amortization that begins in 2004, you must complete and attach Form 4562.

You can amortize:

● The cost of pollution-control facilities.

● Amounts paid for research and experimentation.

● Qualified revitalization expenditures.

● Amounts paid to acquire, protect, expand, register, or defend trademarks or trade names.

● Goodwill and certain other intangibles.

In general, you cannot amortize real property construction period interest and taxes. Special rules apply for allocating interest to real or personal property produced in your trade or business.

At-risk loss deduction. Any loss from this activity that was not allowed as a deduction last year because of the at-risk rules is treated as a deduction allocable to this activity in 2004.

Business start-up costs. You can elect to amortize certain business start-up costs paid or incurred before October 23, 2004, over 60 months or more, beginning with the month your business began. For certain business start-up costs paid or incurred after October 22, 2004, you can elect to deduct up to $5,000 for the year your business began. This limit is reduced by the amount by which your start-up costs exceed

$50,000. You can elect to amortize any remaining business start-up costs over 15 years. For details, see Pub. 535. For amortization that begins in 2004, you must complete and attach Form 4562.

Capital construction fund. Do not claim on Schedule C or C-EZ the deduction for amounts contributed to a capital construction fund set up under the Merchant Marine Act of 1936. Instead, reduce the amount you would otherwise enter on Form 1040, line 42, by the amount of the deduction. Next to line 42, enter "CCF" and the amount of the deduction. For details, see Pub. 595.

Clean-fuel vehicles and clean-fuel vehicle refueling property. You may be able to deduct part of the cost of qualified clean-fuel vehicle property used in your business and qualified clean-fuel vehicle refueling property. See Pub. 535 for details.

Disabled access credit and the deduction for removing barriers to individuals with disabilities and the elderly. You may be able to claim a tax credit of up to $5,000 for eligible expenditures paid or incurred in 2004 to provide access to your business for individuals with disabilities. See Form 8826 for details. You can also deduct up to $15,000 of costs paid or incurred in 2004 to remove architectural or transportation barriers to individuals with disabilities and the elderly. However, you cannot take both the credit and the deduction on the same expenditures.

Film and television production expenses. You can elect to deduct costs of certain qualified film and television productions that begin after October 22, 2004. For details, see Pub. 535.

Forestation and reforestation costs. You can elect to amortize certain forestation and reforestation costs over 84 months. You can also elect to expense up to $10,000 ($5,000 if married filing separately) of certain forestation and reforestation costs paid or incurred after October 22, 2004, for each qualified timber property. The amortization election does not apply to trusts and the expense election does not apply to estates and trusts. For details, see Pub. 535. For amortization that begins in 2004, you must complete and attach Form 4562.

Principal Business or Professional Activity Codes

These codes for the Principal Business or Professional Activity classify sole proprietorships by the type of activity they are engaged in to facilitate the administration of the Internal Revenue Code. These six-digit codes are based on the North American Industry Classification System (NAICS).

Select the category that best describes your primary business activity (for example, Real Estate). Then select the activity that best identifies the principal source of your sales or receipts (for example, real estate agent). Now find the six-digit code assigned to this activity (for example, 531210, the code for offices

of real estate agents and brokers) and enter it on Schedule C or C-EZ, line B.

Note. If your principal source of income is from farming activities, you should file Schedule F.

Accommodation, Food Services, & Drinking Places		
Accommodation		
721310	Rooming & boarding houses	
721210	RV (recreational vehicle) parks & recreational camps	
721100	Travel accommodation (including hotels, motels, & bed & breakfast inns)	
Food Services & Drinking Places		
722410	Drinking places (alcoholic beverages)	
722110	Full-service restaurants	
722210	Limited-service eating places	

722300	Special food services (including food service contractors & caterers)
Administrative & Support and Waste Management & Remediation Services	
Administrative & Support Services	
561430	Business service centers (including private mail centers & copy shops)
561740	Carpet & upholstery cleaning services
561440	Collection agencies
561450	Credit bureaus

561410	Document preparation services
561300	Employment services
561710	Exterminating & pest control services
561210	Facilities support (management) services
561600	Investigation & security services
561720	Janitorial services
561730	Landscaping services
561110	Office administrative services
561420	Telephone call centers (including telephone answering services & telemarketing bureaus)

561500	Travel arrangement & reservation services
561490	Other business support services (including repossession services, court reporting, & stenotype services)
561790	Other services to buildings & dwellings
561900	Other support services (including packaging & labeling services, & convention & trade show organizers)

C-7

Waste Management & Remediation Services
562000 Waste management & remediation services

Agriculture, Forestry, Hunting, & Fishing
112900 Animal production (including breeding of cats and dogs)
114110 Fishing
113000 Forestry & logging (including forest nurseries & timber tracts)
114210 Hunting & trapping

Support Activities for Agriculture & Forestry
115210 Support activities for animal production (including farriers)
115110 Support activities for crop production (including cotton ginning, soil preparation, planting, & cultivating)
115310 Support activities for forestry

Arts, Entertainment, & Recreation
Amusement, Gambling, & Recreation Industries
713100 Amusement parks & arcades
713200 Gambling industries
713900 Other amusement & recreation services (including golf courses, skiing facilities, marinas, fitness centers, bowling centers, skating rinks, miniature golf courses)

Museums, Historical Sites, & Similar Institutions
712100 Museums, historical sites, & similar institutions

Performing Arts, Spectator Sports, & Related Industries
711410 Agents & managers for artists, athletes, entertainers, & other public figures
711510 Independent artists, writers, & performers
711100 Performing arts companies
711300 Promoters of performing arts, sports, & similar events
711210 Spectator sports (including professional sports clubs & racetrack operations)

Construction of Buildings
236200 Nonresidential building construction
236100 Residential building construction

Heavy and Civil Engineering Construction
237310 Highway, street, & bridge construction
237210 Land subdivision
237100 Utility system construction
237990 Other heavy & civil engineering construction

Specialty Trade Contractors
238310 Drywall & insulation contractors
238210 Electrical contractors
238350 Finish carpentry contractors
238330 Flooring contractors
238130 Framing carpentry contractors
238150 Glass & glazing contractors
238140 Masonry contractors
238320 Painting & wall covering contractors
238220 Plumbing, heating & air-conditioning contractors
238110 Poured concrete foundation & structure contractors
238160 Roofing contractors
238170 Siding contractors

238910 Site preparation contractors
238120 Structural steel & precast concrete construction contractors
238340 Tile & terrazzo contractors
238290 Other building equipment contractors
238390 Other building finishing contractors
238190 Other foundation, structure, & building exterior contractors
238990 All other specialty trade contractors

Educational Services
611000 Educational services (including schools, colleges, & universities)

Finance & Insurance
Credit Intermediation & Related Activities
522100 Depository credit intermediation (including commercial banking, savings institutions, & credit unions)
522200 Nondepository credit intermediation (including sales financing & consumer lending)
522300 Activities related to credit intermediation (including loan brokers)

Insurance Agents, Brokers, & Related Activities
524210 Insurance agencies & brokerages
524290 Other insurance related activities

Securities, Commodity Contracts, & Other Financial Investments & Related Activities
523140 Commodity contracts brokers
523130 Commodity contracts dealers
523110 Investment bankers & securities dealers
523210 Securities & commodity exchanges
523120 Securities brokers
523900 Other financial investment activities (including investment advice)

Health Care & Social Assistance
Ambulatory Health Care Services
621610 Home health care services
621510 Medical & diagnostic laboratories
621310 Offices of chiropractors
621210 Offices of dentists
621330 Offices of mental health practitioners (except physicians)
621320 Offices of optometrists
621340 Offices of physical, occupational & speech therapists, & audiologists
621111 Offices of physicians (except mental health specialists)
621112 Offices of physicians, mental health specialists
621391 Offices of podiatrists
621399 Offices of all other miscellaneous health practitioners
621400 Outpatient care centers
621900 Other ambulatory health care services (including ambulance services, blood, & organ banks)

Hospitals
622000 Hospitals

Nursing & Residential Care Facilities
623000 Nursing & residential care facilities

Social Assistance
624410 Child day care services
624200 Community food & housing, & emergency & other relief services
624100 Individual & family services
624310 Vocational rehabilitation services

Information
511000 Publishing industries (except Internet)

Broadcasting (except Internet) & Telecommunications
515000 Broadcasting (except Internet)
517000 Telecommunications

Internet Publishing & Broadcasting
516110 Internet publishing & broadcasting

Internet Service Providers, Web Search Portals, & Data Processing Services
518210 Data processing, hosting, & related services
518111 Internet service providers
518112 Web search portals
519100 Other information services (including news syndicates and libraries)

Motion Picture & Sound Recording
512100 Motion picture & video industries (except video rental)
512200 Sound recording industries

Manufacturing
315000 Apparel mfg.
312000 Beverage & tobacco product mfg.
334000 Computer & electronic product mfg.
335000 Electrical equipment, appliance, & component mfg.
332000 Fabricated metal product mfg.
337000 Furniture & related product mfg.
333000 Machinery mfg.
339110 Medical equipment & supplies mfg.
322000 Paper mfg.
324100 Petroleum & coal products mfg.
326000 Plastics & rubber products mfg.
331000 Primary metal mfg.
323100 Printing & related support activities
313000 Textile mills
314000 Textile product mills
336000 Transportation equipment mfg.
321000 Wood product mfg.
339900 Other miscellaneous mfg.

Chemical Manufacturing
325100 Basic chemical mfg.
325500 Paint, coating, & adhesive mfg.
325300 Pesticide, fertilizer, & other agricultural chemical mfg.
325410 Pharmaceutical & medicine mfg.
325200 Resin, synthetic rubber, & artificial & synthetic fibers & filaments mfg.

325600 Soap, cleaning compound, & toilet preparation mfg.
325900 Other chemical product & preparation mfg.

Food Manufacturing
311110 Animal food mfg.
311800 Bakeries & tortilla mfg.
311500 Dairy product mfg.
311400 Fruit & vegetable preserving & speciality food mfg.
311200 Grain & oilseed milling
311610 Animal slaughtering & processing
311710 Seafood product preparation & packaging
311300 Sugar & confectionery product mfg.
311900 Other food mfg. (including coffee, tea, flavorings, & seasonings)

Leather & Allied Product Manufacturing
316210 Footwear mfg. (including leather, rubber, & plastics)
316110 Leather & hide tanning & finishing
316990 Other leather & allied product mfg.

Nonmetallic Mineral Product Manufacturing
327300 Cement & concrete product mfg.
327100 Clay product & refractory mfg.
327210 Glass & glass product mfg.
327400 Lime & gypsum product mfg.
327900 Other nonmetallic mineral product mfg.

Mining
212110 Coal mining
212200 Metal ore mining
212300 Nonmetallic mineral mining & quarrying
211110 Oil & gas extraction
213110 Support activities for mining

Other Services
Personal & Laundry Services
812111 Barber shops
812112 Beauty salons
812220 Cemeteries & crematories
812310 Coin-operated laundries & drycleaners
812320 Drycleaning & laundry services (except coin-operated) (including laundry & drycleaning dropoff & pickup sites)
812210 Funeral homes & funeral services
812330 Linen & uniform supply
812113 Nail salons
812930 Parking lots & garages
812910 Pet care (except veterinary) services
812920 Photofinishing
812190 Other personal care services (including diet & weight reducing centers)
812990 All other personal services

Repair & Maintenance
811120 Automotive body, paint, interior, & glass repair
811110 Automotive mechanical & electrical repair & maintenance
811190 Other automotive repair & maintenance (including oil change & lubrication shops & car washes)

C-8

196

811310	Commercial & industrial machinery & equipment (except automotive & electronic) repair & maintenance
811210	Electronic & precision equipment repair & maintenance
811430	Footwear & leather goods repair
811410	Home & garden equipment & appliance repair & maintenance
811420	Reupholstery & furniture repair
811490	Other personal & household goods repair & maintenance

Professional, Scientific, & Technical Services
541100	Legal services
541211	Offices of certified public accountants
541214	Payroll services
541213	Tax preparation services
541219	Other accounting services

Architectural, Engineering, & Related Services
541310	Architectural services
541350	Building inspection services
541340	Drafting services
541330	Engineering services
541360	Geophysical surveying & mapping services
541320	Landscape architecture services
541370	Surveying & mapping (except geophysical) services
541380	Testing laboratories

Computer Systems Design & Related Services
| 541510 | Computer systems design & related services |

Specialized Design Services
| 541400 | Specialized design services (including interior, industrial, graphic, & fashion design) |

Other Professional, Scientific, & Technical Services
541800	Advertising & related services
541600	Management, scientific, & technical consulting services
541910	Market research & public opinion polling
541920	Photographic services
541700	Scientific research & development services
541930	Translation & interpretation services
541940	Veterinary services
541990	All other professional, scientific, & technical services

Real Estate & Rental & Leasing
Real Estate
531100	Lessors of real estate (including miniwarehouses & self-storage units)
531210	Offices of real estate agents & brokers
531320	Offices of real estate appraisers
531310	Real estate property managers
531390	Other activities related to real estate

Rental & Leasing Services
532100	Automotive equipment rental & leasing
532400	Commercial & industrial machinery & equipment rental & leasing
532210	Consumer electronics & appliances rental
532220	Formal wear & costume rental
532310	General rental centers
532230	Video tape & disc rental
532290	Other consumer goods rental

Religious, Grantmaking, Civic, Professional, & Similar Organizations
| 813000 | Religious, grantmaking, civic, professional, & similar organizations |

Retail Trade
Building Material & Garden Equipment & Supplies Dealers
444130	Hardware stores
444110	Home centers
444200	Lawn & garden equipment & supplies stores
444120	Paint & wallpaper stores
444190	Other building materials dealers

Clothing & Accessories Stores
448130	Children's & infants' clothing stores
448150	Clothing accessories stores
448140	Family clothing stores
448310	Jewelry stores
448320	Luggage & leather goods stores
448110	Men's clothing stores
448210	Shoe stores
448120	Women's clothing stores
448190	Other clothing stores

Electronic & Appliance Stores
443130	Camera & photographic supplies stores
443120	Computer & software stores
443111	Household appliance stores
443112	Radio, television, & other electronics stores

Food & Beverage Stores
445310	Beer, wine, & liquor stores
445220	Fish & seafood markets
445230	Fruit & vegetable markets
445100	Grocery stores (including supermarkets & convenience stores without gas)
445210	Meat markets
445290	Other specialty food stores

Furniture & Home Furnishing Stores
| 442110 | Furniture stores |
| 442200 | Home furnishings stores |

Gasoline Stations
| 447100 | Gasoline stations (including convenience stores with gas) |

General Merchandise Stores
| 452000 | General merchandise stores |

Health & Personal Care Stores
446120	Cosmetics, beauty supplies, & perfume stores
446130	Optical goods stores
446110	Pharmacies & drug stores

| 446190 | Other health & personal care stores |

Motor Vehicle & Parts Dealers
441300	Automotive parts, accessories, & tire stores
441222	Boat dealers
441221	Motorcycle dealers
441110	New car dealers
441210	Recreational vehicle dealers (including motor home & travel trailer dealers)
441120	Used car dealers
441229	All other motor vehicle dealers

Sporting Goods, Hobby, Book, & Music Stores
451211	Book stores
451120	Hobby, toy, & game stores
451140	Musical instrument & supplies stores
451212	News dealers & newsstands
451220	Prerecorded tape, compact disc, & record stores
451130	Sewing, needlework, & piece goods stores
451110	Sporting goods stores

Miscellaneous Store Retailers
453920	Art dealers
453110	Florists
453220	Gift, novelty, & souvenir stores
453930	Manufactured (mobile) home dealers
453210	Office supplies & stationery stores
453910	Pet & pet supplies stores
453310	Used merchandise stores
453990	All other miscellaneous store retailers (including tobacco, candle, & trophy shops)

Nonstore Retailers
454112	Electronic auctions
454111	Electronic shopping
454310	Fuel dealers
454113	Mail-order houses
454210	Vending machine operators
454390	Other direct selling establishments (including door-to-door retailing, frozen food plan providers, party plan merchandisers, & coffee-break service providers)

Transportation & Warehousing
481000	Air transportation
485510	Charter bus industry
484110	General freight trucking, local
484120	General freight trucking, long distance
485210	Interurban & rural bus transportation
486000	Pipeline transportation
482110	Rail transportation
487000	Scenic & sightseeing transportation
485410	School & employee bus transportation
484200	Specialized freight trucking (including household moving vans)
485300	Taxi & limousine service
485110	Urban transit systems
483000	Water transportation
485990	Other transit & ground passenger transportation

| 488000 | Support activities for transportation (including motor vehicle towing) |

Couriers & Messengers
| 492000 | Couriers & messengers |

Warehousing & Storage Facilities
| 493100 | Warehousing & storage (except leases of miniwarehouses & self-storage units) |

Utilities
| 221000 | Utilities |

Wholesale Trade
Merchant Wholesalers, Durable Goods
423600	Electrical & electronic goods
423200	Furniture & home furnishing
423700	Hardware, & plumbing & heating equipment & supplies
423940	Jewelry, watch, precious stone, & precious metals
423300	Lumber & other construction materials
423800	Machinery, equipment, & supplies
423500	Metal & mineral (except petroleum)
423100	Motor vehicle & motor vehicle parts & supplies
423400	Professional & commercial equipment & supplies
423930	Recyclable materials
423910	Sporting & recreational goods & supplies
423920	Toy & hobby goods & supplies
423990	Other miscellaneous durable goods

Merchant Wholesalers, Nondurable Goods
424300	Apparel, piece goods, & notions
424800	Beer, wine, & distilled alcoholic beverage
424920	Books, periodicals, & newspapers
424600	Chemical & allied products
424210	Drugs & druggists' sundries
424500	Farm product raw materials
424910	Farm supplies
424930	Flower, nursery stock, & florists' supplies
424400	Grocery & related products
424950	Paint, varnish, & supplies
424100	Paper & paper products
424700	Petroleum & petroleum products
424940	Tobacco & tobacco products
424990	Other miscellaneous nondurable goods

Wholesale Electronic Markets and Agents & Brokers
| 425110 | Business to business electronic markets |
| 425120 | Wholesale trade agents & brokers |

| 999999 | **Unclassified establishments (unable to classify)** |

SCHEDULE C-EZ
(Form 1040)

Department of the Treasury
Internal Revenue Service

Net Profit From Business
(Sole Proprietorship)

▶ Partnerships, joint ventures, etc., must file Form 1065 or 1065-B.

▶ Attach to Form 1040 or 1041. ▶ See instructions on back.

OMB No. 1545-0074

2004

Attachment
Sequence No. **09A**

Name of proprietor

Social security number (SSN)

Part I   **General Information**

**You May Use
Schedule C-EZ
Instead of
Schedule C
Only If You:**

- Had business expenses of $5,000 or less.
- Use the cash method of accounting.
- Did not have an inventory at any time during the year.
- Did not have a net loss from your business.
- Had only one business as a sole proprietor.

And You:

- Had no employees during the year.
- Are not required to file **Form 4562,** Depreciation and Amortization, for this business. See the instructions for Schedule C, line 13, on page C-4 to find out if you must file.
- Do not deduct expenses for business use of your home.
- Do not have prior year unallowed passive activity losses from this business.

A   Principal business or profession, including product or service

B   Enter code from pages C-7, 8, & 9
▶

C   Business name. If no separate business name, leave blank.

D   Employer ID number (EIN), if any

E   Business address (including suite or room no.). Address not required if same as on Form 1040, page 1.

City, town or post office, state, and ZIP code

Part II   **Figure Your Net Profit**

1 **Gross receipts. Caution.** If this income was reported to you on Form W-2 and the "Statutory employee" box on that form was checked, see **Statutory Employees** in the instructions for Schedule C, line 1, on page C-3 and check here . . . . ▶ ☐ | **1** |

2 **Total expenses** (see instructions). If more than $5,000, you **must** use Schedule C. . . . . . | **2** |

3 **Net profit.** Subtract line 2 from line 1. If less than zero, you **must** use Schedule C. Enter on **Form 1040, line 12,** and **also** on **Schedule SE, line 2.** (Statutory employees **do not** report this amount on Schedule SE, line 2. Estates and trusts, enter on Form 1041, line 3.) . . . . . | **3** |

Part III   **Information on Your Vehicle.** Complete this part **only** if you are claiming car or truck expenses on line 2.

4   When did you place your vehicle in service for business purposes? (month, day, year) ▶ ..../.........../........ .

5   Of the total number of miles you drove your vehicle during 2004, enter the number of miles you used your vehicle for:

a Business .... **b** Commuting .... **c** Other ....

6   Do you (or your spouse) have another vehicle available for personal use? . . . . ☐ **Yes**   ☐ **No**

7   Was your vehicle available for personal use during off-duty hours? . . . . ☐ **Yes**   ☐ **No**

8a   Do you have evidence to support your deduction? . . . . ☐ **Yes**   ☐ **No**

b   If "Yes," is the evidence written? . . . . ☐ **Yes**   ☐ **No**

For Paperwork Reduction Act Notice, see Form 1040 instructions.   Cat. No. 14374D   Schedule C-EZ (Form 1040) 2004

Instructions

You can use Schedule C-EZ instead of Schedule C if you operated a business or practiced a profession as a sole proprietorship and you have met all the requirements listed in Schedule C-EZ, Part I.

Line A

Describe the business or professional activity that provided your principal source of income reported on line 1. Give the general field or activity and the type of product or service.

Line B

Enter the six-digit code that identifies your principal business or professional activity. See pages C-7 through C-9 of the Instructions for Schedule C for the list of codes.

Line D

You need an employer identification number (EIN) only if you had a qualified retirement plan or were required to file an employment, excise, estate, trust, or alcohol, tobacco, and firearms tax return. If you need an EIN, see the Instructions for Form SS-4. If you do not have an EIN, leave line D blank. Do not enter your SSN.

Line E

Enter your business address. Show a street address instead of a box number. Include the suite or room number, if any.

Line 1

Enter gross receipts from your trade or business. Include amounts you received in your trade or business that were properly shown on Forms 1099-MISC. If the total amounts that were reported in box 7 of Forms 1099-MISC are more than the total you are reporting on line 1, attach a statement explaining the difference. You must show all items of taxable income actually or constructively received during the year (in cash, property, or services). Income is constructively received when it is credited to your account or set aside for you to use. Do not offset this amount by any losses.

Line 2

Enter the total amount of all deductible business expenses you actually paid during the year. Examples of these expenses include advertising, car and truck expenses, commissions and fees, insurance, interest, legal and professional services, office expense, rent or lease expenses, repairs and maintenance, supplies, taxes, travel, the allowable percentage of business meals and entertainment, and utilities (including telephone). For details, see the instructions for Schedule C, Parts II and V, on pages C-3 through C-7. If you wish, you can use the optional worksheet below to record your expenses.

If you claim car or truck expenses, be sure to complete Schedule C-EZ, Part III.

Optional Worksheet for Line 2 (keep a copy for your records)

		a				
a	Business meals and entertainment	a				
b	Enter nondeductible amount included on line **a** (see the instructions for Schedule C, lines 24b and 24c, on page C-5)	b				
c	Deductible business meals and entertainment. Subtract line **b** from line **a**			c		
d	....			d		
e	....			e		
f	....			f		
g	....			g		
h	....			h		
i	....			i		
j	**Total.** Add lines **c** through **i**. Enter here and on line 2			j		

Form **8829**

Department of the Treasury
Internal Revenue Service   (99)

Expenses for Business Use of Your Home

▶ File only with Schedule C (Form 1040). Use a separate Form 8829 for each home you used for business during the year.

▶ See separate instructions.

OMB No. 1545-1266

20**04**

Attachment
Sequence No. **66**

Name(s) of proprietor(s)

Your social security number

Part I   Part of Your Home Used for Business

1	Area used regularly and exclusively for business, regularly for day care, or for storage of inventory or product samples (see instructions)	1	
2	Total area of home	2	
3	Divide line 1 by line 2. Enter the result as a percentage	3	%

- For day-care facilities not used exclusively for business, also complete lines 4–6.
- All others, skip lines 4–6 and enter the amount from line 3 on line 7.

4	Multiply days used for day care during year by hours used per day	4	hr.
5	Total hours available for use during the year (366 days × 24 hours) (see instructions)	5	8,784 hr.
6	Divide line 4 by line 5. Enter the result as a decimal amount	6	
7	Business percentage. For day-care facilities not used exclusively for business, multiply line 6 by line 3 (enter the result as a percentage). All others, enter the amount from line 3 ▶	7	%

Part II   Figure Your Allowable Deduction

		(a) Direct expenses	(b) Indirect expenses	
8	Enter the amount from Schedule C, line 29, **plus** any net gain or (loss) derived from the business use of your home and shown on Schedule D or Form 4797. If more than one place of business, see instructions			8
	See instructions for columns (a) and (b) before completing lines 9–20.			
9	Casualty losses (see instructions)			
10	Deductible mortgage interest (see instructions)			
11	Real estate taxes (see instructions)			
12	Add lines 9, 10, and 11			
13	Multiply line 12, column (b) by line 7		13	
14	Add line 12, column (a) and line 13			14
15	Subtract line 14 from line 8. If zero or less, enter -0-			15
16	Excess mortgage interest (see instructions)	16		
17	Insurance	17		
18	Repairs and maintenance	18		
19	Utilities	19		
20	Other expenses (see instructions)	20		
21	Add lines 16 through 20	21		
22	Multiply line 21, column (b) by line 7		22	
23	Carryover of operating expenses from 2003 Form 8829, line 41		23	
24	Add line 21 in column (a), line 22, and line 23			24
25	Allowable operating expenses. Enter the **smaller** of line 15 or line 24			25
26	Limit on excess casualty losses and depreciation. Subtract line 25 from line 15			26
27	Excess casualty losses (see instructions)		27	
28	Depreciation of your home from Part III below		28	
29	Carryover of excess casualty losses and depreciation from 2003 Form 8829, line 42		29	
30	Add lines 27 through 29			30
31	Allowable excess casualty losses and depreciation. Enter the **smaller** of line 26 or line 30			31
32	Add lines 14, 25, and 31			32
33	Casualty loss portion, if any, from lines 14 and 31. Carry amount to **Form 4684,** Section B			33
34	Allowable expenses for business use of your home. Subtract line 33 from line 32. Enter here and on Schedule C, line 30. If your home was used for more than one business, see instructions ▶			34

Part III   Depreciation of Your Home

35	Enter the **smaller** of your home's adjusted basis or its fair market value (see instructions)	35	
36	Value of land included on line 35	36	
37	Basis of building. Subtract line 36 from line 35	37	
38	Business basis of building. Multiply line 37 by line 7	38	
39	Depreciation percentage (see instructions)	39	%
40	Depreciation allowable (see instructions). Multiply line 38 by line 39. Enter here and on line 28 above	40	

Part IV   Carryover of Unallowed Expenses to 2005

41	Operating expenses. Subtract line 25 from line 24. If less than zero, enter -0-	41	
42	Excess casualty losses and depreciation. Subtract line 31 from line 30. If less than zero, enter -0-	42	

For Paperwork Reduction Act Notice, see page 4 of separate instructions.   Cat. No. 13232M   Form **8829** (2004)

2004

 Department of the Treasury
Internal Revenue Service

Instructions for Form 8829

Expenses for Business Use of Your Home

Section references are to the Internal Revenue Code.

General Instructions

Note. If you are claiming expenses for business use of your home as an employee or a partner, or you are claiming these expenses on Schedule F (Form 1040), do not use Form 8829. Instead, complete the worksheet in Pub. 587, Business Use of Your Home (Including Use by Daycare Providers).

Purpose of Form

Use Form 8829 to figure the allowable expenses for business use of your home on Schedule C (Form 1040) and any carryover to 2005 of amounts not deductible in 2004.

If all of the expenses for business use of your home are properly allocable to inventory costs, do not complete Form 8829. These expenses are figured in Schedule C, Part III, and not on Form 8829.

You must meet specific requirements to deduct expenses for the business use of your home. Even if you meet these requirements, your deductible expenses may be limited. Part IV is used to figure any allowable carryover of expenses that are more than the limit. For details, see Publication 587.

Who Can Deduct Expenses for Business Use of a Home

Generally, you can deduct business expenses that apply to a part of your home only if that part is exclusively used on a regular basis:
• As your principal place of business for any of your trades or businesses,
• As a place of business used by your patients, clients, or customers to meet or deal with you in the normal course of your trade or business, or
• In connection with your trade or business if it is a separate structure that is not attached to your home.

As explained on this page, exceptions to this rule apply to space used on a regular basis for:
• Storage of inventory or product samples, and
• Certain daycare facilities.

Principal Place of Business

In determining whether the office in your home qualifies as your principal place of business, you must consider the following two items.
• The relative importance of the activities performed at each place where you conduct business, and
• The amount of time spent at each place where you conduct business.

Your home office will qualify as your principal place of business if you meet the following requirements.
• You use it exclusively and regularly for administrative or management activities of your trade or business.
• You have no other fixed location where you conduct substantial administrative or management activities of your trade or business.

Administrative or management activities. There are many activities that are administrative or managerial in nature. The following are a few examples.
• Billing customers, clients, or patients.
• Keeping books and records.
• Ordering supplies.
• Setting up appointments.
• Forwarding orders or writing reports.

Administrative or management activities performed at other locations. The following activities performed by you or others will not disqualify your home office from being your principal place of business.
• You have others conduct your administrative or management activities at locations other than your home. (For example, another company does your billing from its place of business.)
• You conduct administrative or management activities at places that are not fixed locations of your business, such as in a car or a hotel room.
• You occasionally conduct minimal administrative or management activities at a fixed location outside your home.
• You conduct substantial nonadministrative or nonmanagement business activities at a fixed location outside your home. (For example, you meet with or provide services to customers, clients, or patients at a fixed location of the business outside your home.)
• You have suitable space to conduct administrative or management activities outside your home, but choose to use your home office for those activities instead.

More information. For information on other ways to qualify to deduct business use of the home expenses, see Pub. 587.

Storage of Inventory or Product Samples

You can also deduct expenses that apply to space within your home used on a regular basis to store inventory or product samples from your trade or business of selling products at retail or wholesale. Your home must be the only fixed location of your trade or business.

Daycare Facilities

If you use space in your home on a regular basis in the trade or business of providing daycare, you may be able to deduct the business expenses even though you use

Cat. No. 15683B

the same space for nonbusiness purposes. To qualify for this exception, you must have applied for (and not have been rejected), been granted (and still have in effect), or be exempt from having a license, certification, registration, or approval as a daycare center or as a family or group daycare home under state law.

Expenses Related to Tax-Exempt Income

Generally, you cannot deduct expenses that are allocable to tax-exempt income. However, if you receive a tax-exempt parsonage allowance or a tax-exempt military housing allowance, your expenses for mortgage interest and real property taxes are deductible under the normal rules. No deduction is allowed for other expenses allocable to the tax-exempt allowance.

Specific Instructions

Part I

Lines 1 and 2

To determine the area on lines 1 and 2, you can use square feet or any other reasonable method if it accurately figures your business percentage on line 7.

Do not include on line 1 the area of your home you used to figure any expenses allocable to inventory costs. The business percentage of these expenses should have been taken into account in Schedule C, Part III.

Special Computation for Certain Daycare Facilities

If the part of your home used as a daycare facility included areas used exclusively for business as well as other areas used only partly for business, you cannot figure your business percentage using Part I. Instead, follow these three steps:

1. Figure the business percentage of the part of your home used exclusively for business by dividing the area used exclusively for business by the total area of the home.
2. Figure the business percentage of the part of your home used only partly for business by following the same method used in Part I of the form, but enter on line 1 of your computation only the area of the home used partly for business.
3. Add the business percentages you figured in the first two steps and enter the result on line 7. Attach your computation and enter "See attached computation" directly above the percentage you entered on line 7.

Line 4

Enter the total number of hours the facility was used for daycare during the year.

Example. Your home is used Monday through Friday for 12 hours per day for 250 days during the year. It is also used on 50 Saturdays for 8 hours per day. Enter 3,400 hours on line 4 (3,000 hours for weekdays plus 400 hours for Saturdays).

Line 5

If you started or stopped using your home for daycare in 2004, you must prorate the number of hours based on the number of days the home was available for daycare. Cross out the preprinted entry on line 5. Multiply 24 hours by the number of days available and enter the result.

Part II

Line 8

If all the gross income from your trade or business is from the business use of your home, enter on line 8 the amount from Schedule C, line 29, plus any net gain or (loss) derived from the business use of your home and shown on Schedule D or Form 4797. If you file more than one Form 8829, include only the income earned and the deductions attributable to that income during the period you owned the home for which Part I was completed.

If some of the income is from a place of business other than your home, you must first determine the part of your gross income (Schedule C, line 7, and gains from Schedule D and Form 4797) from the business use of your home. In making this determination, consider the amount of time you spend at each location as well as other facts. After determining the part of your gross income from the business use of your home, subtract from that amount the total expenses shown on Schedule C, line 28, plus any losses from your business shown on Schedule D or Form 4797. Enter the result on Form 8829, line 8.

Columns (a) and (b)

Enter as direct or indirect expenses only expenses for the business use of your home (that is, expenses allowable only because your home is used for business). If you did not operate a business for the entire year, you can deduct only the expenses paid or incurred for the portion of the year you used your home for business. Other expenses not allocable to the business use of your home, such as salaries, supplies, and business telephone expenses, are deductible elsewhere on Schedule C and should not be entered on Form 8829.

Direct expenses benefit only the business part of your home. They include painting or repairs made to the specific area or rooms used for business. Enter 100% of your direct expenses on the appropriate line in column (a).

Indirect expenses are for keeping up and running your entire home. They benefit both the business and personal parts of your home. Generally, enter 100% of your indirect expenses on the appropriate line in column (b).

Exception. If the business percentage of an indirect expense is different from the percentage on line 7, enter only the business part of the expense on the appropriate line in column (a), and leave that line in column (b) blank. For example, your electric bill is $800 for lighting, cooking, laundry, and television. If you reasonably estimate $300 of your electric bill is for lighting and you use 10% of your home for business, enter $30 on line 19 in column (a). Do not make an entry on line 19 in column (b) for any part of your electric bill.

-2-

Lines 9, 10, and 11

Enter only the amounts that would be deductible whether or not you used your home for business (that is, amounts allowable as itemized deductions on Schedule A (Form 1040)).

Treat casualty losses as personal expenses for this step. Figure the amount to enter on line 9 by completing Form 4684, Section A. When figuring Form 4684, line 17, enter 10% of your adjusted gross income excluding the gross income from business use of your home and the deductions attributable to that income. Include on Form 8829, line 9, the amount from Form 4684, line 18. See *Line 27* below to deduct part of the casualty losses not allowed because of the limits on Form 4684.

Do not file or use that Form 4684 to figure the amount of casualty losses to deduct on Schedule A. Instead, complete a separate Form 4684 to deduct the personal portion of your casualty losses.

On line 10, include only mortgage interest that would be deductible on Schedule A and that qualifies as a direct or indirect expense. Do not include interest on a mortgage loan that did not benefit your home (for example, a home equity loan used to pay off credit card bills, to buy a car, or to pay tuition costs).

If you itemize your deductions, be sure to claim only the personal portion of your deductible mortgage interest and real estate taxes on Schedule A. For example, if your business percentage on line 7 is 30%, you can claim 70% of your deductible mortgage interest and real estate taxes on Schedule A.

Line 16

If the amount of home mortgage interest you deduct on Schedule A is limited, enter the part of the excess mortgage interest that qualifies as a direct or indirect expense. Do not include mortgage interest on a loan that did not benefit your home (explained earlier).

Line 20

Include on this line any 2004 operating expenses not included on lines 9 through 19.

If you rent rather than own your home, include the rent you paid on line 20, column (b). If your housing is provided free of charge and the value of the housing is tax exempt, you cannot deduct the rental value of any portion of the housing.

Line 27

Multiply your casualty losses in excess of the amount on line 9 by the business percentage of those losses and enter the result.

Line 34

Part III

Lines 35 Through 37

Enter on line 35 the cost or other basis of your home, or, if less, the fair market value of your home on the date you first used the home for business. Do not adjust this amount for depreciation claimed or changes in fair market value after the year you first used your home for business. Allocate this amount between land and building values on lines 36 and 37.

Attach your own schedule showing the cost or other basis of additions and improvements placed in service after you began to use your home for business. Do not include any amounts on lines 35 through 38 for these expenditures. Instead, see the instructions for line 40.

Line 39

IF you first used your home for business in the following month in 2004...	THEN enter the following percentage on line 39*...
January	2.461%
February	2.247%
March	2.033%
April	1.819%
May	1.605%
June	1.391%
July	1.177%
August	0.963%
September	0.749%
October	0.535%
November	0.321%
December	0.107%

IF you first used your home for business...	THEN the percentage to enter on line 39 is...
after May 12, 1993, and before 2004 (except as noted below),	2.564%*.
after May 12, 1993, and before 1994, and you either started construction or had a binding contract to buy or build that home before May 13, 1993,	the percentage given in Pub. 946.
after May 12, 1993, and you stopped using your home for business before the end of the year,	the percentage given in Pub. 946 as adjusted by the instructions under *Sale or Other Disposition Before the*

IF you first used your home for business...	THEN the percentage to enter on line 39 is...
before 1987,	the percentage given in Pub. 534, Depreciating Property Placed in Service Before 1987.

*Exception. If the business part of your home is qualified Indian reservation property (as defined in section 168(j)(4)), see Pub. 946, How To Depreciate Property, to figure the depreciation.

Line 40

If no additions and improvements were placed in service after you began using your home for business, multiply line 38 by the percentage on line 39. Enter the result on lines 40 and 28.

IF additions and improvements were placed in service...	THEN figure the depreciation allowed on these expenditures by multiplying the business part of their cost or other basis by...
during 2004 (but after you began using your home for business),	the percentage in the line 39 instructions for the month placed in service*.
after May 12, 1993, and before 2004 (except as noted below),	2.564%*.
after May 12, 1993, and before 1994, and you either started construction or had a binding contract to buy or build that home before May 13, 1993,	the percentage given in Pub. 946.
after May 12, 1993, and you stopped using your home for business before the end of the year,	the percentage given in Pub. 946 as adjusted by the instructions under *Sale or Other Disposition Before the Recovery Period Ends* in that publication.
after 1986 and before May 13, 1993,	the percentage given in Pub. 946.
before 1987,	the percentage given in Pub. 534.

*See the *Exception* on page 3.

Attach a schedule showing your computation and include the amount you figured in the total for line 40. Enter "See attached" below the entry space.

Complete and attach Form 4562, Depreciation and Amortization, only if:
- You first used your home for business in 2004, or
- You are depreciating additions and improvements placed in service in 2004.

If you first used your home for business in 2004, enter the amounts from Form 8829, lines 38 and 40, in columns (c) and (g) of line 19i, Form 4562. In column (b) of line 19i, enter the month and year you first used your home for business. Do not include the amount from Form 8829, line 40, on Schedule C, line 13.

If you are depreciating additions and improvements placed in service in 2004, enter in column (b) of line 19i on Form 4562 the month and year the additions or improvements were placed in service. Enter the business basis of the additions or improvements in column (c) and the depreciation allowable on the additions or improvements in column (g). Do not include the amount entered in column (g) on Schedule C, line 13.

Part IV

If your expenses are greater than the current year's limit, you can carry over the excess to 2005. The carryover will be subject to the deduction limit for that year, whether or not you live in the same home during that year.

Line 41

Figure the amount of operating expenses you can carry over to 2005 by subtracting line 25 from line 24. If the result is zero or less, you have no amount to carry over.

Line 42

Figure the amount of excess casualty losses and depreciation you can carry over to 2005 by subtracting line 31 from line 30. If the result is zero or less, you have no amount to carry over.

Paperwork Reduction Act Notice. We ask for the information on this form to carry out the Internal Revenue laws of the United States. You are required to give us the information. We need it to ensure that you are complying with these laws and to allow us to figure and collect the right amount of tax.

You are not required to provide the information requested on a form that is subject to the Paperwork Reduction Act unless the form displays a valid OMB control number. Books or records relating to a form or its instructions must be retained as long as their contents may become material in the administration of any Internal Revenue law. Generally, tax returns and return information are confidential, as required by section 6103.

The time needed to complete and file this form will vary depending on individual circumstances. The estimated average time is: **Recordkeeping,** 52 min.; **Learning about the law or the form,** 7 min.; **Preparing the form,** 1 hr., 15 min.; and **Copying, assembling, and sending the form to the IRS,** 20 min.

If you have comments concerning the accuracy of these time estimates or suggestions for making this form simpler, we would be happy to hear from you. See the Instructions for Form 1040.

Additional Legal Forms

This chapter includes an array of various legal forms that may be useful to a sole proprietor in the operation of his or her business. These forms may be prepared easily from the accompanying Forms-on-CD. They include various forms dealing with contracts, releases, receipts, leases, bills of sale, and real estate transactions. They are intended to be used in general commonly-occurring situations that a small business owner may confront. They are written in plain English and may be carefully altered by business owners to reflect the actual agreements that are intended to be made. As long as the parties to the agreement are clearly specified and identified and the terms of the agreement are noted in sufficient detail so that there will be no disagreements over what was intended, the careful tailoring of these forms is appropriate. If you are in doubt as to the legal effect, or ramifications of a particular form or its altered format, please consult a competent legal professional.

Contract

This Contract is made on _____ , 20 __ , between _____ ,
of_____ , City of _____ , State of _____ ,
and _____ , of _____ , City of_____ , State
of_____ .

For valuable consideration, the parties agree as follows:

1.

2.   No modification of this Contract will be effective unless it is in writing and is signed by
both parties. This Contract binds and benefits both parties and any successors. Time is of the
essence of this contract. This document, including any attachments, is the entire agreement
between the parties. This Contract is governed by the laws of the State of _____ .

The parties have signed this Contract on the date specified at the beginning of this Contract.

_____
Signature

_____
Printed Name

_____
Signature

_____
Printed Name

Extension of Contract

This Extension of Contract is made on _____ , 20 __ , between _____ , of _____ , City of _____ _____ , State of _____ , and _____ , of _____ , City of _____ , State of _____ .

For valuable consideration, the parties agree as follows:

1.   The following described contract will end on _____ , 20 __ :

This contract is attached to this Extension and is a part of this Extension.

2.   The parties agree to extend this contract for an additional period, which will begin immediately on the expiration of the original time period and will end on _____ , 20 __ .

3.   The Extension of this contract will be on the same terms and conditions as the original contract. This Extension binds and benefits both parties and any successors. This document, including the attached original contract, is the entire agreement between the parties.

The parties have signed this Extension on the date specified at the beginning of this Extension.

_____
Signature

_____
Printed Name

_____
Signature

_____
Printed Name

Modification of Contract

This Modification of Contract is made on _____ , 20 ___ , between
_____ , of _____ , City of _____ _____ ,
State of _____ , and _____ , of _____ ,
City of _____ , State of _____ .

For valuable consideration, the parties agree as follows:

1.   The following described contract is attached to this Modification and is made a part of this Modification:

2.   The parties agree to modify this contract as follows:

3.   All other terms and conditions of the original contract remain in effect without modification. This Modification binds and benefits both parties and any successors. This document, including the attached contract, is the entire agreement between the parties.

The parties have signed this modification on the date specified at the beginning of this Modification.

_____
Signature

_____
Printed Name

_____
Signature

_____
Printed Name

Termination of Contract

This Termination of Contract is made on _____ , 20 __ ,
between _____ , of _____ , City of _____ , State
of _____ , and _____ , of _____ , City of _____ ,
State of _____ .

For valuable consideration, the parties agree as follows:

1.   The parties are currently bound under the terms of the following described contract, which is attached and is part of this Termination:

2.   They agree to mutually terminate and cancel this contract effective on this date. This Termination Agreement will act as a mutual release of all obligations under this contract for both parties, as if the contract has not been entered into in the first place.

3.   This Termination binds and benefits both parties and any successors. This document, including the attached contract being terminated, is the entire agreement between the parties.

The parties have signed this Termination on the date specified at the beginning of this Termination.

_____
Signature

_____
Printed Name

_____
Signature

_____
Printed Name

Assignment of Contract

This Assignment is made on _____, 20 ___ , between _____ ,
Assignor , of _____ , City of _____ , State of
_____ , and _____ , Assignee, of _____ ,
City of _____ , State of _____ .

For valuable consideration, the parties agree to the following terms and conditions:

1.   The Assignor assigns all interest, burdens, and benefits in the following described contract to the Assignee:

This contract is attached to this Assignment and is a part of this Assignment.

2.   The Assignor warrants that this contract is in effect, has not been modified, and is fully
assignable. If the consent of a third party is necessary for this Assignment to be effective,
such consent is attached to this Assignment and is a part of this Assignment. Assignor agrees
to indemnify and hold the Assignee harmless from any claim which may result from the
Assignor's failure to perform under this contract prior to the date of this Assignment.

3.   The Assignee agrees to perform all of the obligations of the Assignor and receive all of
the benefits of the Assignor under this contract. Assignee agrees to indemnify and hold the
Assignor harmless from any claim which may result from the Assignee's failure to perform
under this contract after the date of this Assignment.

4.   This Assignment binds and benefits both parties and any successors. This document,
including any attachments, is the entire agreement between the parties.

_____
Signature of Assignor

_____
Printed Name of Assignor

_____
Signature of Assignee

_____
Printed Name of Assignee

Consent to Assignment of Contract

Date: _____

To: _____

1. I am a party to the following described contract:

This contract is the subject of the attached Assignment of Contract.

I consent to the Assignment of this Contract as described in the attached Assignment, which provides that the Assignee is substituted for the Assignor.

_____
Signature

_____
Printed Name

Notice of Assignment of Contract

Date: _____

To: _____

RE: Assignment of Contract

Dear _____ :

This notice is in reference to the following described contract:

Please be advised that as of _____ , 20 __ , all interest and rights under this contract which were formerly owned by _____ ,of _____ , City of _____ , State of _____ , have been permanently assigned to _____ , of _____ , City of _____ , State of _____ .

Please be advised that all of the obligations and rights of the former party to this contract are now the responsibility of the new party to this contract.

_____
Signature

_____
Printed Name

Notice of Breach of Contract

Date: _____

To: _____

RE: Breach of Contract

Dear _____ :

This notice is in reference to the following described contract:

Please be advised that as of _____ , 20 __ , we are holding you in BREACH OF CONTRACT for the following reasons:

If this breach of contract is not corrected within ____ days of this notice, we will take further action to protect our rights, which may include the right to obtain a substitute service and charge you for any additional costs. This notice is made under the Uniform Commercial Code and any other applicable laws. All of our rights are reserved under this notice.

_____
Signature

_____
Printed Name

General Release

For consideration, _____ , of _____ , City of _____ , State of _____ , releases _____ ,of _____ , City of _____ , State of _____ , from all claims and obligations, known or unknown, to this date arising from the following transaction or incident:

The party signing this release has not assigned any claims or obligations covered by this release to any other party.

The party signing this release intends that it both bind and benefit itself and any successors.

Dated: _____

_____
Signature

_____
Printed Name

Mutual Release

For consideration, _____ , of _____ ,
City of _____ , State of _____ ,
and _____ , of _____ , City of
_____ , State of _____ , release each other from all
claims and obligations, known or unknown, to this date that they may have against each
other arising from the following transaction or incident:

Neither party has assigned any claims or obligations covered by this release to any other
party.

Both parties signing this release intend that it both bind and benefit themselves and any
successors.

Dated: _____

_____
Signature

_____
Printed Name

_____
Signature

_____
Printed Name

Specific Release

For consideration, _____ , of _____ ,
City of _____ , State of _____ ,
releases _____ , of _____ ,
City of _____ , State of _____ , from the following
specific claims and obligations:

arising from the following transaction or incident:

Any claims or obligations that not specifically mentioned are not released by this Specific Release.

The party signing this release has not assigned any claims or obligations covered by this release to any other party.

The party signing this release intends that it both bind and benefit itself and any successors.

Dated: _____

_____
Signature

_____
Printed Name

Release of Mechanic's Lien

The following contractors or subcontractors have furnished materials, labor, or both for construction at the property owned by _____ , and located at _____ , City of _____ , State of _____ .

Contractor/Subcontractor	Address	City	State/Zip
_____	_____	_____	_____
_____	_____	_____	_____
_____	_____	_____	_____
_____	_____	_____	_____

These contractors or subcontractors hereby release all liens and the right to file any liens against this property for material or labor provided as of this date. This release does not, however, constitute a release of any sums which may be due to these contractors or subcontractors for materials or labor.

The parties signing this release intend that it both bind and benefit themselves and any successors.

Dated: _____

_____
Signature

_____
Printed Name

_____
Signature

_____
Printed Name

_____
Signature

_____
Printed Name

_____
Signature

_____
Printed Name

State of _____

County of _____

On _____ , 20 __ , _____ personally came before me and, being duly sworn, did state that he/she is the person described in the above document and that he/she signed the above document in my presence.

_____
Notary signature
Notary Public, in and for the County of _____ ,
State of _____
My commission expires: _____   Seal

State of _____

County of _____

On _____ , 20 __ , _____ personally came before me and, being duly sworn, did state that he/she is the person described in the above document and that he/she signed the above document in my presence.

_____
Notary signature
Notary Public, in and for the County of _____ ,
State of _____
My commission expires: _____   Seal

State of _____

County of _____

On _____ , 20 __ , _____ personally came before me and, being duly sworn, did state that he/she is the person described in the above document and that he/she signed the above document in my presence.

_____
Notary signature
Notary Public, in and for the County of _____ ,
State of _____
My commission expires: _____   Seal

State of _____

County of _____

On _____ , 20 __ , _____ personally came before me and, being duly sworn, did state that he/she is the person described in the above document and that he/she signed the above document in my presence.

_____
Notary signature
Notary Public, in and for the County of _____ ,
State of _____
My commission expires: _____   Seal

Receipt in Full

The undersigned acknowledges receipt of the sum of $ _____ paid by
_____ . This payment constitutes full payment and satisfaction
of the following obligation:

Dated: _____

_____
Signature of person receiving payment

_____
Printed Name

Receipt on Account

The undersigned acknowledges receipt of the sum of $ _____ paid by
_____ . This payment will be applied and credited to the following account:

Dated: _____

_____
Signature of person receiving payment

_____
Printed Name

Receipt for Goods

The undersigned acknowledges receipt of the goods which are described on the
attached purchase order. The undersigned also acknowledges that these goods
have been inspected and found to be in conformance with the purchase order
specifications.

Dated: _____

_____
Signature of person receiving goods

_____
Printed Name

Commercial Lease

This Lease is made on _____ , 20 ___ , between _____ ,
Landlord, of _____ , City of _____ , State of
_____ , and _____ , Tenant, of _____ ,
City of _____ , State of _____ .

1. The Landlord agrees to rent to the Tenant and the Tenant agrees to rent from the Landlord the following commercial property:

This property contains _____ square feet of interior floor space.

2. The term of this lease will be from _____ , 20 ___ , until _____ _____ , 20 ___ . If the Tenant continues to occupy the property, with the consent of the Landlord, after the expiration of the original term of this lease, the rental will continue on a month-to-month basis with all of the other terms of this lease continuing unchanged.

3. The rental payments will be $ _____ per _____ and will be payable by the Tenant to the Landlord on the _____ day of each month, beginning on _____ , 20 ___ . If any rental payment is not paid within five (5) days of its due date, the Tenant agrees to pay an additional late charge of five (5) percent (%) of the rental due.

4. The Tenant agrees to use the property only for the purpose of carrying on the following business:

5. The Tenant has paid the Landlord a security deposit of $ _____ . This security deposit will be held as security for the repair of any damages to the property by the Tenant. This deposit will be returned to the Tenant within 10 days of the termination of this lease, minus any amounts needed to repair the property.

6. The Tenant has paid the Landlord an additional month's rent in the amount of $ _____ . This rent payment deposit will be held as security for the payment of rent by the Tenant. This rent payment deposit will be returned to the Tenant within 10 days of the termination of this lease, minus any rent still due upon termination.

7. Tenant agrees to maintain the property in a clean and sanitary manner and not to make any alterations to the property without the Landlord's written consent. At the termination of this lease, the Tenant agrees to leave the residence in the same condition as when it was received, except for normal wear and tear.

8. The Landlord agrees to supply the following utilities to the Tenant:

9. The Tenant agrees to obtain and pay for the following utilities:

10. Tenant agrees not to sub-let the property or assign this lease without the Landlord's written consent. Tenant agrees to allow the Landlord reasonable access to the property for inspection and repair. Landlord agrees to only enter the property after notifying the Tenant in advance, except in an emergency.

11. The Tenant has inspected the property and has found it satisfactory.

12. If the Tenant fails to pay the rent on time or violates any other terms of this lease, the Landlord will have the right to terminate this lease in accordance with state law. The Landlord will also have the right to re-enter the residence and take possession of it and to take advantage of any other legal remedies available.

13. The Landlord is responsible for the repair and upkeep of the exterior of the property and the Tenant is responsible for the repair and upkeep of the interior of the property. The Landlord agrees that the Tenant may install the following equipment and fixtures for the purpose of operating the Tenant's business:

14. The Landlord agrees to carry fire and casualty insurance on the property, but does not have any liability for the operation of the Tenant's business. The Tenant agrees not to do anything that will increase the Landlord's insurance premiums and, further, agrees to indemnify and hold the Landlord harmless from any liability caused by Tenant's operations. The Tenant agrees to carry casualty insurance on any equipment or fixtures that Tenant installs at the property. In addition, the Tenant agrees to carry business liability insurance covering Tenant's business operations in the amount of $ _____ with the Landlord named as a co-insured party. Tenant agrees to furnish Landlord copies of the insurance policies and to not cancel the policies without notifying the Landlord in advance.

15. This lease is subject to any mortgage or deed of trust currently on the property or which may be made against the property at any time in the future. The Tenant agrees to sign any

documents necessary to subordinate this lease to a mortgage or deed of trust for the Landlord.

16. The following are additional terms of this Lease:

17. The parties agree that this lease is the entire agreement between them. This Lease binds and benefits both the Landlord and Tenant and any successors.

_____
Signature of Landlord

_____
Printed Name of Landlord

_____
Signature of Tenant

_____
Printed Name of Tenant

Assignment of Lease

This Assignment is made on _____ , 20 ___ , between _____ , Assignor, of _____ , City of _____ , State of _____ , and _____ , Assignee, of _____ , City of _____ , State of _____ .

For valuable consideration, the parties agree to the following terms and conditions:

1.   The Assignor assigns all interest, burdens, and benefits in the following described lease to the Assignee:

     This lease is attached to this Assignment and is a part of this Assignment.

2.   The Assignor warrants that this lease is in effect, has not been modified, and is fully assignable. If the consent of the Landlord is necessary for this Assignment to be effective, such consent is attached to this Assignment and is a part of this Assignment. Assignor agrees to indemnify and hold the Assignee harmless from any claim which may result from the Assignor's failure to perform under this lease prior to the date of this Assignment.

3.   The Assignee agrees to perform all of the obligations of the Assignor and receive all of the benefits of the Assignor under this lease. Assignee agrees to indemnify and hold the Assignor harmless from any claim which may result from the Assignee's failure to perform under this lease after the date of this Assignment.

4.   This Assignment binds and benefits both parties and any successors. This document, including any attachments, is the entire agreement between the parties.

_____
Signature of Assignor

_____
Printed Name of Assignor

_____
Signature of Assignee

_____
Printed Name of Assignee

Consent to Assignment of Lease

Date: _____

To: _____

1. I am the Landlord under the following described Lease:

This Lease is the subject of the attached Assignment of Lease.

I consent to the Assignment of this Lease as described in the attached Assignment, which provides that the Assignee is fully substituted for the Assignor.

_____
Signature of Landlord

_____
Printed Name of Landlord

Notice of Assignment of Lease

Date: _____

To: _____

RE: Assignment of Lease

Dear _____ :

This notice is in reference to the following described lease:

Please be advised that as of _____ , 20 __ , all interest and rights under this lease which were formerly owned by _____ _____ , of _____ , City of _____ , State of _____ , have been permanently assigned to _____ , of _____ , City of _____ , State of _____ .

Please be advised that all of the obligations and rights of the former party to this lease are now the responsibility of the new party to this lease.

_____
Signature

_____
Printed Name

Amendment of Lease

This Amendment of Lease is made on _____ , 20 __ , between
_____ , of _____ , City of _____ ,
State of _____ , and _____ , of _____ ,
City of _____ , State of _____ .

For valuable consideration, the parties agree as follows:

1. The following described lease is attached to this Amendment and is made a part of this Amendment:

2. The parties agree to amend this lease as follows:

3. All other terms and conditions of the original lease remain in effect without modification. This Amendment binds and benefits both parties and any successors. This document, including the attached lease, is the entire agreement between the parties.

The parties have signed this amendment on the date specified at the beginning of this Amendment.

_____
Signature of Landlord

_____
Printed Name of Landlord

_____
Signature of Tenant

_____
Printed Name of Tenant

Extension of Lease

This Extension of Lease is made on _____ , 20 __ , between _____ , of _____ , City of _____ , State of _____ , and _____ , of _____ , City of _____ , State of _____ .

For valuable consideration, the parties agree as follows:

1. The following described lease will end on _____ , 20 __ :

This lease is attached to this Extension and is a part of this Extension.

2. The parties agree to extend this lease for an additional period, which will begin immediately on the expiration of the original time period and will end on _____ , 20 __ .

3. The Extension of this lease will be on the same terms and conditions as the original lease. This Extension binds and benefits both parties and any successors. This document, including the attached lease, is the entire agreement between the parties.

The parties have signed this Extension on the date specified at the beginning of this Extension.

_____
Signature of Landlord

_____
Printed Name of Landlord

_____
Signature of Tenant

_____
Printed Name of Tenant

Sublease

This Sublease is made on _____ , 20 ___ , between _____
, Tenant, of _____ , City of _____ , State of
_____ , and _____ , Sub-tenant, of _____ ,
City of _____ , State of _____ .

For valuable consideration, the parties agree to the following terms and conditions:

1. The Tenant subleases to the Sub-tenant the following described property:

2. This property is currently leased to the Tenant under the terms of the following described
lease:

    This lease is attached to this Sublease and is a part of this Sublease.

3. This Sublease will be for the period from _____ , 20 ___ , to _____ ,
20 ___ .

4. The subrental payments will be $ _____ per _____ and will be payable by the
Subtenant to the Landlord on the _____ day of each month, beginning on _____
_____ , 20 ___ .

5. The Tenant warrants that the underlying lease is in effect, has not been modified, and that the property may be sublet. If the consent of the Landlord is necessary for his Sublease to be effective, such consent is attached to this Sublease and is a part of this Sublease. Tenant agrees to indemnify and hold the Sub-tenant harmless from any claim which may result from the Tenant's failure to perform under this lease prior to the date of this Sublease.

6. The Sub-tenant agrees to perform all of the obligations of the Tenant under the original lease and receive all of the benefits of the Tenant under this lease. Sub-tenant agrees to indemnify and hold the Tenant harmless from any claim which may result from the Sub-tenant's failure to perform under this lease after the date of this Sublease.

7. The Tenant agrees to remain primarily liable to the Landlord for the obligations under the Lease.

8. The parties agree to the following additional terms:

9. This Sublease binds and benefits both parties and any successors. This document, including any attachments, is the entire agreement between the parties.

_____
Signature of Tenant

_____
Printed Name of Tenant

_____
Signature of Sub-tenant

_____
Printed Name of Sub-tenant

Consent to Sublease

Date: _____

To: _____

1. I am the Landlord under the following described Lease:

This Lease is the subject of the attached Sublease.

I consent to the Sublease of this Lease as described in the attached Sublease, which provides that the Sub-tenant is substituted for the Tenant for the period indicated in the Sublease. This consent does not release the Tenant from any obligations under the lease and the Tenant remains fully bound under the Lease.

_____
Signature of Landlord

_____
Printed Name of Landlord

Notice of Breach of Lease

Date: _____

To: _____

RE: Breach of Lease

Dear _____ :

This notice is in reference to the following described lease:

Please be advised that as of _____ , 20 ___ , we are holding you in BREACH OF LEASE for the following reasons:

If this breach of lease is not corrected within _____ days of this notice, we will take further action to protect our rights, which may include termination of this lease. This notice is made under all applicable laws. All of our rights are reserved under this notice.

_____
Signature of Landlord

_____
Printed Name of Landlord

Landlord's Notice to Terminate Lease

Date: _____

To: _____

RE: Notice to Terminate Lease

Dear _____ :

This notice is in reference to the following described lease:

Please be advised that as of _____ , 20 __ , you have been in BREACH OF LEASE for the following reasons:

You were previously notified of this breach in the NOTICE dated _____ _____ , 20 __ . At that time you were given _____ days to correct the breach of the lease and you have not complied.

THEREFORE, YOU ARE HEREBY GIVEN NOTICE:

The lease is immediately terminated and you are directed to deliver possession of the property to the Landlord on or before _____ , 20 __ . If you fail to deliver the property by this date, legal action to evict you from the property will be taken. Regardless of your deliverance of the property, you are still responsible for all rent due under the lease.

_____
Signature of Landlord

_____
Printed Name of Landlord

Personal Property Rental Agreement (Simple)

This Agreement is made on _____ , 20 __ , between _____ , Owner, of _____ , City of _____ , State of _____ , and _____ , Renter, of _____ , City of _____ , State of _____ .

1. The Owner agrees to rent to the Renter and the Renter agrees to rent from the Owner the following property:

2. The term of this Agreement will be from __ o'clock __ m., _____ , 20 __ , until __ o'clock __ m., _____ , 20 __ .

3. The rental payments will be $ _____ per _____ and will be payable by the Renter to the Owner as follows:

4. This Agreement may be terminated by either party by giving 24 hours notice to the other party.

5. The parties agree that this Agreement is the entire agreement between them. This Agreement binds and benefits both the Owner and Renter and any successors.

_____
Signature of Owner

_____
Printed Name of Owner

_____
Signature of Renter

_____
Printed Name of Renter

Personal Property Rental Agreement
(Complex)

This Agreement is made on _____ , 20 __ , between _____ ,
Owner, of _____ , City of _____ , State of _____ ,
and _____ , Renter, of _____ , City of _____ ,
State of _____ .

1. The Owner agrees to rent to the Renter and the Renter agrees to rent from the Owner the following property:

2. The term of this Agreement will be from __ o'clock __ m., _____ , 20 __ , until __ o'clock __ m., _____ , 20 __ .

3. The rental payments will be $ _____ per _____ and will be payable by the Renter to the Owner as follows:

4. The Renter agrees to pay a late fee of $ _____ per day that the rental payment is late. If the rental payments are in default for over _____ days, the Owner may immediately demand possession of the property without advance notice to the Renter.

5. The Owner warrants that the property is free of any known faults which would affect its safe operation under normal usage and is in good working condition.

6. The Renter states that the property has been inspected and is in good working condition. The Renter agrees to use the property in a safe manner and in normal usage and to maintain the property in good repair. The Renter further agrees not to use the property in a negligent manner or for any illegal purpose.

7. The Renter agrees to fully indemnify the Owner for any damage to or loss of the property during the term of this Agreement, unless such loss or damage is caused by a defect of the rented property.

8. The Owner shall not be liable for any injury, loss, or damage caused by any use of the property.

9.   The Renter has paid the Owner a security deposit of $ _____ . This security deposit will be held as security for payments of the rent and for the repair of any damages to the property by the Renter. This deposit will be returned to the Renter upon the termination of this Agreement, minus any rent still owed to the Owner and minus any amounts needed to repair the property, beyond normal wear and tear.

10. The Renter may not assign or transfer any rights under this Agreement to any other person, nor allow the property to be used by any other person, without the written consent of the Owner.

11. Renter agrees to obtain insurance coverage for the property during the term of this rental agreement in the amount of $ _____ . Renter agrees to provide the Owner with a copy of the insurance policy and to not cancel the policy during the term of this rental agreement.

12. This Agreement may be terminated by either party by giving 24 hours written notice to the other party.

13. Any dispute related to this agreement will be settled by voluntary mediation. If mediation is unsuccessful, the dispute will be settled by binding arbitration using an arbitrator of the American Arbitration Association.

14. The following are additional terms of this Agreement:

15. The parties agree that this Agreement is the entire agreement between them. This Agreement binds and benefits both the Owner and Renter and any successors. Time is of the essence of this Agreement.

16. This Agreement is governed by the laws of the State of _____ .

_____

Signature of Owner

_____

Printed Name of Owner

_____

Signature of Renter

_____

Printed Name of Renter

Contract for Sale of Personal Property

This Contract is made on _____ , 20 __ , between _____ , Seller, of _____ , City of _____ , State of _____ , and _____ , Buyer, of _____ , City of _____ , State of _____ .

1. The Seller agrees to sell to the Buyer, and the Buyer agrees to buy the following personal property:

2. The Buyer agrees to pay the Seller $ _____ for the property. The Buyer agrees to pay this purchase price in the following manner:

3. The Buyer will be entitled to possession of this property on _____ , 20 __ .

4. The Seller represents that it has legal title to the property and full authority to sell the property. Seller also represents that the property is sold free and clear of all liens, indebtedness, or liabilities. Seller agrees to provide Buyer with a Bill of Sale for the property.

5. This Contract binds and benefits both the Buyer and Seller and any successors. This document, including any attachments, is the entire agreement between the Buyer and Seller. This Agreement is governed by the laws of the State of _____ .

_____
Signature of Seller

_____
Printed Name of Seller

_____
Signature of Buyer

_____
Printed Name of Buyer

Bill of Sale, with Warranties

This Bill of Sale is made on _____ , 20 ___ , between
_____ , Seller, of _____ , City of
_____ , State of _____ , and _____ ,
Buyer, of _____ , City of _____ , State
of _____ .

In exchange for the payment of $ _____ , received from the Buyer, the Seller sells and transfers possession of the following property to the Buyer:

The Seller warrants that it owns this property and that it has the authority to sell the property to the Buyer. Seller also warrants that the property is sold free and clear of all liens, indebtedness, or liabilities.

The Seller also warrants that the property is in good working condition as of this date.

Signed and delivered to the Buyer on the above date.

_____
Signature of Seller

_____
Printed Name of Seller

Bill of Sale, without Warranties

This Bill of Sale is made on _____ , 20 __ , between
_____ , Seller, of _____ , City
of _____ , State of _____ , and _____ ,
Buyer, of _____ , City of _____ , State of
_____ .

In exchange for the payment of $ _____ , received from the Buyer, the Seller sells and transfers possession of the following property to the Buyer:

The Seller disclaims any implied warranty of merchantability or fitness and the property is sold in its present condition, "as is."

Signed and delivered to the Buyer on the above date.

_____
Signature of Seller

_____
Printed Name of Seller

Bill of Sale, Subject to Debt

This Bill of Sale is made on _____ , 20 __ ,
between _____ , Seller, of _____ , City of
_____ , State of _____ , and _____ , Buyer,
of _____ , City of _____ , State of _____ .

In exchange for the payment of $ _____ , received from the Buyer, the Seller sells and transfers possession of the following property to the Buyer:

The Seller warrants that it owns this property and that it has the authority to sell the property to the Buyer. Seller also states that the property is sold subject to the following debt:

The Buyer buys the property subject to the above debt and agrees to pay the debt. Buyer also agrees to indemnify and hold the Seller harmless from any claim based on failure to pay off this debt.

The Seller also warrants that the property is in good working condition as of this date.

Signed and delivered to the Buyer on the above date.

_____
Signature of Seller

_____
Printed Name of Seller

_____
Signature of Buyer

_____
Printed Name of Buyer

Contract for Sale of Real Estate

This Contract is made on _____ , 20 ___ , between _____ , Seller, of _____ , City of _____ , State of _____ , and _____ , Buyer, of _____ , City of _____ , State of _____ .

The Seller now owns the following described real estate which is located at _____ , City of _____ , State of _____ :

For valuable consideration, the Seller agrees to sell and the Buyer agrees to buy this property for the following price and on the following terms:

1.   The Seller will sell this property to the Buyer, free from all claims, liabilities, and indebtedness. The following personal property is included in this sale:

2.   The Buyer agrees to pay the Seller the sum of $ _____ , which the Seller agrees to accept as full payment. This Agreement, however, is conditional upon the Buyer being able to arrange suitable financing on the following terms 30 days prior to the closing date for this agreement:

3.   The purchase price will be paid as follows:

4.   The Seller acknowledges receiving the Earnest money deposit of $ _____ from the Buyer. If this sale is not completed for any valid reason, this money will be returned to the Buyer without penalty or interest.

5.   This agreement will close on _____ , 20 ___ , at _____ o'clock ____ m., at _____ , City of _____ , State of _____ .

At that time, and upon payment by the Buyer of the portion of the purchase price then due, the Seller will deliver to Buyer the following documents:
 (a) A Bill of Sale for all personal property
 (b) A Warranty Deed for the real estate.

6.   At closing, pro-rated adjustments to the purchase price will be made for the following items:

(a) Utilities,
(b) Property taxes, and
(c) The following other items: (list other items)

7   The following closing costs will be paid by the Seller:

8. The following closing costs will be paid by the Buyer:

9. Seller represents that it has good and marketable title to the property, and will supply the Buyer with either an abstract of title or a standard policy of title insurance. Seller further represents that the property is free and clear of any restrictions on transfer, claims, indebtedness, or liabilities except the following:

Seller also warrants that all personal property included in this sale will be delivered in working order on the date of closing.

10. The parties also agree to the following additional terms:

11. No modification of this Contract will be effective unless it is in writing and is signed by both the Buyer and Seller. This Contract binds and benefits both the Buyer and Seller and any successors. Time is of the essence of this contract. This document, including any attachments, is the entire contract between the Buyer and Seller. This Contract is governed by the laws of the State of _____ .

_____
Signature of Seller

_____
Printed Name of Seller

_____
Signature of Buyer

_____
Printed Name of Buyer

Option to Buy Real Estate Agreement

This Agreement is made on _____ , 20 _____ , between _____ , Seller, of _____ , City of _____ , State of _____ ____ , and _____ , Buyer, of _____ , City of _____ , State of _____ .

The Seller now owns the following described real estate, which is located at _____ , City of _____ , State of _____ :

For valuable consideration, the Seller agrees to give the Buyer an exclusive option to buy this property for the following price and on the following terms:

1.   The Buyer will pay the Seller $ _____ for this option. This amount will be credited against the purchase price of the property if this option is exercised by the Buyer. If the option is not exercised, the Seller will retain this payment.

2.   The option period will begin on the date of this Agreement and run until _____ , 20 _____ , at which time it will expire unless exercised.

3.   During this period, the Buyer has the option and exclusive right to buy the Seller's property mentioned above for the purchase price of $ _____ . The Buyer must notify the Seller, in writing, of the decision to exercise this option.

4.   Attached to this Option Agreement is a completed Contract for the Sale of Real Estate. If the Buyer notifies the Seller, in writing, of the decision to exercise the option within the option period, the Seller and Buyer agree to sign the Contract for the Sale of Real Estate and complete the sale on the terms contained in the Contract.

5.   No modification of this Agreement will be effective unless it is in writing and is signed by both the Buyer and Seller. This Agreement binds and benefits both the Buyer and Seller and any successors. Time is of the essence of this agreement. This document, including any attachments, is the entire agreement between the Buyer and Seller. This Agreement is governed by the laws of the State of _____ .

_____

Signature of Seller

_____

Printed Name of Seller

_____

Signature of Buyer

_____

Printed Name of Buyer

Quitclaim Deed

This Quitclaim Deed is made on _____ , 20 _____ , between _____ , Grantor, of _____ , City of _____ , State of _____ , and _____ , Grantee, of _____ , City of _____ , State of _____ .

For valuable consideration, the Grantor hereby quitclaims and transfers the following described real estate to the Grantee to have and hold forever, located at _____ _____ , City of _____ , State of _____ :

Dated _____ , 20 ____ .

_____
Signature of Grantor

_____
Printed Name of Grantor

State of _____
County of _____

On _____ , 20 ____ , _____ personally came before me and, being duly sworn, did state that he/she is the person described in the above document and that he/she signed the above document in my presence.

_____
Notary signature
Notary Public
In and for the County of _____
State of _____
My commission expires: _____   Seal

Warranty Deed

This Warranty Deed is made on _____ , 20 ___ , between _____ , Grantor, of _____ , City of _____ , State of _____ , and _____ , Grantee, of _____ , City of _____ , State of _____ .

For valuable consideration, the Grantor hereby sells, grants, and conveys the following described real estate, in fee simple, to the Grantee to have and hold forever, along with all easements, rights, and buildings belonging to the above property, located at _____ _____ , City of _____ , State of _____ :

The Grantor warrants that it is lawful owner and has full right to convey the property, and that the property is free from all claims, liabilities, or indebtedness, and that the Grantor and its successors will warrant and defend title to the Grantee against the lawful claims of all persons.

Dated _____ , 20 ___ .

_____
Signature of Grantor

_____
Printed Name of Grantor

State of _____
County of _____

On _____ , 20 ___ , _____ personally came before me and, being duly sworn, did state that he/she is the person described in the above document and that he/she signed the above document in my presence.

_____
Notary signature
Notary Public
In and for the County of _____
State of _____
My commission expires: _____   Seal

Appendix:
State Business Name Registration

On the following pages are found state listings containing relevant information regarding the registration of business names. You are advised to check your state's listing carefully to determine the particular requirements in your jurisdiction. You are also advised to write to the appropriate state office for information on name registration. They will provide you with any necessary updates on the information in this Appendix, any useful forms, and details of the fees required for name registration. Following is an explanation of the components of each listing:

State website: This listing provide the location of the official state website on the internet. The addresses were current at the time of this books publication; however, like most websites, the page addresses are subject to change. If an expired state's webpage is not automatically redirected to a new site, state laws can be searched at www.findlaw.com.

Registration of business name requirements: Here is noted whether the state's name registration requirements are mandatory or voluntary. In addition, it is noted whether registration of business names is as trade names or as fictitious names.

Online form: This listing shows the location of official state online forms if they are available. Generally, this is the state Secretary of State's office website in a state.

Registration fee: This is the amount it costs to file your name registration.

Term of registration: This listing specifies the length of time that the registration of the business name will be valid.

Name requirements: Under this listing are any state requirements regarding the choice of a business name.

Registration application requirements: The application generally must include the name of the owner(s), business address of the owner(s), a description of the type of business intended, and the fictitious or trade name to be used.

Publication requirements: A few states require that a notice of the intention to conduct business under an assumed or fictitious name be published in a newspaper.

Office for registration: Here is listed the name and address or reference to the particular state or county office that handles business name registration.

Alabama

State website: www.alabama.gov

State law reference for name registration: Code of Alabama, Title 8, Sections 8-12-7+.

Registration of business name requirements: Registration is optional. Alabama does not have a fictitious name statute, but has a trade name statute. A trade name is essentially a business name other than the owner's name. The applicant must register with the Secretary of State. (Section 8-12-7).

Online form: www.sos.state.al.us/business/land.htm

Registration fee: $30.00

Term of registration: None stated in statute.

Name requirements: The statute is exhaustive, stating that the trade name can not be immoral, deceptive, or scandalous. Please refer directly to the statute. (Section 8-12-7).

Registration application requirements: The application must include the name of the owner(s), business address of the owner(s), a description of the type of business the person is or intends to conduct, the date when the name was first used, a statement that the owner(s) is the only person with the right to use that name, three copies or specimens of the mark. The application must be signed and verified. (Section 8-12-8).

Publication requirements: None stated.

Office for registration:
Alabama Secretary of State
PO Box 5616
Montgomery AL 36103-5616

Alaska

State website: www.state.ak.us

State law reference for name registration: Alaska Statutes, Sections 10.35.010+.

Registration of business name requirements: Registration is voluntary. Any person may register a business name by filing an application with the Commissioner of Corporations. Registration gives the person the exclusive right to use the name. (Sections 10.35.040-10.35.070).

Online form: www.commerce.state.ak.us/bsc/pub/08-575.pdf

Registration fee: $25.00

Term of registration: Five years. (Section 10.35.070).

Name requirements: The intended name must not be the same as or deceptively similar to a corporation or other reserved or registered name and must not give the impression that the business is incorporated. (Section 10.35.040).

Registration application requirements: The application must be signed by the business owner(s) and contain the owner's name and address, the name and addresses of the business, the name and address of each person having an interest in the business, a statement that the owner(s) is doing business, and a brief statement of the nature of the business. (Section 10.35.050).

Publication requirements: None stated.

Office for registration:
Alaska Department of Commerce and Economic Development
PO Box 110800
Juneau, AK 99811-0800

Arizona

State website: www.azleg.state.az.us

State law reference for name registration: Arizona Revised Statutes, Sections 44-1460+.

Registration of business name requirements: Registration is voluntary. Any person, partnership, corporation, firm, association, society, foundation, federation, or organization doing business in Arizona may register the name of the business. (Section 44-1460).

Online form: www.azsos.gov/business_services/Forms/Tradename/apptn.pdf

Registration fee: $10.00

Term of registration: Five years. (Section 44-1460.02).

Name requirements: The name to be registered must be distinguishable from other business names and not misleading to the public. (Section 44-1460.1(b)).

Registration application requirements: The application must state the name and address of the applicant, the name to be registered, the nature of the business, and the length of time the name has been used. The applicant must sign the application. The Secretary of State will issue a Certificate of Registration upon compliance with the requirements. (Sections 44-1460-1460.1).

Publication requirements: None stated.

Office for registration:
Arizona Secretary of State
1700 West Washington, 7th floor
Phoenix AZ 85007

Arkansas

State website: www.arkleg.state.ar.us

State law reference for name registration: Arkansas Code of 1987 Annotated, Sections 4-70-203+.

Registration of business name requirements: Registration is mandatory. The applicant must register in the office of the County Clerk in the county in which the person conducts or intends to conduct business. (Section 4-70-203).

Online form: not available online

Registration fee: not available

Term of registration: Perpetual until withdrawn. (Section 4-70-204).

Name requirements: None stated in statute.

Registration application requirements: The certificate shall set forth the name under which the applicant intends to conduct business, and the full name and post office address of each person conducting the business. (Section 4-70-203).

Publication requirements: None stated.

Office for registration: The applicant must register with the County Clerk in the counties in which the applicant will conduct business.

California

State website: www.state.ca.us

State law reference for name registration: California Codes Annotated, Business and Professional Code, Sections 17900+.

Registration of business name requirements: Registration is mandatory. The applicant must register with the County Clerk in the county where the person conducts or intends to conduct business. (Sections 17910, 17915).

Online form: Form located in Business and Professional Code, Sections 17913.

Registration fee: not available

Term of registration: Five years. (Section 17913).

Name requirements: None stated in statute.

Registration application requirements: The applicant must file a statement within forty days after the person begins to conduct business. The statement shall contain the fictitious business name, the street address of the place of business, the name and address of the individual filing the statement, and the nature of the business (for example: sole proprietorship or partnership). (Section 17913).

Publication requirements: Within thirty days of filing the statement, the applicant must publish the name in the newspaper of general circulation in the county in which the applicant's principal place of business is located. (Section 17917).

Office for registration: The applicant must register with the County Clerk of the county in which the registrant has his principal place of business. (Section 17915).

Colorado

State website: www.leg.state.co.us

State law reference for name registration: Colorado Revised Statutes Annotated, Sections 7-71-101+.

Registration of business name requirements: Colorado does not have a statute for registration of assumed names for sole proprietors, However, tradenames for other business organization forms are registerable. The applicant must register with the Secretary of State and record a statement of trade name with the clerk in any county in which real estate is held. (Section 7-71-101).

Online form: www.revenue.state.co.us/PDF/dr0592.pdf

Registration fee: $8.00

Term of registration: None stated in statute.

Name requirements: The name cannot be the same as or deceptively similar to any other registered name, or the name of a dissolved corporation within 120 days of dissolution. (Section 7-71-101).

Registration application requirements: The certificate must state the name of the entity, the location of the principal office, any other name the business is transacted under, and the type of business transacted. (Section 7-7-101).

Publication requirements: None stated.

Office for registration:
Colorado Secretary of State
1700 Broadway Ste 200
Denver, CO 80290

Connecticut

State website: www.cga.ct.gov

State law reference for name registration: Connecticut General Statutes Annotated, Sections 35-1+.

Registration of business name requirements: Registration is mandatory. The applicant must register with the Town Clerk where the business is or where the person intends to conduct business. (Section 35-1).

Online form: not available online

Registration fee: not available

Term of registration: None stated in statute.

Name requirements: None stated in statute.

Registration application requirements: The certificate must include the name of the business, and the full name, and the post-office address of the individuals transacting the business. (Section 35-1).

Publication requirements: None stated.

Office for registration: The applicant must register with the Town Clerk in the town where the applicant intends to conduct business. (Section 35-1).

Delaware

State website: www.delaware.gov

State law reference for name registration: Delaware Code Annotated, Title 6, Chapter 31, Sections 3101+.

Registration of business name requirements: Registration is mandatory. The applicant must register with the office of the Prothonotary in the county where the person is transacting business. (Section 3101).

Online form: not available online

Registration fee: not available

Term of registration: None stated in statute.

Name requirements: None stated in statute.

Registration application requirements: The certificate shall contain the trade name, the Christian name and the surname of the persons transacting business, the date when the business was organized. The person signing shall attach an affidavit affirming that everything included is true. (Section 3101).

Publication requirements: None stated.

Office for registration: The applicant must register with the office of the Prothonotary in the county where the applicant is transacting business. (Section 3101).

District of Columbia (Washington D.C.)

State website: dccouncil.washington.dc.us

State law reference for name registration: District of Columbia Code 1981, Title 47, Sections 47-2855.2+.

Registration of business name requirements: Registration is mandatory. The applicant must register with the Department of Consumer and Regulatory affairs. (Section 47-2855.2).

Online form: mblr.dc.gov/services/trade_name/appl.shtm

Registration fee: $50.00

Term of registration: None stated in statute.

Name requirements: None stated in statute.

Registration application requirements: The certificate shall contain the name of the business, the name of the owner(s), and the address of the person conducting business. (Section 47-2855.2).

Publication requirements: None stated.

Office for registration:
Department of Consumer and
Regulatory Affairs -
Trade Name Registration
941 N. Capitol St. NE, Rm 7200
Washington DC, 20002

Florida

State website: www.leg.state.fl.us

State law reference for name registration: Florida Statutes, Chapter 865. Sections 865.09+.

Registration of business name requirements: Registration is mandatory. The applicant must register with the Department of State. (Section 865.09).

Online form: www.dos.state.fl.us/doc/pdf/CR4E001.pdf

Registration fee: $50.00

Term of registration: Five years. (Section 865.09).

Name requirements: The name may not contain the words *incorporated* or *corporation* in the name. (Section 865.09).

Registration application requirements: Before conducting the business, the person must file a sworn statement. The sworn statement must contain the name to be registered, the mailing address of the business, the name and address of the owner(s), and certification that the fictitious name has been published in a newspaper in the county where the principal place of business is located. (Section 865.09).

Publication requirements: The applicant must certify that the fictitious name has been published in a newspaper in the county in which the applicant's principal place of business is located. (Section 865.09).

Office for registration:
Fictitious Name Registration
P O Box 1300
Tallahassee, FL 32302-1300

Georgia

State website: www.legis.state.ga.us

State law reference for name registration: Official Code of Georgia Annotated, Title 10, Chapter 1, Sections 10-1-490+.

Registration of business name requirements: Registration is mandatory. The applicant must register with the Clerk of the superior court in the county in which the person conducts the business. (Section 10-1-490).

Online form: not available online

Registration fee: not available

Term of registration: None stated in statute.

Name requirements: None stated in statute.

Registration application requirements: The applicant must file a statement within thirty days before the person intends to begin conducting the business. The statement is to include the name of the owner(s), the address of the owner(s), the nature of the business (for example: sole proprietorship or partnership), and the business name used. (Section 10-1-490).

Publication requirements: The name shall be published once a week for two weeks in paper in which the sheriff's advertisements are printed. (Section 10-1-490).

Office for registration: The applicant must register with the Clerk of the Superior Court in the county in which the applicant conducts business. (Section 10-1-490).

Hawaii

State website: www.capitol.hawaii.gov

State law reference for name registration: Hawaii Revised Statutes Annotated, Title 482, Sections 482-2+.

Registration of business name requirements: Registration is optional. Hawaii does not have a fictitious name statute, but has a trade name statute. A trade name is essentially a business name other than the owner's name. The applicant must register with the Director of Commerce and Consumer Affairs. (Section 482-2).

Online form: www.hawaii.gov/dcca/areas/breg/registration/trade/forms

Registration fee: $50.00

Term of registration: None stated in statute.

Name requirements: None stated in statute.

Registration application requirements: The application shall state that the person is the proprietor, or the assign of the proprietor, and shall state the nature of the business. (Section 482-2).

Publication requirements: None stated.

Office for registration:
Hawaii Department of Commerce and Consumer Affairs
P O Box 40
Honolulu, HI 96810

Idaho

State website: www.state.id.us

State law reference for name registration: Idaho Code, Title 53, Sections 53-503+.

Registration of business name requirements: Registration is mandatory. The applicant must register with the Secretary of State. (Section 53-504).

Online form: www.idsos.state.id.us/corp/ABNform.htm

Registration fee: $25.00

Term of registration: Five years. (Section 53-506).

Name requirements: None stated in statute.

Registration application requirements: The applicant must file a certificate before the person intends to conduct business. The certificate must include the assumed business name, the true name of the owner(s), the address of the owner(s), and the general type of business conducted. (Section 53-505).

Publication requirements: None stated.

Office for registration:
Idaho Secretary of State
P O Box 83720
Boise, ID 83720-0080

Illinois

State website: www.ilga.gov

State law reference for name registration: Illinois Compiled Statutes, Chapter 805, Sections 405+.

Registration of business name requirements: Registration is mandatory. The applicant must register in the office of the County Clerk of the county in which the person conducts or intends to conduct business. (Section 805 ILCS 405/1).

Online form: not available online

Registration fee: not available

Term of registration: None stated in statute.

Name requirements: None stated in statute.

Registration application requirements: The registration is to include the name of the business, the real name of the owner(s), the post office address of the owner(s), and the post office address of every business location. (Section 805 ILCS 405/1).

Publication requirements: The owner(s) is required to file proof of publication for three consecutive weeks in the newspaper of general circulation in the county in which the applicant conducts the business. (Section 805 ILCS 405/1).

Office for registration: The applicant must register in the office of the County Clerk of the county in which the person conducts or intends to conduct business. (Section 805 ILCS 405/1).

Indiana

State website: www.state.in.us

State law reference for name registration: Indiana Code, Chapter 23, Sections 23-15-1-1+.

Registration of business name requirements: Registration is mandatory. The applicant must register with the office of the Recorder in the county in which business is conducted. (Section 23-15-1-1).

Online form: not available online

Registration fee: not available

Term of registration: None stated in statute.

Name requirements: None stated in statute.

Registration application requirements: The certificate must state the name of the business, the full name of the owner(s), and the address of the owner(s). (Section 23-15-1-1).

Publication requirements: None stated.

Office for registration: The applicant must register with the office of the Recorder in the county where the applicant conducts business. (Section 23-15-1-1).

Iowa

State website: www.legis.state.ia.us

State law reference for name registration: Iowa Annotated Code, Sections 547.1+.

Registration of business name requirements: Registration is mandatory. The applicant must register with the county Recorder in the county in which the person intends to conduct business. (Section 547.1).

Online form: not available online

Registration fee: not available

Term of registration: None stated in statute.

Name requirements: None stated in statute.

Registration application requirements: The applicant must file a statement before the person intends to conduct business. The statement must include the name of the owner(s), the post office address of the owner(s), the residence address of the owner(s), and the address where the person intends to conduct business. (Section 547.1).

Publication requirements: None stated.

Office for registration: The applicant must register with the county Recorder in the county in which the applicant intends to conduct business. (Section 547.1).

Kansas

State website: www.accesskansas.org

State law reference for name registration: Kansas Revised Statutes, Sections 81-205+.

Registration of business name requirements: Registration is optional. Kansas does not have a fictitious name statute, but has a trade name statute. A trade name is essentially a business name other than the owner(s)'s name. The applicant must register with the Secretary of State.

Online form: www.kssos.org/forms/business_services/TM.pdf

Registration fee: $40.00

Term of registration: Ten years. (Section 81-215).

Name requirements: None stated in statute.

Registration application requirements: The signed and verified registration must include the name of the owner(s), the business address of the owner(s), a description of the type of business, three copies or specimens of the trade name, and a statement that the owner(s) is the exclusive user of the name. (Section 81-213).

Publication requirements: None stated.

Office for registration:
Office of the Secretary of State
First Floor, Memorial Hall
120 S.W. 10th Ave.
Topeka, KS 66612-1594

Kentucky

State website: www.lrc.state.ky.us

State law reference for name registration: Kentucky Revised Statutes Annotated, Chapter 365, Sections 365.015+.

Registration of business name requirements: Registration is mandatory. The applicant must file the certificate with the County Clerk where the person resides. (Section 365.015).

Online form: not available online

Registration fee: not available

Term of registration: Five years. (Section 365.015).

Name requirements: None stated in statute.

Registration application requirements: The applicant must file a certificate before the person intends to conduct business. The certificate must state the assumed name of the business, the name of the owner(s), and the address of the owner(s). (Section 365.015).

Publication requirements: None stated.

Office for registration: The applicant must file the certificate with the County Clerk where the person resides. (Section 365.015).

Louisiana

State website: www.legis.state.la.us

State law reference for name registration: Louisiana Statutes Annotated, Sections 51:281+.

Registration of business name requirements: Registration is mandatory. The applicant must register with the Clerk of the court in the parish or parishes in which the person intends to or conducts the business. (Section 51:281).

Online form: www.sec.state.la.us/comm/cforms/f-309.pdf

Registration fee: $50.00

Term of registration: None stated in statute.

Name requirements: The name can be in any language, but must be in English on the certificate. The name shall not suggest that the business is a government agency. The name also shall not contain the name of a public facility. In addition, the name must not falsely suggest that the business is incorporated. (Sections 51:281, 281.2).

Registration application requirements: The applicant must file a certificate before the person intends to conduct business. The certificate must set forth the name of the business, the real full name of the owner(s), and the post office address of the owner(s). (Section 51:281).

Publication requirements: None stated.

Office for registration: The applicant must register with the Clerk of the Court in the parish or parishes in which the person intends to or conducts the business and with the Secretary of States office. (Section 51:281).

Sec. of State Commercial Division
P O Box 94125
Baton Rouge, LA 70804-9125

Maine

State website: janus.state.me.us/legis/ros/meconlaw.htm

State law reference for name registration: Maine Revised Statutes Annotated, Sections 31-2+.

Registration of business name requirements: Registration is mandatory. The applicant must register with the office of the Clerk in the city or town where the person intends to conduct business. (Section 31-2).

Online form: not available online

Registration fee: not available

Term of registration: None stated in statute.

Name requirements: The name must not contain the words or abbreviations of: *corporation*, *incorporated*, or *limited*. (Section 31-6).

Registration application requirements: The applicant must file a certificate before the person intends to conduct business. The signed certificate shall state the name of the owner, the residential address of the owner, the name of the business, the style or designation under which the business is to be conducted, and that the owner is a sole proprietor. (Section 31-2).

Publication requirements: None stated.

Office for registration: The applicant must register with the office of the Clerk in the city or town where the applicant intends to conduct business. (Section 31-2).

Maryland

State website: mlis.state.md.us/index.html

State law reference for name registration: Annotated Code of Maryland, Business Regulation, Sections 1-406+.

Registration of business name requirements: Registration is mandatory. The applicant must register with the Department of Assessments and Taxation. (Section 1-406).

Online form: www.dat.state.md.us/sdatweb/nameappl.pdf

Registration fee: $25.00

Term of registration: Five years. (Section 1-406).

Name requirements: None stated in statute.

Registration application requirements: The certificate must be in writing, affirmed under oath, and it must state the true name of the owner(s), the address of the owner(s), the character of the business, the street address of the business, and the name the business is going to be conducted under. (Section 1-406).

Publication requirements: None stated.

Office for registration:
Maryland State Department of Assessments and Taxation
301 West Preston Street
Baltimore, MD 21201-2305

Massachusetts

State website: www.mass.gov

State law reference for name registration: Annotated Laws of Massachusetts, Sections 110:5+.

Registration of business name requirements: Registration is mandatory. The applicant must register with the office of the Clerk in every city where the business has an office. (Section 110:5).

Online form: not available online

Registration fee: not available

Term of registration: Four years. (Section 110:5).

Name requirements: None stated in statute.

Registration application requirements: The certificate must include the full name of the owner(s), the residence address of the owner(s), the street address of the business, and the name of the business. (Section 110:5).

Publication requirements: None stated.

Office for registration: The applicant must register with the office of the Clerk in every city where the business has an office. (Section 110:5).

Michigan

State website: www.legislature.mi.gov

State law reference for name registration: Michigan Compiled Laws Annotated, Sections 445.1+.

Registration of business name requirements: Registration is mandatory. The applicant must register with the office of the Clerk in the county or counties where the business is or where the applicant intends to conduct business. (Section 445.1).

Online form: not available online

Registration fee: not available

Term of registration: Five years.

Name requirements: The statute does not set guidelines. However, the County Clerk can reject an assumed name that is likely to mislead the public or a name that is similar to another business name. (Section 445.2).

Registration application requirements: The applicant must file a certificate before the person intends to conduct business. The certificate shall state the name of the business, the real full name of the owner(s), and the address of the owner(s). (Section 445.1).

Publication requirements: None stated.

Office for registration: The applicant must register with the office of the Clerk in the county or counties where the business is or where the applicant intends to conduct business. (Section 445.1).

Minnesota

State website: www.leg.state.mn.us

State law reference for name registration: Minnesota Statutes Annotated, Section 333.01+.

Registration of business name requirements: Registration is mandatory. The applicant must register with the Secretary of State. (Section 333.01).

Online form: Certificate of Assumed Name
http://www.sos.state.mn.us/business/forms.html

Registration fee: $25.00

Term of registration: Ten years. (Section 333.055).

Name requirements: The name shall not include any of these words or their abbreviations: *corporation, incorporated, limited, chartered, professional, cooperative, association, limited partnership, limited liability company, professional limited liability company, limited liability partnership,* or *professional limited liability partnership.* (Section 333.01).

Registration application requirements: The certificate must state the name of the business, the address of the business, the true name of the owner(s), and the address of the owner(s). (Section 333.01).

Publication requirements: The applicant must publish the certificate for two consecutive issues in a qualified newspaper where the principal place of business is located. (Section 333.01).

Office for registration:
Minnesota Secretary of State
Business Services Division
180 State Office Building, 100 Rev.
Dr. Martin Luther King Jr. Blvd
St. Paul, MN 55155-1299

Mississippi

State website: www.mscode.com
State law reference for name registration: Mississippi Code Annotated, Sections 75-25-3+.
Registration of business name requirements: Registration is optional. Mississippi does not have a fictitious name statute, but the name of a business is registerable as a service mark or trademark. The applicant must register with the Secretary of State. (Sections 75-25-3, 75-25-5).
Online form: not available online
Registration fee: not available
Term of registration: None stated in statute.
Name requirements: The statute is exhaustive, stating that the trade name cannot be immoral, deceptive, or scandalous. Please refer directly to the statute. (Section 75-25-3).
Registration application requirements: The signed and verified application must include the name of the owner(s), business address of the owner(s), a description of the type of business the person intends to conduct, the date when the name was first used, and a statement that the owner(s) is the only person with the right to use that name. The applicant must provide three examples of the name in use. (Section 75-25-5).
Publication requirements: None stated.
Office for registration:
Mississippi Secretary of State
P O Box 136
Jackson, MS 39205-0136

Missouri

State website: ww.moga.state.mo.us
State law reference for name registration: Missouri Statutes, Sections 417.200+.
Registration of business name requirements: Registration is mandatory. The applicant must register with the Secretary of State. (Section 417.200).
Online form: http://www.sos.mo.gov/forms/corp/corp56.pdf
Registration fee: $7.00
Term of registration: None stated in statute.
Name requirements: None stated in statute.
Registration application requirements: The applicant must file a statement within five days after the person begins to conduct business. The statement must contain the fictitious business name, the name of the owner(s), and the residence address of the owner(s). (Section 417.210).
Publication requirements: None stated.
Office for registration:
Missouri Secretary of State
P O Box 778
Jefferson City, MO 65102

Montana

State website: leg.state.mt.us

State law reference for name registration: Montana Code Annotated, Sections 30-13-201+.

Registration of business name requirements: Registration is mandatory. The applicant must register with the Secretary of State. (Section 30-13-203).

Online form: Application for Registration of Assumed Business Name: www.sos.state.mt.us/css/BSB/Filing_Forms.asp#LIMITED%20PARTNERSHIPS

Registration fee: $20.00

Term of registration: Five years. (Section 30-13-206).

Name requirements: None stated in statute.

Registration application requirements: The form must contain the name of the owner(s), the street address of the owner(s), the proposed business name, the date of first use of the name, a description of the business, and the name of the county or counties where the business is being conducted. (Section 30-13-203).

Publication requirements: None stated.

Office for registration:
Secretary of State
P O Box 202801
Helena, MT 59620-2801

Nebraska

State website: www.unicam.state.ne.us

State law reference for name registration: Revised Statutes of Nebraska, Sections 87-209+.

Registration of business name requirements: Registration is optional. Nebraska does not have a fictitious name statute, but has a trade name statute. A trade name is essentially a business name other than the owner(s)'s name. The applicant must register with the Secretary of State. (Section 87-219).

Online form: www.sos.state.ne.us/business/corp_serv/pdf/210_219.pdf

Registration fee: $100.00

Term of registration: Ten years. (Section 87-211).

Name requirements: The statute is exhaustive, stating that the trade name cannot be immoral, deceptive, or scandalous. Please refer directly to the statute. (Section 87-209).

Registration application requirements: The registrant must provide the name of the business owner(s), the street address of the business owner(s), the trade name, the general nature of the business, the length of time the business has been operating, and the notarized signature of the owner(s). (Section 87-210).

Publication requirements: None stated.

Office for registration:
Secretary of State
P O Box 94608
Lincoln, NE 68509

Nevada

State website: www.leg.state.nv.us

State law reference for name registration: Nevada Revised Statutes, Sections 600.310+.

Registration of business name requirements: Registration is optional. Nevada does not have a fictitious name statute, but has a trade name statute. A trade name is essentially a business name other than the owner(s)'s name. The applicant must register with the Secretary of State. (Section 600.340).

Online form: sos.state.nv.us/comm_rec/trademk/mark_pk.pdf

Registration fee: $100.00

Term of registration: Five years. (Section 600.360).

Name requirements: The statute is exhaustive, stating that the trade name cannot be immoral, deceptive, or scandalous. Please refer directly to the statute. (Section 600.330).

Registration application requirements: The application for registration must set forth that the person is applying for trade name, a description of the name. It must include the name of the owner(s), the business address of the owner(s), the type of business being conducted, the date when the name was first used, a statement that the owner(s) is the only person with the right to use that name. The application must be signed and verified, and contain three copies of the trade name. (Section 600.340).

Publication requirements: None stated.

Office for registration:
Nevada Secretary of State
555 E. Washington Ave. #4000
Las Vegas, NV 89101

New Hampshire

State website: www.nh.gov

State law reference for name registration: New Hampshire Revised Statutes Annotated, Sections 349:1+.

Registration of business name requirements: Registration is mandatory. The applicant must register with the Secretary of State. (Sections 349:1, 349:5).

Online form: www.sos.nh.gov/corporate/PDF/TN-1%20V-1.0.pdf

Registration fee: $50.00

Term of registration: Five years. (Section 349:6).

Name requirements: The name cannot be deceptively similar to any instrumentality of the United States or New Hampshire government, or any recognized political party. (Section 349:1).

Registration application requirements: The signed certificate must state the principal place of the business, a brief description of the business, the name of the owner(s), the address of the owner(s), the date when the business was established, and the date when the business will end if anticipated. (Section 349:5).

Publication requirements: None stated.

Office for registration:
New Hampshire Secretary of State
107 North Main Street
Concord, NH 03301-4989

New Jersey

State website: www.njleg.state.nj.us

State law reference for name registration: New Jersey Statutes, Sections 56: 1-2+.

Registration of business name requirements: Registration is mandatory. The applicant must register with the Clerk of the county or counties where the business is or the person intends to conduct business. In addition, the applicant must register with the Secretary of State. (Section 56:1-2).

Online form: not available online

Registration fee: $50.00

Term of registration: None stated in statute.

Name requirements: None stated in statute.

Registration application requirements: The certificate must contain the name of the business, the true name of the owner(s), the post-office address of the owner(s). The certificate must be sworn to by the owner(s). In addition, if the person filing for the certificate is not a resident, then the owner(s) must give a power of attorney to the County Clerk for service of process. (Section 56:1-2).

Publication requirements: None stated.

Office for registration: The applicant must register with the Clerk of the county or counties where the business is or the applicant intends to conduct business. In addition, the applicant must register with the Secretary of State. (Section 56:1-2).

New Jersey Secretary of State
125 West State Street
Trenton, NJ 08608-1101

New Mexico

State website: legis.state.nm.us

State law reference for name registration: New Mexico Statutes Annotated, Sections 57-3B-1+.

Registration of business name requirements: Registration is optional. New Mexico's statute is for trade names which are names used to identify a person's business. The applicant must register with the Secretary of State. (Section 57-3B-2).

Online form: Application for registration of Trademark: www.sos.state.nm.us/ ucc/tmapplication.pdf

Registration fee: $25.00

Term of registration: Ten years. (Section 57-3B-7).

Name requirements: None stated in statute.

Registration application requirements: The application must include the type of business, a sworn statement that the owner(s) is claiming the exclusive right to use. The owner(s) shall sign the certificate. (Section 57-3B-2).

Publication requirements: None stated.

Office for registration:
Office of the Secretary of State
Operations Division
325 Don Gaspar, Suite 300
Santa Fe, NM 87503

New York

State website: assembly.state.ny.us
State law reference for name registration: New York General Business Law, Article 9B, Sections 130+.
Registration of business name requirements: Registration is mandatory. The applicant must register with the Clerk of the county or counties where the business is or the applicant intends to conduct business. (Section 130).
Online form: Certificate of Assumed Name: www.dos.state.ny.us/corp/pdfs/dos1338.pdf
Registration fee: $25.00
Term of registration: None stated in statute.
Name requirements: The name cannot appear to be the full name, the initials, or a word that appears to be a real name. The exception to that law is if the owners are the successors of the person for which the business was originally named. (Section 130).
Registration application requirements: The certificate must include the name of the business, the address of the business, the full name of the person conducting the business, the residence address of the person conducting the business, and the age of the owner(s), if under eighteen. (Section 130).
Publication requirements: None stated.
Office for registration: The applicant must register with the Clerk of the county or counties where the business is or the applicant intends to conduct business (Section 130).and with the:
NYS Department of State
Division of Corporations, State Records
41 State Street,
Albany, NY 12231-0001.

North Carolina

State website: www.ncga.state.nc.us
State law reference for name registration: General Statutes of North Carolina, Sections 66-68+.
Registration of business name requirements: Registration is mandatory. The applicant must register with the office of the Register of Deeds in the county or counties where the person intends to conduct business. (Section 66-68).
Online form: not available online
Registration fee: not available
Term of registration: None stated in statute.
Name requirements: None stated in statute.
Registration application requirements: The applicant must file a certificate before transacting the business. The Certificate must state the name of the business, the name of the owner(s), the address of the owner(s), and the applicant must sign the certificate. (Section 66-68).
Publication requirements: None stated.
Office for registration: The applicant must register with the office of the Register of Deeds in the county or counties where the person intends to conduct business. (Section 66-68).

North Dakota

State website: www.nd.gov

State law reference for name registration: North Dakota Century Code, Sections 47-25-01+.

Registration of business name requirements: Registration is mandatory. North Dakota's statute is for trade names which is a name other than the owner(s)'s name used to identify a person's business. The applicant must register with the Secretary of State. (Section 47-25-02).

Online form: www.state.nd.us/eforms/Doc/sfn13401.pdf

Registration fee: $25.00

Term of registration: Five years. (Section 47-25-04).

Name requirements: A trade name can not be deceptively similar to the name of any other registered business name in the state. (Section 47-25-03).

Registration application requirements: The applicant must file a statement before the person intends to conduct business. The statement must state the name of the business, the name of the owner(s), the address of the owner(s), the address of the principal place of business, and the nature of the business. (Section 47-25-02).

Publication requirements: None stated.

Office for registration:
North Dakota Secretary of State
600 East Boulevard Avenue, Dept 108
Bismarck, ND 58505-0500

Ohio

State website: www.ohio.gov

State law reference for name registration: Ohio Revised Code, Sections 1329.01+.

Registration of business name requirements: Registration is optional. Ohio's statute is for trade names. Generally, a trade name is a name used to identify a person's business, and to which the owner(s) asserts the exclusive right to use. The applicant must register with the Secretary of State. (Section 1329.01).

Online form: www.sos.state.oh.us/SOS/Forms/BusinessServices/534.pdf

Registration fee: $50.00

Term of registration: Five years. (Section 1329.04).

Name requirements: The name can not imply that the business is connected with a government entity if not so connected, the name can not imply that the business is incorporated if not incorporated, and the name shall not be indistinguishable from any other previously registered business name. (Section 1329.02).

Registration application requirements: The application must state the name of the owner(s), the business address of the owner(s), the trade name to be registered, the general nature of the business, and the length of time the name has been in use. (Section 1329.01).

Publication requirements: None stated.

Office for registration:
Ohio Secretary of State
P O Box 670
Columbus, OH 43216

Oklahoma

State website: www.ok.gov

State law reference for name registration: Oklahoma Statutes, Sections 18-1140+.

Registration of business name requirements: Registration is mandatory. The applicant must register with the Secretary of State. (Section 18-1140).

Online form: Trade Name Report: www.sos.state.ok.us/forms/ FM0021.PDF

Registration fee: $25.00

Term of registration: None stated in statute.

Name requirements: The name must be distinguishable from the registered name of other business entities, and foreign business entities qualified to do business in Oklahoma, or if either of the above existed within the last three years the name is also barred. The name must also be distinguishable from names reserved with the Secretary of State. These restrictions are avoidable with the written consent of a registered business entity, or if the applicant establishes prior right to a registered name. (Sections 18-1140, 1141).

Registration application requirements: The report must include the trade name, the type of business, and the address where the business will be conducted. (Section 18-1140).

Publication requirements: None stated.

Office for registration:
Oklahoma Secretary of State
2300 North Lincoln Blvd. #101
Oklahoma City, OK 73105-4897

Oregon

State website: www.leg.state.or.us

State law reference for name registration: Oregon Revised Statutes, Sections 648.005+.

Registration of business name requirements: Registration is mandatory. The applicant must register with the Secretary of State. (Section 648.010).

Online form: www.filinginoregon.com/ forms/pdf/bizreg/101.pdf

Registration fee: $50.00

Term of registration: Two years. (Section 648.017).

Name requirements: The name must be distinguishable from any other registered name. (Section 648.051).

Registration application requirements: The applicant must file an application before the person intends to conduct business. The application must include the name of the business, the real name of the owner(s), the street address of the owner(s), the address of the principal place of business, the mailing address of the authorized agent for transactions with the Secretary of State, and the applicant's primary business activity. (Section 648.010).

Publication requirements: None stated.

Office for registration:
Oregon Secretary of State
255 Capitol Street NE, Ste 151
Salem, OR 97310-1327

Pennsylvania

State website: www.state.pa.us

State law reference for name registration: Pennsylvania Consolidated Statutes, Sections 54:301+.

Registration of business name requirements: Registration is optional. The applicant must register with the Department of State. (Section 54:311).

Online form: www.dos.state.pa.us/ corps/LIB/corps/20/7/311.pdf

Registration fee: $70.00

Term of registration: Ten years. (Section 54:321).

Name requirements: The statute is exhaustive, the name cannot imply that the business is incorporated or that the business is a professional organization. Please refer directly to the statute. (Section 54:311).

Registration application requirements: The application must include the business name, the nature of the business, the street address of the principal place of business, the name of the owner(s), and the street address of the owner(s). (Section 54:311).

Publication requirements: The applicant must publish the fictitious name in the county in which the applicant conducts or intends to conduct business. The notice must contain the fictitious name, street address of the principal place of business, name of the owner(s), statement that an application for fictitious name is or was filed. (Section 54: 311).

Office for registration:
Pennsylvania Department of State
P O Box 8722
Harrisburg, PA 17105-8722

Rhode Island

State website: www.state.ri.us

State law reference for name registration: General Laws of Rhode Island, Sections 6-1-1+.

Registration of business name requirements: Registration is mandatory. The applicant must register with the Clerk in the town or city where the person conducts business. (Section 6-1-1).

Online form: not available online

Registration fee: not available

Term of registration: None stated in statute.

Name requirements: None stated in statute.

Registration application requirements: The certificate must state the name of the business, the full name of the owner(s), and the post office address of the owner(s). The certificate must be sworn to by the owner(s). (Section 6-1-1).

Publication requirements: None stated.

Office for registration: The applicant must register with the Clerk in the town or city where the person conducts conduct business. (Section 6-1-1).

South Carolina

State website: www.scstatehouse.net

State law reference for name registration: Code of Laws of South Carolina, Sections 39-13-10+.

Registration of business name requirements: Repealed 2004. Check statutes for updates. (Section 39-13-10).

Online form: not available online

Registration fee: Not available.

Term of registration: None stated in statute.

Name requirements: None stated in statute.

Registration application requirements: Repealed 2004. Check statutes for updates. (Section 39-13-10).

Publication requirements: None stated.

Office for registration: Repealed 2004. Check statutes for updates.(Section 39-13-10).

South Dakota

State website: www.state.sd.us

State law reference for name registration: South Dakota Compiled Laws, Sections 37-11-1+.

Registration of business name requirements: Registration is mandatory. The applicant must register electronically with the Office of the Secretary of State or with the office of the Register of Deeds in each county where the person intends to conduct business. (Section 37-11-1).

Online form: www.state.sd.us/ Applications/st08bnrs/secure/BNRS_ Process.asp

Registration fee: $10.00

Term of registration: Five years. (Section 37-11-1).

Name requirements: None stated in statute.

Registration application requirements: The applicant must file a statement before the person intends to conduct business. The statement must contain the name of the owner(s), the post office address of the owner(s), the residence address of the owner(s), and the address where the principal place of business is located. (37-11-1).

Publication requirements: The applicant is not required to publish the fictitious name. However, the Register of Deeds does have the fictitious name published. (Section 37-11-1).

Office for registration: The applicant must register with the office of the Register of Deeds in each county where the person intends to conduct business or electronically on the Secretary of State web site. www.sdsos.gov/(Section 37-11-1).

Tennessee

State website: www.michie.com

State law reference for name registration: Tennessee Code Annotated. Sections 47-25-501+.

Registration of business name requirements: Registration is optional. Tennessee does not have a fictitious name statute, but allows an individual to register a business name under the trademark statute. The applicant must register with the Secretary of State. (Section 47-25-503).

Online form: Application for Registration of Trademark: www.state.tn.us/sos/forms/ss-4264.pdf

Registration fee: $20.00

Term of registration: Ten years. (Section 47-25-505).

Name requirements: The statute is exhaustive, stating that the trade name cannot be immoral, deceptive, or scandalous. Please refer directly to the statute. (Section 47-25-502).

Registration application requirements: The signed and verified application must include the name of the owner(s), the business address of the owner(s), the type of business transacted, the date when the name was first used, a statement that the owner(s) has the exclusive right to use the name, and three copies or specimens of the name. (Section 47-25-503).

Publication requirements: None stated.

Office for registration:
Tennessee Department of State
312 8th Ave. North
6th Floor, Snodgrass Tower
Nashville, TN 37243

Texas

State website: www.state.tx.us

State law reference for name registration: Vernon's Texas Business and Commerce Code, Sections 36.02+.

Registration of business name requirements: Registration is mandatory. The applicant must register with the County Clerk in each county where the person intends to conduct business. (Section 36.10).

Online form: www.sos.state.tx.us/corp/forms/502.pdf

Registration fee: Check with County Clerk

Term of registration: Ten years. (Section 36.13).

Name requirements: None stated in statute.

Registration application requirements: The sworn certificate must include the business name, the full name of the owner(s), and the residence address of the owner(s). (Section 36.10).

Publication requirements: None stated.

Office for registration:
Secretary of State, Statutory Filings Division, Corporations Section,
P O Box 13697,
Austin, Texas 78711-3697

Utah

State website: www.utah.gov

State law reference for name registration: Utah Code Annotated, Sections 42-2-5+.

Registration of business name requirements: Registration is mandatory. The applicant must register with the Division of Corporations and Commercial Code. (Section 42-2-5).

Online form: ww.commerce.utah.gov /cor/pdfforms/nmrserv.pdf

Registration fee: $22.00

Term of registration: None stated in statute.

Name requirements: Basically, the name cannot imply a type of business organization that the business is not, or be the name of any already registered trade name. The statute is exhaustive. Please refer directly to the statute. (Section 42-2-6.6).

Registration application requirements: The certificate must state the name of the business, the full true name of the owner(s), the street address of the owner(s), and the location of the principal place of business. It must be filed within 30 days after beginning to conduct business. (Section 42-2-5).

Publication requirements: None stated.

Office for registration:
Utah Division of Corporations and Commercial Code
P O Box 146705
Salt Lake City, UT 84114-6705

Vermont

State website: www.leg.state.vt.us

State law reference for name registration: Vermont Statutes Annotated, Sections 11: 1621+.

Registration of business name requirements: Registration is mandatory. The applicant must register with the Secretary of State. (Section 11:1621).

Online form: not available online

Registration fee: not available

Term of registration: None stated in statute.

Name requirements: The name cannot be deceptively similar to any other previously registered name. (Section 11:1621).

Registration application requirements: The applicant must file a sworn statement within ten days after the person begins to conduct business. The sworn statement must include the name of the business, the name of the town where the business is located, a description of the type of business, the name of the owner(s), and the address of the owner(s). (Section 11:1621).

Publication requirements: None stated.

Office for registration:
Vermont Secretary of State
26 Terrace Street
Montpelier, VT 05602-2972

Virginia

State website: www.virginia.gov

State law reference for name registration: Code of Virginia, Sections 59.1-69+.

Registration of business name requirements: Registration is mandatory. The applicant must register with the Clerk of the Court for deeds in the county or city where the person intends to conduct business. (Section 59.1-69).

Online form: Trademark Application: www.wvsos.com/forms/business/2004/tm1.pdf

Registration fee: $50.00

Term of registration: None stated in statute.

Name requirements: None stated in statute.

Registration application requirements: The signed and acknowledged certificate must state the name of the business, the name of the owner(s), the post office address of the owner(s), and the residence address of the owner(s). (Section 59.1-69).

Publication requirements: None stated.

Office for registration: The applicant must register with the Clerk of the Court for deeds in the county or city where the person intends to conduct business. (Section 59.1-69).

Washington

State website: www.leg.wa.gov

State law reference for name registration: Revised Code of Washington, Sections 19.80.010+.

Registration of business name requirements: Registration is mandatory. The applicant must register with the Department of Licensing. (Section 19.80.010).

Online form: Master Application: www.dol.wa.gov/forms/700028fillable.pdf

Registration fee: $5.00

Term of registration: None stated in statute, but the Department of Licensing may have rules. (Section 19.80.040).

Name requirements: None stated in statute, but the Department of Licensing may have rules. (Section 19.80.040).

Registration application requirements: The registration must state the true full name of the owner(s), and the post office address of the owner(s). (Section 19.80.010).

Publication requirements: None stated.

Office for registration: The applicant must register with the Department of Licensing Master License Service, PO Box 9034, Olympia, WA 98507-9034 (Section 19.80.010).

West Virginia

State website: www.legis.state.wv.us

State law reference for name registration: West Virginia Code, Sections 47-8-2+.

Registration of business name requirements: Registration is mandatory. The applicant must register with the Clerk of the County Commission in the county where the person intends to have the principal place of business. (Section 47-8-2).

Online form: Application for Tradename: www.wvsos.com/forms/business/2004/nr3.pdf

Registration fee: $25.00

Term of registration: None stated in statute.

Name requirements: None stated in statute.

Registration application requirements: The duly acknowledged certificate must state the name of the business, the true full name of the owner(s), the residence address of the owner(s), and the post office address of the owner(s). (Section 47-8-2).

Publication requirements: None stated.

Office for registration: The applicant must register with the Clerk of the County Commission in the county where the person intends to have the principal place of business. (Section 47-8-2).

Wisconsin

State website: www.legis.state.wi.us

State law reference for name registration: Wisconsin Statutes Annotated, Sections 132.001+.

Registration of business name requirements: Registration is optional. Wisconsin does not have a fictitious name statute, but has a tradename statute. A trade name is essentially a business name other than the owner's name. The applicant must register with the Secretary of State. (Section 132.01).

Online form: APPLICATION FOR REGISTRATION OF MARKS: http://www.sos.state.wi.us/pdf/register_marks.pdf

Registration fee: $15.00

Term of registration: Twenty years. (Section 132.01).

Name requirements: The trade name may not consist of any flag, coat of arms, or insignia of the United States, a foreign nation, other state of the Union, or any municipality. (Section 132.01).

Registration application requirements: The sworn statement must include the name(s) of the applicant, type of business conducted, and the residence or business address of the applicant. The applicant must claim the sole right to use of the trade name. (Section 132.01).

Publication requirements: None stated.

Office for registration:
Wisconsin Secretary of State
Trademark Records
P O Box 7848
Madison, WI 53707-7848

Wyoming

State website: legisweb.state.wy.us

State law reference for name registration: Wyoming Statutes, Sections 40-2-102.

Registration of business name requirements: Registration is optional. The applicant must register with the Secretary of State. (Section 40-2-104).

Online form: APPLICATION FOR REGISTRATION OF TRADE NAME: soswy.state.wy.us/corporat/forms/new/tnreg.pdf

Registration fee: $100.00

Term of registration: Ten years. (Section 40-2-105).

Name requirements: Basically, the name can not imply a type of business organization that the business is not or be the name of any already registered trade name. The statute is exhaustive. Please refer directly to the statute. (Section 42-2-6.6).

Registration application requirements: The application, in duplicate, must contain the name of the owner(s), the business address of the owner(s), the name of the business, the general nature of the business The signature of the owner(s) must be notarized. (Section 40-2-104).

Publication requirements: None stated.

Office for registration:
Wyoming Secretary of State
200 West 24th Street
Cheyenne, WY 82001-0020

Glossary of Business, Legal, and Accounting Terms

Account: A separate record of an asset, liability, income, or expense of a business.

Accounting: The process for recording, summarizing, and interpreting business financial records.

Accounting method: The method of recording income and expenses for a business; can be either accrual method or cash method.

Accounting period: A specific time period covered by the financial statements of a business.

Accounting system: The specific system of record-keeping used to set up the accounting records of a business. See also *single-entry accounting* or *double-entry accounting*.

Accounts payable: Money owed by a business to another for goods or services purchased on credit. Money that the business intends to pay to another.

Accounts receivable: Money owed to the business by another for goods or services sold on credit. Money that the business expects to receive.

Accrual method: Accounting method in which all income and expenses are counted when earned or incurred regardless of when the actual cash is received or paid.

Accrued expenses: Expenses that have been incurred but have not yet been paid.

Accrued income: Income that has been earned but has not yet been received.

ACRS: Accelerated Cost Recovery System. Generally, a method of depreciation used for assets purchased between 1980 and 1987.

Agent: A person who is authorized to act on behalf of another. A corporation acts only through its agents, whether they are directors, employees, or officers.

Aging: The method used to determine how long accounts receivable have been owed to a business.

Amend: To alter or change.

Articles of Organization: The charter of the limited liability company, the public filing with a state that requests that the company be allowed to exist. Along with the Operating Agreement, the articles provide details of the organization and structure of the business. The articles must be consistent with the laws of the state of organization.

Assets: Everything a business owns, including amounts of money that are owed to the business.

Assumed name: A name, other than the limited liability company's legal name as shown on the Articles of Organization, under which a company will conduct business. Most states require registration of the fictitious name if a company desires to conduct business under an assumed name. The company's legal name is not an assumed name.

Balance sheet: The business financial statement that depicts the financial status of the business on a specific date by summarizing the assets and liabilities of the business.

Balance sheet accounts: Asset and liability accounts used to prepare business balance sheets.

Balance sheet equation: Assets = Liabilities + Equity, or Equity = Assets − Liabilities.

Bookkeeping: The actual process of recording the figures in accounting records.

Business liabilities: Business debts. Also the value of the owner's equity in his or her business.

C-corporation: A business entity owned by shareholders that is not an S-corporation. Subject to double taxation, unlike S-corporations.

Calendar year: Year consisting of 12 consecutive months ending on December 31st.

Capital: Initially, the actual money or property that shareholders transfer to the limited liability company to allow it to operate. Once in operation, capital also consists of accumulated profits. The net worth of the company, the owner's equity in a business, and/or the ownership value of the business.

Capital expense: An expense for the purchase of a fixed asset; an asset with a useful life of over one year. Generally, must be depreciated rather than deducted as a business expense.

Capital surplus: Corporation owner's equity. See also *retained capital*.

Cash: All currency, coins, and checks that a business has on hand or in a bank account.

Cash method: Accounting method in which income and expenses are not counted until the actual cash is received or paid.

Cash out: Cash paid out for business purposes, such as a refund.

Certificate of Organization: Another name for Articles of Organization, used by some states. See *Articles of Organization*.

Chart of Accounts: A listing of the types and numbers of the various accounts that a business uses for its accounting records.

Check register: A running record of checks written, deposits made, and other transactions for a bank account.

Close corporation: Corporation with less than 50 shareholders that has elected to be treated as a close corporation. Not all states have close corporation statutes. (For information regarding close corporations, please consult a competent attorney.)

Closely held corporation: Not a specific state-sanctioned type of corporation, but rather a designation of any corporation in which the stock is held by a small group of people or entities and is not publicly traded.

Common stock: The standard stock of a corporation that includes the right to vote the shares and the right to proportionate dividends.

Company record book: Contains all the records of the limited liability company (except accounting records).

Consent Resolution: Any resolution signed by all of the directors or shareholders of a corporation authorizing an action, without the necessity of a meeting.

Corporate bylaws: Internal rules governing management of a corporation, containing procedures for holding meetings, appointments, elections, and other matters.

Corporation: A business entity owned by shareholders; can be a C-corporation or an S-corporation.

Cost basis: Total cost to a business of a fixed asset.

Cost of goods sold: The amount that a business has paid for the inventory that it has sold during a specific period. Calculated by adding beginning inventory and additions to inventory and then deducting the ending inventory value.

Credit: In double-entry accounting, an increase in liability or income accounts or a decrease in asset or expense accounts.

Current assets: Cash and any other assets that can be converted to cash or consumed by the business within one year.

Current debt: Debt that will normally be paid within one year.

Current liabilities: Debts of a business that must be paid within one year.

Current ratio: A method of determining the liquidity of a business. Calculated by dividing current assets by current liabilities.

Debit: In double-entry accounting, a decrease in liability or income accounts or an increase in asset or expense accounts.

Debt: The amount that a business owes to another. Also known as "liability."

Debt ratio: A method of determining the indebtedness of a business. Calculated by dividing total liabilities by total assets.

Default rules: Rules set by statute in each state that define the actual operational characteristics of limited liability companies.

Depreciation: Cost of fixed asset deductible proportionately over time.

Dissolution: Methods by which a limited liability company concludes its business and liquidates. Dissolutions may be involuntary because of bankruptcy or credit problems, or voluntary on the initiation of the members of the company.

Dividend: A distribution of money or property paid by a corporation to a shareholder based on the amount of shares held. A proportionate share of the net profits of a business that the board of directors has determined should be paid out to shareholders, rather than held as retained earnings. Dividends must be paid out of the corporation's net earnings and profits. The board of directors has the authority to declare or withhold dividends based on sound business discretion.

Domestic company: A limited liability company is a domestic company in the state in which it is organized. See also *foreign company*.

Double-entry accounting: An accounting system under which each transaction is recorded twice: as a credit and as a debit. A very difficult system of accounting to learn and understand.

Equity: Any debt that a business owes. It is owner's equity if owed to the business owners and liabilities if owed to others.

Expenses: The costs to a business of producing its income. Any money that it has paid or will pay out during a certain period

FEIN: Federal Identification Number, used for tax purposes.

FICA: Federal Insurance Contributions Act. Taxes withheld from employees and paid by employers for Social Security and Medicare.

Fictitious name: See *assumed name*.

Fiduciary duty: A duty to act with reasonable care and prudence.

FIFO: First-in, first-out method of accounting for inventory. The inventory value is based on the cost of the latest items purchased.

Financial statements: Reports that summarize the finances of a business; generally a profit and loss statement and a balance sheet.

Fiscal year: A 12-month accounting period used by a business.

Fiscal-year reporting: For income tax purposes, reporting business taxes for any 12-month period that does not end on December 31 of each year.

Fixed assets: Assets of a business that will not be sold or consumed within one year. Generally, fixed assets (other than land) must be depreciated.

Foreign company: A limited liability company is referred to as a foreign company in all states other than the one in which it is actually organized. In order to conduct active business affairs in a different state, a foreign company must be registered with the other state for the authority to transact business and it must pay an annual fee for this privilege.

FUTA: Federal Unemployment Tax Act. Federal business unemployment taxes.

General journal: In double-entry accounting, used to record all of the transactions of a business in chronological order. Transactions are then posted (or transferred) to the appropriate accounts in the general ledger.

General ledger: In double-entry accounting, the central listing of all accounts of a business.

Gross pay: The total amount of an employee's compensation before the deduction of any taxes or benefits.

Gross profit: Gross sales minus the cost of goods sold.

Gross sales: The total amount received for goods and services during an accounting period.

Gross wages: The total amount of an employee's compensation before the deduction of any taxes or benefits.

Income: Any money that a business has received or will receive during a certain period.

Income statement: Financial statement that shows the income and expenses for a business. Also referred to as an "operating statement" or "profit and loss statement."

Indemnify: To reimburse or compensate. Members and managers of limited liability companies are often reimbursed or indemnified for all the expenses they may have incurred in organizing a company.

Initial capital: The money or property that an owner or owners contribute to starting a business.

Intangible personal property: Generally, property not attached to land that you cannot hold or touch (for example: copyrights, business goodwill, etc.).

Inventory: Goods that are held by a business for sale to customers.

Invoice: A bill for the sale of goods or services that is sent to the buyer.

Ledgers: The accounting books for a business. Generally, refers to the entire set of accounts for a business.

Liabilities: The debts of a business.

LIFO: Last-in, first-out method of valuing inventory. Total value is based on the cost of the earliest items purchased.

Liquidity: The ability of a company to convert its assets to cash and meet its obligations with that cash.

Long-term assets: The assets of a business that will be held for over one year. Those assets of a business that are subject to depreciation (except for land).

Long-term debts: Debts that will not be paid off in one year.

Long-term liabilities: The debts of a business that will not be due for over one year.

Long-term loans payable: Money due on a loan more than one year in the future.

Long-term notes payable: Money due more than one year in the future.

MACRS: Modified accelerated cost recovery system. A method of depreciation for use with assets purchased after January 1, 1987.

Managers: In a limited liability company, those persons selected by the members of the company to handle the management functions of the company. Managers of limited liability companies may or may not be members/owners of the company. Managers are roughly analogous to the officers of a corporation.

Members: In a limited liability company, those persons who have ownership interests (equivalent to shareholders in a corporation). Most states allow single-member limited liability companies.

Minutes: A written record of the activities of a meeting.

Natural person: An actual human being, not a business entity.

Net income: The amount of money that a business has after deducting the cost of goods sold and the cost of all expenses. Also referred to as "net profit."

Net loss: The amount by which a business has expenses and costs of goods sold greater than income.

Net pay: The amount of compensation that an employee actually will be paid after the deductions for taxes and benefits.

Net profit: The amount by which a business has income greater than expenses and cost of goods sold. Also referred to as "net income."

Net sales: The value of sales after deducting the cost of goods sold from gross sales.

Net wages: The amount of compensation that an employee will actually be paid after the deductions for taxes and benefits.

Net worth: The value of the owner's share in a business. The value of a business determined by deducting the debts of a business from the assets of a business. Also referred to as "owner's equity."

Nontaxable income: Income that is not subject to any state or local sales tax.

Not-for-profit corporation: A corporation formed under state law that exists for a socially worthwhile purpose. Profits are not distributed but retained and used for corporate purposes. May be tax-exempt. Also referred to as "nonprofit."

Officers: Manage the daily operations of a corporation. Generally consists of a president, vice president, secretary, and treasurer. Appointed by the board of directors.

Operating Agreement: The internal rules that govern the management of the limited liability company. The agreement contains the procedures for holding meetings, appointments, elections and other management matters. If this agreement conflicts with the Articles of Organization, the provision in the articles will be controlling.

Operating margin: Net sales divided by gross sales. The actual profit on goods sold, before deductions for expenses.

Operating statement: Financial statement that shows the income and expenses for a business. Also referred to as "income statement" or "profit and loss statement."

Owner's equity: The value of an owner's share in a business. Also referred to as "capital."

Paid-in capital: Total amount of money or property transferred to the limited liability company upon its beginning business.

Partnership: An unincorporated business entity that is owed by two or more persons.

Payee: Person or business to whom a payment is made.

Payor: Person or business that makes a payment.

Per capita: One vote per member.

Perpetual duration: Existence of a limited liability company forever.

Personal property: All business property other than land and the buildings that are attached to the land.

Petty cash: Cash that a business has on hand for payment of minor expenses when use of a business check is not convenient. Not to be used for handling sales revenue.

Petty cash fund: A cash fund. Considered part of cash on hand.

Petty cash register: The sheet for recording petty cash transactions.

Physical inventory: The actual process of counting and valuing the inventory on hand at the end of an accounting period.

Plant assets: Long-term assets of a business. Those business assets that are subject to depreciation (other than land).

Posting: In double-entry accounting, the process of transferring data from journals to ledgers.

Pre-paid expenses: Expenses that are paid for before they are used (for example: insurance, rent, etc.).

Profit and loss statement: Financial statement that shows the income and expenses for a business. Also referred to as an "income statement" or "operating statement."

Proxy: A written member authorization to vote shares on behalf of another.

Qualify: Having a Certificate of Authority to Transact Business from another state in order to actively conduct business in that state.

Quorum: The percentage of ownership shares in the limited liability company that must be represented at a members meeting in order to officially transact any company business.

Real property: Land and any buildings or improvements that are attached to the land.

Reconciliation: The process of bringing a bank statement into agreement with the business check register.

Recovery period: Specific time period for dividing up the cost into proportionate amounts.

Registered agent: The person designated in the Articles of Organization who will be available to receive service of process (summons, subpoena, etc.) on behalf of the limited liability company. A limited liability company must always have a registered agent.

Registered office: The actual physical location of the registered agent. Need not be the actual principal place of business of the limited liability company.

Resolution: A formal decision that has been adopted by either the shareholders or the board of directors of a corporation.

Retail price: The price for which a product is sold to the public.

Retained capital: Limited liability company member/owner's equity. See also *capital surplus*.

Retained earnings: In a limited liability company, the portion of the annual profits of a business that are kept and reinvested in the company, rather than paid to the members/owners.

Revenue: Income that a business brings in from the sale of goods or services or from investments.

S-corporation: A type of business corporation in which all of the expenses and profits are passed through to its shareholders to be accounted for at tax time individually in the manner of partnerships. A specific IRS designation that allows a corporation to be taxed similarly to a partnership, yet retain limited liability for its shareholders.

Salary: Fixed weekly, monthly, or annual compensation for an employee.

Sales: Money brought into a business from the sale of goods or services.

Sales income: Revenue derived from selling a product of some type

Salvage value: The value of an asset after it has been fully depreciated.

Service income: Income derived from performing a service for someone.

Service of process: To accept subpoenas or summonses for a company.

Shareholders: Owners of issued stock of a corporation and, therefore, owners of an interest in the corporation. They elect the board of directors and vote on major corporate issues.

Short-term loans payable: Money due on a loan within one year.

Short-term notes payable: Money due within one year.

Single-entry accounting: A business recordkeeping system that generally tracks only income and expense accounts. Used generally by small businesses, it is much easier to use and understand than double-entry accounting.

Sole proprietorship: An unincorporated business entity in which one person owns the entire company.

Straight-line depreciation: Spreads the deductible amount equally over the recovery period.

Supplies: Materials used in conducting the day-to-day affairs of a business (as opposed to raw materials used in manufacturing).

Tangible personal property: Property not attached to land that you can hold and touch (for example: machinery, furniture, equipment).

Taxes payable: Total of all taxes due but not yet paid.

Termination: End of legal existence of company.

Trial balance: In double-entry accounting, a listing of all the balances in the general ledger in order to show that debits and credits balance.

Wages: Hourly compensation paid to employees, as opposed to salary.

Wages payable: Total of all wages and salaries due to employees but not yet paid out.

Wholesale price: The cost to a business of goods purchased for later sale to the public.

Working capital: The money available for immediate business operations. Current assets minus current liabilities.

Index

☆ Nova Publishing Company ☆
Small Business and Consumer Legal Books and Software

Law Made Simple Series
Basic Wills Simplified
ISBN 0-935755-90-X	Book only	$22.95
ISBN 0-935755-89-6	Book w/Forms-on-CD	$28.95

Divorce Agreements Simplified
ISBN 0-935755-87-X	Book only	$24.95
ISBN 0-935755-86-1	Book w/Forms-on-CD	$29.95

Estate Planning Simplified
ISBN 1-892949-10-5	Book w/Forms-on-CD	$34.95

Living Trusts Simplified
ISBN 0-935755-53-5	Book only	$22.95
ISBN 0-935755-51-9	Book w/Forms-on-CD	$28.95

Living Wills Simplified
ISBN 0-935755-52-7	Book only	$22.95
ISBN 0-935755-50-0	Book w/Forms-on-CD	$28.95

Personal Legal Forms Simplified (3rd Edition)
ISBN 0-935755-97-7	Book w/Forms-on-CD	$28.95

Personal Bankruptcy Simplified (4th Edition)
ISBN 1-892949-34-2	Book w/Forms-on-CD	$29.95

Small Business Made Simple Series
Corporation: Small Business Start-up Kit (2nd Edition)
ISBN 1-892949-06-7	Book w/Forms-on-CD	$29.95

Limited Liability Company: Small Business Start-up Kit (2nd Edition)
ISBN 1-892949-04-0	Book w/Forms-on-CD	$29.95

Partnership: Small Business Start-up Kit (2nd Edition)
ISBN 1-892949-07-5	Book w/Forms-on-CD	$29.95

Real Estate Forms Simplified
ISBN 1-892949-09-1	Book w/Forms-on-CD	$29.95

S-Corporation: Small Business Start-up Kit (2nd Edition)
ISBN 1-892949-05-9	Book w/Forms-on-CD	$29.95

Small Business Accounting Simplified (3rd Edition)
ISBN 0-935755-91-8	Book only	$22.95

Small Business Bookkeeping Systems Simplified
ISBN 0-935755-74-8	Book only	$14.95

Small Business Legal Forms Simplified (4th Edition)
ISBN 0-935755-98-5	Book w/Forms-on-CD	$29.95

Small Business Payroll Systems Simplified
ISBN 0-935755-55-1	Book only	$14.95

Sole Proprietorship: Small Business Start-up Kit (2nd Edition)
ISBN 1-892949-08-3	Book w/Forms-on-CD	$29.95

Legal Self-Help Series
Divorce Yourself: The National Divorce Kit (6th Edition)
ISBN 1-892949-11-3	Book only	$29.95
ISBN 1-892949-12-1	Book w/Forms-on-CD	$39.95

Incorporate Now!: The National Corporation Kit (4th Edition)
ISBN 1-892949-00-8	Book w/Forms-on-CD	$29.95

Prepare Your Own Will: The National Will Kit (6th Edition)
ISBN 1-892949-14-8	Book only	$19.95
ISBN 1-892949-15-6	Book w/Forms-on-CD	$29.95

National Legal Kits
Simplified Divorce Kit (2nd Edition)
ISBN 1-892949-20-2	Book only	$19.95

Simplified Family Legal Forms Kit
ISBN 1-892949-18-0	Book only	$18.95

Simplified Living Will Kit
ISBN 1-892949-22-9	Book only	$15.95

Simplified Will Kit   (2nd Edition)
ISBN 1-892949-21-0	Book only	$16.95

☆ Ordering Information ☆

Distributed by:
National Book Network
4501 Forbes Blvd. Suite 200
Lanham MD 20706

Shipping: $4.50 for first & $.75 for each additional
Phone orders with Visa/MC: (800) 462-6420
Fax orders with Visa/MC: (800) 338-4550
Internet: www.novapublishing.com
Free shipping on all internet orders